Education for a Civil Society

Teaching Young Children to Gain Five Democratic Life Skills

Second Edition

DAN GARTRELL

National Association for the Education of Young Children
Washington, DC

National Association for the Education of Young Children

1401 H Street NW, Suite 600
Washington, DC 20005
202-232-8777 • 800-424-2460
NAEYC.org

NAEYC Books

Senior Director, Publishing and Content Development
Susan Friedman

Director, Books
Dana Battaglia

Senior Editor
Holly Bohart

Editor II
Rossella Procopio

Senior Creative Design Manager
Charity Coleman

Senior Creative Design Specialist
Gillian Frank

Creative Design Specialist
Makayla Johnson

Creative Design Specialist
Ashley McGowan

Publishing Business Operations Manager
Francine Markowitz

Through its publications program, the National Association for the Education of Young Children (NAEYC) provides a forum for discussion of major issues and ideas in the early childhood field, with the hope of provoking thought and promoting professional growth. The views expressed or implied in this book are not necessarily those of the Association.

Contents

For Sharon Hoverson,

who has spent her career teaching kindergarten at the Community School in Ponemah,

the traditional village of the Red Lake Nation in northern Minnesota.

Leaving Bemidji every morning before six; returning every evening not before five.

Waase giizis, waabanoo anang, gagiibaatis chii ikwezens

"Shining Sun, Morning Star, Crazy Big Girl"

Sharon's half-humorous, half-serious Ojibwe name,

a unique honor given to her by

Ponemah Elders

of the Red Lake Nation

Acknowledgments

Endless gratitude goes to my friend, partner, and wife, Dr. Julie Jochum Gartrell. Dr. J. was a longtime faculty member at Bemidji State University and an emeritus professor in special education at Concordia University, St. Paul. Julie assisted with about every aspect of preparation of this book. During the daytime, she even let me sit in her favorite reclining chair to do the writing. Thanks, You!

A note of gratitude also goes to my high school classmate and longtime good friend to Julie and me, Merrilee Brown. A retired writer and editor for a local newspaper in Maine, Merrilee aided Julie in the final proofreading of the book.

Thanks go to former students and colleagues who over the years have shared their anecdotal stories with me. That these folks have recognized the power of real-life stories from classrooms and have sent them to me to curate is humbling.

I would like to thank the staffs at all of my publishers who edited and published my previous books. Working with them has prepared me for my magnum opus, which is this book.

Finally, much appreciation is expressed to the publications staff at NAEYC. Many thanks to my good editor, Holly Bohart. Holly, you made teaming for a common goal a very natural task. And thanks to each of the following: Susan Friedman and Dana Battaglia, publications staff who saw the value of this new edition, and the talented Creative Services team who brought these words to life.

About the Author

Dan Gartrell is a former Head Start teacher for the Red Lake Band of Ojibwe in northern Minnesota. During the 1970s, Dan completed his master's degree at Bemidji State University in northern Minnesota, where he was a CDA (Child Development Associate) credential adviser for the Child Development Training Program. Dan received his EdD from the University of North Dakota in 1977. For 40 years, Dan was director of the Child Development Training Program and professor of early childhood education at Bemidji State University. He is now a professor emeritus.

Dan has written 30 articles that have appeared in *Young Children, Teaching Young Children, The SAGE Encyclopedia of Contemporary Early Childhood Education,* and *Exchange.* His column, Guidance Matters, appeared in *Young Children* from 2004 to 2015.

Dan is the author of seven books, including six editions of his textbook, *A Guidance Approach for the Encouraging Classroom,* and two NAEYC comprehensive membership selection books: *The Power of Guidance: Teaching Social-Emotional Skills in Early Childhood Classrooms* (2004) and *Education for a Civil Society: How Guidance Teaches Young Children Democratic Life Skills* (2012).

Two of his books, on guidance in early childhood education and guidance for early childhood leaders, were published in 2017 and 2020 by Redleaf Press.

Dan has led over 300 presentations, keynotes, and master classes in 23 states; Washington, DC; Germany; and Mexico. About 20 times Dan has presented at NAEYC annual conferences and professional learning institutes. Dan is a member of two families that include wife, Dr. Julie Jochum, five adult children, and fifteen grandchildren.

Website

www.dangartrell.net

Contact information

Email: gartrell@paulbunyan.net

Address: 535A Laurel Ave, St. Paul, Minnesota 55102

Greetings, readers. Welcome to this child-friendly book for adults. Although technically it is a second edition of *Education for Civil Society: How Guidance Teaches Young Children Democratic Life Skills* (2012), the book is essentially new. The first edition explored the traditions of European and American education, as well as the work of twentieth-century psychologists, that led to the development of the five Democratic Life Skills (referred to as the DLS in this edition). The first edition stressed the roots of the DLS in progressive education. I made the case (now as then) that the largest platform for progressive education in the United States is the field of early childhood education. Only the last part of the first edition addressed in practical terms teaching for the DLS in early childhood programs. At the time, I felt a stronger need to justify the skills than to explain how they are taught for.

Since that edition, folks have let me know that they want more about practice in regard to teaching for the DLS. A second loud and clear message has been that civility in society is a heightened urgency now—compared to more "innocent" times back in 2012. These are reasons for the new edition, which NAEYC's senior director of publishing and content development, Susan Friedman, and director of books, Dana Battaglia, agreed should be written (happily for me). Reflecting these changes, the book's title is slightly different from that of the previous edition.

The book is my seventh on guidance in early childhood education, with the most recent published in 2020 by Redleaf Press. As well, from 2005 to 2015, I wrote the column Guidance Matters for *Young Children*, the peer-reviewed early childhood education journal of NAEYC. What is guidance? As I see it, guidance is intentionally teaching for healthy emotional-social development in young children. Guidance involves leading by building secure relationships with children *outside of conflicts* and, during conflicts, calming and teaching rather than disciplining. The goals of guidance are the five DLS. These skills evolve from centuries of progressive education and from the writing of psychologist Abraham Maslow ([1962] 1999).

The five DLS first appeared in the third edition of my textbook, *A Guidance Approach for the Encouraging Classroom*, which is now in its sixth edition (Gartrell 2014). The skills are formally introduced in Chapter 1. So the suspense doesn't overwhelm, they are:

DLS 1: Finding acceptance as a member of the group and as a worthy individual

DLS 2: Expressing strong emotions in nonhurting ways

DLS 3: Solving problems creatively—independently and in cooperation with others

DLS 4: Accepting differing human qualities in others

DLS 5: Thinking intelligently and ethically

The Author

The author would be me, this gnarly old duffer, Dan Gartrell—professor emeritus in early childhood and foundations education from Bemidji State University in Minnesota.

In my first year of teaching, sixth grade in Ohio, the principal unexpectedly issued paddles to the teaching staff. I didn't take a paddle, but what an introduction to the profession that year was! In my second year, at the Red Lake Ojibwe Head Start program in Minnesota, I found that the adults there really loved those kids. The Red Lakers on the staff took wounded pride that their Head Start program was in the old boarding school where the janitor and others had been forced to live as children. (Red Lake Head Start has long since moved to its own building, and the old boarding school has been torn down.) Age restrictions in the program were informal back then, and in our group we had children from 2½ to 6. Our Head Start was year-round, and a favorite summer activity was wading in the shallows of the mighty Red Lake. My years there were a joy, and at Red Lake (named for its iron deposits) I found my true calling: preparing adults from low-income communities to be early childhood teachers.

After the Red Lake experience, over the next 40 years I did CDA (Child Development Associate) training, got advanced degrees, taught teacher education classes (many off campus), supervised student teachers, and coached teaching staff in prekindergarten classrooms and, late in my career, family child care homes. The arc of my career began with those two night-and-day first teaching experiences.

. . . .

Where did my interest in children's emotional-social development first come from? A lot probably from my mom, Beth Twiggar Goff. For my first nine years and my brother's first seven, Bethy was a single mom. In midlife, she studied and became a psychiatric social worker, specializing in therapy with children. From her sessions with one child, Bethy wrote one of the first books for helping the very young cope with divorce, *Where Is Daddy?* (1969). (Unlike one of my books, *Where Is Daddy?* is still available.)

. . . .

Writing Style

Some would say that my writing style is a creative mix (others would say funky mix) of vignettes, big words, long sentences, references where needed, everyday plain language, and a sprinkling of friendly humor—all intended to present big ideas in engaging ways. (I also include occasional asides to readers in parentheses or sidebars.)

Complex sentences appear a lot in the book. When I'm writing a complex sentence and I hear a pause point before a *but* or *and,* a comma often gets plopped in. I hear written language as much as see it. For the same reason, key words are italicized or bolded more than is customary (words that appear in the glossary are bolded in the text). I hope that readers won't mind these personal touches. The beginning paragraphs of Chapter 1 provide an open window into my combination formal-informal writing style.

Also, for the most part I refer to young children's ages not in years but in months. As early childhood education professionals know, there is a big difference between a "just 3" (36-month-old) and an "almost 4" (47-month-old).

Anecdotes

There are many anecdotes in the book. An anecdote is a classroom story used for instructional purposes. My preference is to use anecdotal stories that are grounded in actual observations of child-teacher events. As such, the anecdotes are more specific and (I think) more authentic than invented vignettes used to illustrate predetermined points. Important to note, the anecdotes are not intended to connote normative research findings but to illustrate specific examples of good teaching practice.

Some anecdotes have been consolidated, with material added to maximize their instructional value. An example is in Chapter 6 about Head Start teacher Deb's effort to bring healing to a four-child conflict involving three fairy wands. (It can happen!) Because the incident might have been symptomatic of a class-wide problem with sharing and taking turns, I added material from another anecdote to include a large group meeting that Deb's teaching team *might* have held. (I knew Deb, and I had a pretty good idea of how her teaching team would handle the matter.) Watch for the two bears and a frog puppet play in that anecdote. The few anecdotes that are "value added" like this are identified.

A past source for anecdotes was *What the Kids Said Today: Using Classroom Conversations to Become a Better Teacher* (Gartrell 2000). Now out of print, the book included 145 stories shared with me by "students, assistant teachers, teachers, professors, and directors in prekindergarten settings and primary grade classrooms in six different states" (vi). Some anecdotal stories from that book have traveled with me across publications. Since 2000, teachers and former students have continued to share their anecdotal observations for use in my writing. Names have been changed for all children and most adults. Thank you once more to these many early childhood educators.

Particular Use of Key Terms

Children. I prefer this term to *students,* which for me reduces children to a single restrictive role. Whole children come into learning settings. Occasionally, to provide variety in wording, I use *kids.* I have always thought that the transmogrification of this term from the young of quadrupedal, ruminant mammals to young humans is (honestly) endearing. But for the sake of professional writing standards, I use *kids* sparingly.

The five Democratic Life Skills (DLS). The heart of the book, the skills are the goals of using guidance with children, and what adults need to civilly converse in today's contentious society. Teachers can guide learners of any age to gain the skills. The skills are derived, in general, from progressive education over the last 500 years—starting with the lifelong refugee (and genius) John Comenius—and most specifically in the 1960s from Abraham Maslow, protégé of the psychiatrist Alfred Adler. Later in the century, Lilian Katz and Mary Ainsworth each developed key concepts that are related to the DLS (Gartrell 2012). Also, the work of social scientists Kenneth and Mamie Clark imbue the spirit of DLS theory.

Developmentally appropriate practice. The DLS rely on developmentally appropriate practice (DAP). The go-to reference book for us all on the subject is the fourth edition of *Developmentally Appropriate Practice in Early Childhood Programs Serving Children from Birth Through Age Eight* (NAEYC 2022). DAP provides the foundation for the encouraging early learning community, a term used throughout the book for a setting that is developmentally appropriate for every community member, and so uniquely conducive to teaching for the five DLS.

Early childhood care and education. Early childhood professionals provide care *and* education in whatever setting they are in: family child care, center-based programs, Head Start, nursery school, public preschool, early childhood special education, family education, kindergarten or primary grade classrooms, and so on. For brevity, I use the term *early childhood education* as inclusive of the provision of care and education. I try to write for readers who work in any of these settings.

Emotional-social development. Not the other way around (social-emotional). *Healthy* emotional development can happen only after a child has had the most basic human needs met: physical safety and security, a sense of unconditional belonging, and a profound feeling of being loved. Without adequate emotional support through basic needs being met, children cannot undertake healthy development in the social domain (Dye 2018; Maslow [1962] 1999). So, in my writing beginning a few years ago, the listing is *emotional* first, *social* second.

As a related point, healthy *personal* development in the book refers to a child's having gained in emotional development to the extent that they become willing and able to engage in healthy development in all the other domains. In the terms of the DLS, the child has achieved the safety-needs skills, DLS 1 and 2, sufficiently to pursue the growing-needs skills, DLS 3–5. More on this fundamental idea follows in Chapter 1.

Encouraging early learning community. The community includes young children, the adults who care for and teach them, any other program personnel, volunteers and visitors, and the children's families. Specific to the encouraging early learning community, teachers form secure relationships and use unconditional acceptance, guidance leadership, and teaming with other adults to further the personal development of all children in the community. A simple validator of an encouraging early learning community is that it is a place where people want to be even when sick, as opposed to not wanting to be there when they are well.

Guidance. Guidance is teaching for healthy emotional-social development. Two forms are *developmental guidance* and *intervention guidance* (further explained in Chapter 2), both of which operate within the context of DAP. Primary developmental guidance practices include communication techniques to build secure relationships, friendly large group meetings, and in-depth investigations through emergent curriculum. Major intervention guidance practices include calming methods, guidance talks, mediation, intervention large group meetings, and comprehensive guidance. During conflicts, guidance entails calming and teaching rather than disciplining. Teachers who use *comprehensive guidance* never give up on a child. Guidance within developmentally appropriate settings is how educators teach for the five DLS.

Liberation teaching. I use this term in the context of guidance to refer to guiding a child to gain DLS 1 and 2 and willingly engage with attaining DLS 3, 4, and 5. In everyday language, it refers to never giving up on a child. I explain more about liberation teaching in Chapter 2.

NAEYC (National Association for the Education of Young Children). NAEYC is the largest association of early childhood professionals in the world. I like the association because they take positions on important issues and advocate for good teaching practices. For full disclosure, they also have printed "a big bunch" of my writings. I am member #536.

Parents. I use the term inclusively to refer to birth parents, single or couples, as well as stepparents, in-family surrogate parents, foster parents, and guardians. From experience, I often say that there is no more difficult profession for which there is so little preparation as a parent. Single parents have an especially difficult road, and surrogate parents have an even more difficult road. Whenever grandparents, aunts, uncles, or older siblings are raising children as surrogate parents—or children are in foster care or with guardians—trauma has happened in the family.

Teachers do well to recognize that surrogate parents of any kind have taken on a difficult role and likely need extra support. Teachers also need to consider, and be supportive of, siblings who have major caregiving responsibilities. Due to the diversity in modern family life, in the book I refer to *families* as well as to *parents*.

Progressive education. Progressive education is teaching and learning that focuses on the whole child—on holistic personal development and learning—to further democracy. Reaching back over 100 years, the multistate Progressive Education Network (PEN) promotes a vision of progressive education for the twenty-first century that promotes the kind of education I advocate for in the book. (See further information about PEN's vision and goals in Chapter 1.)

The DLS come out of the same progressive education tradition as PEN does. Moreover, progressive education has great congruence with the guidance approach and DAP. This congruence is why I contend that early childhood education is the largest platform for progressive education in the country. Not in my lifetime, but hopefully in yours, the trifecta of DAP, the DLS, and the guidance approach in progressive early childhood education will percolate upward in our K–12 education institutions. Why? So a new generation of citizens can continue to make our complex, modern democracy a "more perfect union."

Stress-conflict-punishment syndrome. Many children who encounter adverse experiences and trauma suffer the consequence of feeling unmanageable (toxic) stress. In early childhood settings, unmanageable stress can cause children to show mistaken survival behaviors, including aggression. Although for them the intent is defense of the self, some adults react to disruptive acting out with punishment. Punishment intensifies already high stress and causes children to internalize negative messages about themselves and the setting, perpetuating the stress-conflict-punishment cycle. Studies of the condition (see Chapter 2) indicate that this cycle too often follows children into other levels of schooling and adulthood.

Teachers. To a child, anyone bigger than they are is a teacher. In this book, a teacher is a professional specializing in early childhood care and education, operating as a member of a team whenever possible. For variety, I use *early childhood professionals, educators, providers,* and occasionally *adults* as informally synonymous terms.

Teaching teams (TTs). There are team teachers, and then there are teaching teams. TTs are professionals of different backgrounds, educations, and experiences who work together on behalf of all in the encouraging early learning community. In standard educational jargon, what TTs use is sometimes defined as *differentiated staffing.* TTs practice friendly differentiated staffing in their roles. Together, members of the TT accomplish what individual teachers have difficulty accomplishing alone. For this reason, a prominent term throughout the book is the *TT.*

Some family child care providers have teaching assistants—and so they can team. Many do not. Support can come in other forms; a Head Start agency in northern Minnesota contracted with and provided advisers and resources for their satellite family child care providers. These family child care providers served Head Start children whose family members were working. Such systems are needed nationwide, as they can help alleviate the challenges so many family child care providers face of going it alone with very limited resources.

Format of the Book

> Each chapter begins with a list of suggested goals for readers.

> References to works follow standard in-text citation and are listed at the end of the book by chapter.

> In each chapter, points of emphasis are italicized, and key concepts are in boldface. The terms in boldface are listed at the end of each chapter and defined in an end-of-book glossary.

> Each chapter concludes with an overview statement or a summary grid.

> Each chapter includes discussion questions to help readers digest and apply information.

> End matter for the book includes an appendix of key lists of principles and practices, the glossary of terms, the list of references, and an index.

A note about the references: Many are recent, within the last few years. Many others are circa 2010; these references served the first edition of the book well and to my knowledge have not been outdated by more recent information. A few are older foundation references, the work of originating authorities like Abraham Maslow, whose work has proven indispensable to authors since and to this book. Being an older septuagenarian, I enjoy referring to older authorities whose works might guide us today more than we realize. (A grandkid once referred to us "septageraniums," then looked at my wife and me and grinned. We did too.)

Chapters 1–3 focus on the big picture relating to education for a civil society. In the opening chapters, I make the case that teaching for the five DLS is our essential task in early childhood education to promote healthy personal development—and to sustain a civil, democratic society. Working for these ideas throughout all levels of American education, to the extent we can, seems to me to be part of this calling.

Chapters 5–9 focus on teaching practices for DLS 1 through 5 respectively. For continuity, Chapters 5–8 follow a similar format. Each heading within the chapters serves as a separate analysis point for that skill. Chapter 4 introduces and discusses these headings along with content foundational to the discussion of the skills.

Discussed in Chapter 9, Skill 5—thinking intelligently and ethically—is an expression of children who have gained DLS 1 through 4. When children show Skill 5, the result is aspirational for the immediate parties present, and should be for all humankind! Chapter 9 uses a few headings that appear in the other DLS chapters, but the organization is more free flowing.

Chapter 10, "Teachers and the Democratic Life Skills," is the wrap-up chapter. The chapter iterates and reiterates these ideas:

> Early childhood educators need to have adequate resources to be fully effective, and they must have support systems in and outside of the program.

> All benefit when teaming includes administrators and classroom staff together.

> Women and men working together as teachers is a continuing ideal vision.

> TT members lead children to gain the DLS when they themselves have gained them.

> Teaching for the five DLS contributes to a more perfect civil, democratic society.

A Caveat: My Own Bias

A reader of the manuscript has pointed out that my identified theoretical influencers have mainly been White, Western scholars. Yes, there are inherent biases and limitations in their theories, and, when speaking about all children's development, dangers in unexamined application and interpretation. (This observation is underscored in NAEYC's position statements on advancing equity in early childhood education and DAP, works I highly respect.)

In the specific academic sense, I accept this criticism, and I endorse this reader's and NAEYC's urging us to seek diverse voices regarding the evidence base in early childhood (for example, see Farquhar & White [2014] and Broughton [2022]). I think it is worth noting that my broader philosophical underpinnings for DLS theory reflect my liberal upbringing; the diversity inherent in the cultural revolution of the 1960s; baccalaureate education at an ultra-progressive college (Antioch); doctoral education at the quite progressive Center for Teaching and Learning at the University of North Dakota (as it was known then); my work experience; and readings of works including by Harriet Tubman, W.E.B. Du Bois, Malcolm X, Kenneth Clark, and David Treuer.

That the DLS theory is inclusive in nature is further supported by the positive anecdotal feedback to my presentations and writings received over the years by diverse audiences and readers. Still, I wholeheartedly welcome further research, especially on universality versus culture boundedness of DLS ideas.

Contact Information

My website is dangartrell.net. Lots of the content there is available as free downloads, including published pieces, workshop and training handouts, and PowerPoints. My books are also listed on the website, including a sixth edition textbook published by Cengage, a book copublished by Cengage and NAEYC, two other books by NAEYC, and three published by Redleaf Press.

Contact me directly by email at gartrell@paulbunyan.net. (Paul Bunyan is the patron saint of Bemidji—and of countless other towns across the country's northern tier.) Usually, I get back to folks within a day. Being a neanderthal septuagenarian, email is my only electronic social connection.

A few copies of my out-of-print book *What the Kids Said Today: Using Classroom Conversations to Become a Better Teacher* are still available (while supplies last—you are guaranteed a signed copy). Contact me by email for information.

Noncommercial Endnote

Despite the risk of misinterpretation, I have never considered franchising or otherwise commercializing constructs that I have formulated in relation to guidance and the five DLS. An attribution here or there would be appreciated, but that is all I expect. Also, I invite research regarding any concept or construct that I have developed. If I can help such efforts while sitting (with permission) in my wife's favorite chair, I will sure try to provide it.

Cheers and happy reading!

Dan Gartrell

Yes, the old dude professor still does speaking, training, and master classes.

CHAPTER 1

Roots and Shoots

The Democratic Life Skills and Progressive Education

SUGGESTED GOALS FOR READERS

1. Form a working knowledge of the five Democratic Life Skills (DLS).

2. Learn about ways early childhood educators teach for the five DLS.

3. Gain understanding of connections between Dewey's philosophy of democracy, progressive education, and the goal of civility in contemporary democracy.

4. Describe how early childhood education is a major platform for progressive education.

This is a book about bringing things together. If I do my job well, the connections, intersections, nexuses, congruences, harmonious temporal sequences, and efforts at synthesis will be apparent. Readers will be nodding yes and not nodding off. If the book is not clear, it will be due to too many sentences like the second one above. The book has a wee bit of humor sprinkled in, ranging in quality from fairy dust to troll droppings, but always friendly. Along with (1) pursuing intellectual truth, (2) proactively following one's passion, (3) communicating with others in mutually affirming ways, and (4) enjoying the arts, (5) friendly humor gives meaning to our eternal human traffic jam. To me, friendly humor is one of the best assets teachers at any level can cultivate. The book will endeavor to radiate these five values (but probably will not glow in the dark).

In this chapter we take a beginning look at four important concepts and the connections between them:

1. The five DLS
2. John Dewey's philosophy of democracy
3. The congruence of the DLS and progressive education
4. Early childhood education as a platform for progressive education and the DLS

The Five Democratic Life Skills

As I've written about the **Democratic Life Skills (DLS)** across time, they have become ever more clear to me. The five skills are these:

Safety-Needs Skills

DLS 1: Finding acceptance as a member of the group and as a worthy individual

DLS 2: Expressing strong emotions in nonhurting ways

Growing-Needs Skills

DLS 3: Solving problems creatively—independently and in cooperation with others

DLS 4: Accepting unique human qualities in others

DLS 5: Thinking intelligently and ethically

We'll return to the DLS shortly. First, some insight into where they come from.

Dual Motivations Behind the DLS

As catalyst for his iconic hierarchy of needs, psychologist Abraham Maslow ([1962] 1999) wrote about two universal motivational needs, for safety and for growth—a concept that developmental scientists Shonkoff and Phillips (2000) and Benarroch (2020) in their own ways have studied since. The first motivational source, for safety—what Maslow called "deficiency motivation"—is the stronger, especially in young children. By "deficiency," Maslow was not referring to a person's character but to an inability of an individual to have physiological and psychological safety needs met, and the resulting strong motivation to meet them.

Needs or Skills?

People attribute the term *needs* to Maslow, the manifestations of his two motivational sources, for safety and for psychological growth. As educators, we tend to speak more of skills, the particular abilities people need to meet the needs. Even with DLS 1, where dependence on significant others to meet their needs is high, children must develop skills that allow them to take the steps to find a place of acceptance in the group and to muster self-esteem. Teachers do all they can do to ready children to take the active step, but children must take the step on their own.

Because of children's basic needs for belonging, security, and affection, work on gaining DLS 1, the ability to gain affirming acceptance, precedes work on gaining DLS 2, the ability to express emotions in nonhurting ways. Due to adverse experiences (more in the next chapter), children who are emotionally adrift have difficulty learning to manage their strong emotions with respect for themselves and others. Even more so than adults, children besieged by unmet safety needs may experience unmanageable **toxic stress.** To relieve the stress, children show survival behaviors—often aggression through unintentional or intentional **conflicts,** but also through psychological withdrawal.

As children often experience with caregivers, *conflicts* are expressed disagreements between individuals. Because each person is unique, conflicts are a normal part of life. From when an infant feels discomfort and cries, to when an elderly person in care would rather watch the snow fall than come to lunch, conflicts mark the intersection of one life with another, every minute of every day.

The central question in teaching for the five DLS is how we humans learn to handle conflicts. Children struggling with DLS 1 and 2 need gentle but sometimes firm guidance leadership within the context of a secure relationship. As they mostly achieve Skills 1 and 2, children organically switch to the work of the young, making gains with Skills 3, 4, and 5. Children busy with the **growing-needs skills** still require nudging and support, and still from the context of secure relationships, but they need less guidance leadership. Most of us adults struggle to attain a mature comprehension of the role of conflicts in life. I hope the book helps early childhood professionals to progress with this understanding—perhaps a task easier for us old-timers who have mostly "graduated" (in one way or another) from the fray.

To attain the first two **safety-needs skills,** young children depend on caring, supportive adults. Secure relationships and the use of **guidance**—adult responses to conflicts that calm and teach rather than punish—are key. Gaining DLS 1 and 2 lets children shift attention to the second motivational source—Maslow's "growth motivation"—for learning and psychological growing. In the book's terms, this means DLS 3, 4, and 5: learning to solve problems creatively, independently and in cooperation with others; accepting differing human qualities in others; and thinking intelligently and ethically. In line with his mentor Alfred Adler, Maslow wrote that the state of mind for being able to actualize one's potential is essentially positive—for me, *an enjoyment of life.*

The Democratic Life Skills, Introduced

In future chapters I discuss the specifics of each skill, but this section provides an introduction by illustration. For each DLS, an anecdote offers an informal case study of educators guiding children to attain that skill; this is followed by a brief author reflection.

Across a Common Bridge

As a matter of spiritual faith for some, humanistic psychology for others, there seems to be a common thread among the scholars cited in the book. I have found this to be articulated exquisitely in the writings of Maslow: a life force in the form of a dynamic for development powers the brain. This life force is fragile, especially in the early years. Maslow's contribution—that healthy psychological growing can occur only when psychological safety is attained—has been corroborated (as mentioned) by developmental scientists since the advent of the concept over 60 years ago.

When the motivation for psychological growing is released (made free or, in my wording, supported and nudged), the intrinsic life force, which some call *mastery motivation,* comes to the fore. Amazing, child-generated learning then takes place—such as by Cynthia, just 5, who one afternoon completed five class puzzles simultaneously. When children walk a hard road to reach this space, a common term for their state of mind is **resilience**. DLS theory is only a current iteration of this miraculous but vulnerable guiding force within everyone, which, if empowered, potentially leads to individual fulfillment and the betterment of democratic society.

Skill 1: Finding Acceptance as a Member of the Group and as a Worthy Individual

Composite anecdote/case study. Rahmi, 40 months, had just joined the child care community. The teaching team (TT), with Morgan as lead, could not miss that Rahmi was showing a particular pattern of behavior. He played alone; tended to reject social initiatives made by other children and the TT; and, when he could, physically or psychologically distanced himself from organized activities. Rahmi sometimes sought to hide when it was time for large groups or sitting at the meal table. When "discovered," he refused to participate. At other times, like cleanup, he seemed to blend in to his surroundings. (The TT noted that he was not grinning when he did this.)

With Morgan's leadership, the TT recognized that punishing Rahmi for not following the routine would only aggravate his isolation from the group. Instead, the TT remained especially matter-of-fact in their interventions, inviting rather than forcing, and emphasized building relationships with the child. They also had built communications with Rahmi's family from the first day and talked with the designated family members who picked Rahmi up each day.

With quiet persistence, individual TT members—especially Claudia, who took particular interest in the child—looked for times during the day to have **contact talks** with Rahmi. (Contact talks are intentional moments of quality time during which a TT member engages a child in friendly conversation. The purpose is for the child and adult to get to know each other better and build mutual trust.) Here's a short contact talk Claudia had one day with Rahmi as he was playing with a truck loaded with "stuff." Claudia had been sitting beside Rahmi, sharing the moment with him.

Claudia: Your truck is really loaded. (*Pausing to give Rahmi time to respond.*)

Rahmi: Yeah, Uncle Cy hauls stuff.

Claudia: Bet you like to ride with him.

Rahmi: (*Smiling slightly.*) Yeah, he got a 150. He takes me sometimes.

Rahmi concentrated on getting his truck onto a rug without "stuff" falling off. Claudia decided to end the conversation, but continued to spend a few more minutes with the child. By building secure relationships with Rahmi outside of conflict situations, Claudia and the TT helped Rahmi gradually decide the community was a safe and welcoming place.

Reflection. Contact talks don't have to be lengthy, but they need to happen with every child, at least every day. With Rahmi and other children struggling to gain DLS 1, the talks need to happen even more than that. Ample individual *choice time* (work time, playtime) afforded by developmentally appropriate programs allows for the talks to happen. Chapter 4 gives further analysis and illustration of contact talks, as well as seven other related communication practices for building secure relationships.

From contacts with the family, the TT surmised that Rahmi was dealing with developmental challenges, and not traumatic challenges outside of the program. Being only months old and just joining a group of unfamiliar peers and adults, Rahmi was reacting with high stress levels. The TT recognized that the 40-month-old needed general affirmation of his acceptance and worth, and so the team coordinated in using contact talks to help him. At the same time, the TT met and began to develop partnerships with Rahmi's family (including his Uncle Cy, who picked up Rahmi some days, always driving his pickup truck). All the team worked to establish the connection with the child that Claudia had, through friendly one-on-one conversations. Over a few weeks, Rahmi came to recognize that the community was a safe place.

Skill 2: Expressing Strong Emotions in Nonhurting Ways

Composite anecdote/case study. From the first day, Caroline (59 months) showed behavior that indicated a high need for attention and to be in control of situations and people, including the TT. Caroline's actions suggested a mistrust of others—evident when it was her turn to catch a bounced ball from the teacher and, instead of throwing it back, she ran off with it. One morning, Caroline was observed crowding out a smaller child who was washing a truck in a dishpan ("like at the car wash") to wash it herself. Caroline seemed to give thought to when she chose to show bullying behavior, appearing to intentionally cause conflicts.

This was also a pattern of behavior the TT could not miss! (Lead teacher Ina said to me that one adult on the team already seemed to harbor negative feelings toward Caroline.) Ina and the team talked. Ina noticed that her colleague Scout (new but catching on) seemed to get along with Caroline. Ina asked Scout to do extra work with the child. With backing from Ina, Scout had frequent, informal contact talks with Caroline (again, when conflicts were not happening). The team agreed that Ina would handle most conflicts involving the child. By playing the "good teacher," Scout became a big sister figure to Caroline, someone the child could go to when things got tough. (With a classroom guideline of "We are friendly to others," Ina consistently intervened when Caroline aggressively asserted her will—and the entire staff encouraged her when she did not.)

Reflection. Like other children who assert their will to get what they want, Caroline had likely learned that people couldn't be trusted to help her meet her safety needs and concluded she must act for herself. She was showing a **mistaken behavior**—which can be intentional as well as reactive. (See Chapter 4 for further information.) Important in helping young children gain DLS 2 is giving them a support system to develop trust while teaching them they needn't bully to find a place in the **encouraging early learning community.** Teaching kids who show intentional mistaken behaviors how to use their ego strength to become community leaders is the challenge. The long-term difference might well be between an adult who is a virtuous civic leader and one who is self-serving.

Skill 3: Solving Problems Creatively—Independently and in Cooperation with Others

Reconstructed anecdote/independent problem solving. Karin (44 months), from the Ojibwe village of Redby, came into the room with even more than her usual enthusiasm. She barely got her coat hung before she raced to the stand-up paint easel and threw on a paint shirt. I watched as Karin painted five large squiggles in blue. "Another one, Dan," she said, and I hung the first picture to dry as she went to work on the second one. This time she made five figures approximating *p*'s and *q*'s. Looking at it, she said, "Another one, Dan." As I hung the second to dry, she was already busy on her third picture. She made five large circles. In each she painted spots for eyes and lines for smiles. She looked at her picture and put down her brush. Smiling, Karin said, "Maze and Luke came home. Ma says we are going to have a real Indian Thanksgiving!" Still beaming, Karin took off her paint shirt and went to find her friends.

Reflection. Until this day in November, I had never seen Karin make anything other than distinct blotches or shapes. The second picture with the letter-like figures made me think she was really trying to say something through her art. She told me what when she finished her third. I had almost said

something to her about wasting paper, but I was glad I didn't. In terms of Rhoda Kellogg's ([1969] 2015) classic stages of art development, Karin went from "controlled scribbling" to "shapes" and "designs" to "early pictorial" within 10 minutes!

Most pictures young children see are in picture books telling stories. It is natural for them to want to tell stories through their art. If we pause to give the child a chance to think, she may tell us how her family has reunited and is going to celebrate "a real Indian Thanksgiving."

Reconstructed anecdote/cooperative problem solving. On this Monday, Brian, Louella, and Darwin (all 52–56 months) were the only ones in the dramatic play area. My teaching teammate Josie and I watched the three take everything out of the wood refrigerator, stove, and wardrobe; place the furniture pieces on their backs on the floor, sit down in them; and make loud machine noises. My teammate started to walk over and remind them of the "correct" way of using the play furniture. I asked Josie to wait, and we went over to ask what they were doing.

"There's a fire across the lake," one child said. "Yeah, we got to get the water and put the fire out," said another. "We gotta get the water in them bucket planes. That's very dangerous," added the third.

I turned to Josie. Resigned, she told me, "Yeah, there was a fire on the west end (of Red Lake) over the weekend. They had to fly a forestry [water scooper] plane up here from Bemidji. They got it out." She told the children that they could use the furniture as planes this once, but they needed to put them back and restock them when they were done. The three played water-scooping planes putting out a wildfire for nearly a half hour—getting out occasionally to fight the fire by hand. Under Josie's watchful eye, they put everything back after they were done.

Reflection. I refer to DLS 3 as the *learning skill.* Of the skills, DLS 3 most directly refers to the implicit mental processes of sizing up an activity, applying oneself to it through mental and physical activity, seeing it through to a conclusion, and cognitively and affectively (if intuitively) evaluating the outcome. In early childhood education, learning activities that afford rich learning opportunities are most appropriately open-ended ones, with children feeling welcome to uniquely engage in them. When involved in developmentally appropriate learning experiences, young children don't think about adults' conventional expectations about materials and the program. Karin was not thinking about paper conservation, and the firefighters were not concerned that they were using play furniture unconventionally.

A guiding insight for me that readers will occasionally come across is from John Dewey, paraphrased like this: curricula are set up logically. Children learn *psychologically,* according to the varying individual patterns of their development. Teachers use responsive leadership to mediate between the fixed logical curriculum and the dynamic psychological child.

Skill 4: Accepting Unique Human Qualities in Others

Reconstructed anecdote. Back in the 1960s, our Ojibwe Head Start program at Red Lake was informal about guidelines like participation age and income eligibility. It was a community program, and besides Red Lake community members, it served a few of the young children of doctors and school officials who lived close by. James Druso was the 50-month-old son of the White school superintendent who lived at Red Lake with his family. James was in our room, one of maybe 18 in the group. The other kids didn't care that he was White or who his father was. James had lots of friends and clearly enjoyed Head Start.

Knowing that the families of some of our kids sang traditional songs at Red Lake dance gatherings (powwows), my teaching teammate Josie and I brought in two 5-gallon plastic buckets, supplied easel brushes for drumsticks, and played a cassette of songs by the Red Lake Singers. We had this powwow activity going outside on a regular basis and, when it got too cold on occasion, in the room.

James danced regularly with his mates and occasionally joined the few who were beating the drums. On a Wednesday after the kids had gone home, I got called to the Head Start director's office. Director Jody grew up in the nearby village of Redby and had worked herself up through the ranks. She was professional and on occasion, especially with the White male

teaching staff (me), formidable. She informed me that the superintendent wanted to meet with her and me that afternoon to discuss whether we were allowing powwows at Head Start. Jody said she had a meeting and sent me.

When I walked into Mr. Druso's office, I saw a picture on the wall of Native Americans attacking a stagecoach! (Remember, this was in the 1960s.) He informed me that the powwows were inappropriate. He asked me if other teachers were doing the same thing in their rooms. I said I didn't know, but they were in my room. Mr. Druso told me then, and the next morning told Jody, that if the powwows did not stop, he would pull his son, James, from the program—and that there might be other ramifications. After talking with me, Jody called Mr. Druso and told him that powwows were a part of Red Lake culture, and Dan would not stop. On Friday, James did not attend.

But something happened in the family over the weekend—perhaps Mrs. Druso and James outvoted Dad—and on Monday James returned. He kept close with his mates but told me he wouldn't dance "Indian" again, and didn't.

Reflection. An intolerance of differing human qualities in others is passed down in families as a part of childrearing and too often is reinforced by media, many schools, and other societal institutions. This is no big news, and neither is pressure from prestigious families to influence a program to make unwarranted changes—ask most directors. Two points of interest strike me in relation to this true story pertaining to DLS 4.

First, James returned to the program he really cared about. His mates probably missed him when "doing powwow," but they welcomed him back, and he was glad to be with us. At his tender age, James apparently had to make a difficult sacrifice in the arrangement that let him return. How this compromise affected him in the long term, I do not know. But one thing is for sure: when children attend inclusive programs, a family member's racism will not be the only influence on a growing child.

Second, the TT and director stood together to remain inclusive, welcoming, and culturally relevant. A school superintendent is a powerful person in the community, but the Head Start program did what was right to support the unique cultural heritage of the community. Within a few years, Mr.Druso and his family moved on, but Head Start continued, and the school district eventually got superintendents who were more attuned to the culture of the families served by the schools. Some years later, the Red Lake High School Pow-Wow Club was invited to the White House!

Skill 5: Thinking Intelligently and Ethically

Teacher Beth Wallace shares this account:

> Jeremiah was almost 3 when I started teaching at the center. He was one of those very physical kids, whose feelings and thoughts always moved through his body first. He'd had a turbulent life and when I came to the center, he was living mostly with his mom, and some with his dad. They were separated, and neither made very much money. Jeremiah was curious about and interested in everything. He loved stories and connected with others with his whole heart. He knew much about the natural world and was observant and gentle with animals, insects, and plants.
>
> When I first started working with Jeremiah, he had a lot of angry outbursts. The center used time-out at that point (the dreaded "green chair") and Jeremiah spent considerable time there. While I was at the center, we moved away from using time-outs. Instead, we introduced a system called "peer problem solving." By the time Jeremiah graduated to kindergarten, we had been using the system for three years, and he was one of the experts.
>
> One day, I overheard a fracas in the block corner. I stood up to see what was going on, ready to intervene. The youngest child in the room, who was just 2 and talking only a little bit, and one of the 4-year-olds were in a dispute over a truck. I took a step forward, ready to go to their aid, and then I saw Jeremiah approach them.
>
> "What's going on?" he asked (my standard opening line). He proceeded to facilitate a discussion between the two children that lasted for five minutes. He made sure both kids got a chance to speak; he interpreted for the little one. "Jordan, what do you think of that idea?" he asked. Jordan shook his head and clutched the truck tighter. "I don't think Jordan's ready to give up the truck yet," he told the 4-year-old.
>
> It was amazing. Jeremiah helped the kids negotiate an agreement, and then he walked away with a cocky tilt to his head I'd never seen before. His competence was without question; his pride was evident. (Gartrell 2000, 131–32).

Reflection. Early childhood educators model and teach for intelligent and ethical decision making every time they interact with others in the encouraging community. Beth did so by not judging Jeremiah and by teaching him to resolve conflicts peaceably within the context of the group's peer mediation program that the teacher had started.

Showing DLS 5 is difficult for all of us and especially for young children who are still only months old in their **personal development.** While we shouldn't try to "boost" young children into consistent intelligent and ethical decision making, we can guide them in this direction. As they gain DLS 3 and 4, children become more able to show DLS 5. In teaching for the DLS, TTs empower the very young to build brain structures and reaction tendencies that make intelligent and ethical decisions possible. Teachers facilitate progress in this direction whenever they view as positive children's efforts to be prosocial and offer them encouragement.

Working Cooperatively with Families

The reality is that a child's basic needs are met primarily via the child's family members. Teachers only help. But, by building secure relationships with children *and* family members, and by using the encouraging communication skills of guidance leadership with both, teachers can be a big help.

In the learning community, guidance leadership assists children by modeling and teaching for the five skills. In building family-teacher connections, as parents learn that the relationship with teachers is authentic and can be trusted, they become open to and feel supported in actively helping children meet their needs (Mancilla & Blanco 2022) and gain the DLS.

In the early and mid-twentieth century, Maria Montessori ([1912] 1964) and James Hymes ([1953] 1974) contributed greatly to the early childhood library by writing about the importance of building positive family-teacher relations. They were among the first to recognize and write about this essentiality in early childhood education. In these times of diverse family life, the fourth edition of *Developmentally Appropriate Practice in Early Childhood Programs Serving Children from Birth Through Age 8* (NAEYC 2022) lists in its index sixteen references to family-teacher relationships, most multipage references. Building the relationships is that important.

So, with the added component of working with families, I say that being an early childhood teacher in a center setting is the second most difficult job in the world. (The first is a three-way tie between being a Head Start home visitor, a family child care provider, and a middle school substitute teacher!) Because they can do so much while children are young, early childhood teachers arguably are the most important teachers in the child's life. Chapters 4–8 have sections on building partnerships with families.

John Dewey, Progressive Education, and Early Childhood Education

One of the iconic cultural philosophers of the twentieth century, John Dewey advocated for *democracy* more in the social sense than the political (Baker 1966). As he saw the matter, democracy empowers the furthering of individual experiences in ways that are productive both for the individual and for groups (Dewey [1916] 1966). Only in a democracy is full and meaningful *experiencing*—which we can think of as *the willingness and capacity to experience*—the rightful currency of life for both children and adults.

For Dewey, classrooms—including at the prekindergarten level—were to be busy, cooperative workshops, with teachers acting as guides in children's efforts to further their development through engagement and learning (Dewey [1897] 1990). Dewey saw unknowable human potential within the intrinsic dynamic in children that needs support and teaching—the key tasks of education

professionals. With an education *for* democracy, individuals and groups could indeed sustain that democracy and, in turn, support that education.

Critics accused Dewey, in his later years, of being a socialist (Westbrook 1995). Beginning in the early 1930s, Dewey, before most others, was vocal in assailing Germany, Japan, and later the Soviet Union for their authoritarian and oppressive—anti-democratic—governments. Authoritarianism of any kind was antithetical to the principles of democracy, and education for democracy, which Dewey stood for.

Dewey believed that more of the diverse groupings of modern society should be democratic (Westbrook 1995). He argued that the institutions and entities of business, government, medicine, religion, and education must have strong leaders, but those leaders should interact with and invite the participation of others—and decidedly refrain from dictatorial behaviors in rigidly vertical structures of operations. For Dewey, social structures enlightened in this way further the well-being of the institution, the whole of democratic society, and its education of the young.

In short, the philosopher abhorred dictators and state-instigated authoritarian "committees" associated with both fascist and communist governments. Dewey was a "small d" democrat in a universal sense, a cultural philosopher for his generation, ours, and those to come.

The Evolution of Progressive Education

In Dewey's time, the term *progressive education* had a different meaning than it does today. **Progressive education** then was considered child centered, which meant that teachers sat back and allowed children to "educate" themselves via their own experiences (Dewey [1938] 1997). Dewey rejected child-centered education, just as he did rigid traditional schooling, and so objected when people wrongly accused his *new education* of so being. Maria Montessori and Friedrich Froebel likewise argued that their programs were not child centered—without adult guidance. Montessori referred to teachers as "directresses" [1912] 1964). All three saw their systems as *teacher centered*, with teachers mediating between the logical curriculum and psychological child.

Today we use the term *progressive education* in a way more congruent with Dewey's approach. In this book, progressive education prepares children, in all domains of development, for civil, productive life in a modern democracy. As it illuminates an essential link to the DLS, let's get a firsthand view of key principles of contemporary progressive education. The Progressive Education Network (PEN) is a multistate affiliation of educators that reaches back over 100 years and projects ahead the education process we need to further our country's democratic ideals. The sidebar on page 16 contains a 2022 posting of PEN's vision statement and education principles. The excerpt makes clear that teaching for the DLS fits perfectly within the vision and mission of schools, pre-K–college, that practice progressive education.

Like earlier educational pillars John Comenius, Friedrich Froebel, and Maria Montessori, Dewey believed in expanding the accessibility of education beyond the traditional notion of who should be a scholar—White male children of affluent families (Gartrell 2012). These educators advocated opening schools to both boys and girls from all walks of life. A half century before the Brown Supreme Court decision making school segregation illegal in 1954, Dewey advocated for education that was racially integrated. In fact, John Dewey was a founding member of the NAACP.

Quality Early Childhood Education: A Platform for Progressive Education

In fall 2021, just before I began work on this book, I gave a virtual presentation on the DLS to the Minnesota Retired Principals' Association. The feedback was unanimous that knowledge of the five skills is vital at all levels of education—especially for prospective teachers—and not just in early childhood. I agree, but early childhood education is where I have given my professional attention for over 50 years.

Besides, early childhood education programs provide the largest platform for progressive education in the country. Nationally, the progressive nature of the field is largely due to Head Start and NAEYC—especially the latter's accreditation efforts and position statements, such as on **developmentally appropriate practice (DAP)**. At a state level, credit for the progressive nature of the field goes to early childhood chapters and associations, to dedicated early childhood professionals, and to early childhood teacher educators—a special group of academics, college trainers, instructors, and professors.

Endnote: Smiling While Teaching for the Skills

> In a church preschool, a student teacher's activity did not go as planned. The teacher kindly asked, "Anything I can do to help?" Overhearing, one of the children suggested, "We could pray!" The student teacher and teacher both smiled.

> When anything goes exactly as you expect in early childhood education, something's wrong.

Notice that the subtitle of the book is *Teaching Young Children* to Gain *Five Democratic Life Skills,* not *Teaching the Five Democratic Life Skills*. Adults prepare an encouraging environment; learn as much as they can about the children; and support, nudge, guide, and cooperate with each small but dynamic being. To the extent that each child can at any minute of any day, it is up to them take it from there. In everyday words, *you do as much as you need to do, but only as much, to motivate the child to do the rest*.

How this leadership happens differs from child to child and with the same child from day to day—the young are that unique and dynamic. Perhaps a key lesson from the DLS for early childhood educators is this: to respond to both motivations of human behavior—for security and psychologically growing—teachers should support but also nudge. Taking cues from the child, the teacher makes the call on the balance in every interaction every day. Being mentally nimble is an important attribute to cultivate. Bet there is a high correlation between being flexible and being able to smile or laugh at unexpected situations.

On the sidewalk in the play yard, for example, one 30-month-old is hesitant to get on a small trike; another 30-month-old is wheeling around on a mini two-wheel bike. Seems like an important thing to do is smile at the wonders of your job. Then figure out who needs support, who needs nudging, and who needs to be left on their own for the moment.

Vision Statement of the Progressive Education Network

PEN believes that the purpose of education transcends preparation for college or career. Schools nurture citizens in an increasingly diverse democracy. Within the complexities of education theory, practice, policy, and politics, we promote a vision of progressive education for the 21st century that

> Engages students as active participants in their learning and in society

> Supports teachers' voice as experienced practitioners and growth as lifelong learners

> Builds solidarity between progressive educators in the public and private sectors

> Advances critical dialogue on the roles of schools in a democratic society

> Responds to contemporary issues from a progressive educational perspective

> Welcomes families and communities as partners in children's learning

> Promotes diversity, equity, and justice in our schools and society

> Encourages progressive educators to play an active role in guiding the educational vision of our society

Educational Principles

Education must

> Amplify students' voice, agency, conscience, and intellect to create a more equitable, just, and sustainable world

> Encourage the active participation of students in their learning, in their communities, and in the world

> Respond to the developmental needs of students, and focus on their social, emotional, intellectual, cognitive, cultural, and physical development

> Honor and nurture students' natural curiosity and innate desire to learn, fostering internal motivation and the discovery of passion and purpose

> Emerge from the interests, experiences, goals, and needs of diverse constituents, fostering empathy, communication, and collaboration across difference

> Foster respectfully collaborative and critical relationships between students, educators, parents/guardians, and the community

"Our Mission," PEN (Progressive Education Network), n.d. https:// progressiveeducationnetwork.org/mission.

DISCUSSION QUESTIONS

1. Identify three key concepts (listed below and in the glossary). If you are a visual learner, write each out with its definition from the glossary. Then, referring to the section of the chapter where the key concept originated, reflect on what the concept means to you now that you have read the chapter.

2. Various anecdotes in the chapter illustrate TT members working with children to gain the DLS. Identify one anecdote (and the author reflection) that has meaning for you. Reflect on how the anecdote enhanced and/or changed your possible response to a similar situation.

3. How are Maslow's intrinsic motivational sources for behavior evident in the five DLS?

4. How have you personally experienced the educational principles of the Progressive Education Network, professionally or in your own education? After reading the chapter, reflect on the meaning of those experienced principles for you as a developing professional.

5. After reading Chapter 1, reflect on how your thinking has developed or changed regarding teaching for the DLS.

6. The book is about education for democracy. Identify a new or newly reinforced idea for you from the chapter. Discuss how that idea contributes to your own approach toward teaching for democracy.

7. How have the thoughts and ideas shared in this chapter impacted your thinking about being a professional working with young children?

Key Concepts

conflict

contact talks

Democratic Life Skills (DLS)

developmentally appropriate practice (DAP)

encouraging early learning community

growing-needs skills

guidance

mistaken behavior

personal development

progressive education

resilience

safety-needs skills

toxic stress

CHAPTER 2

Teaching for Healthy Brain Development

Motivation, Guidance, and Developmentally Appropriate Practice for All

SUGGESTED GOALS FOR READERS

1. Recognize reasons for differing brain function and development patterns in response to the two sources of motivation.

2. Understand how using guidance rather than conventional discipline accommodates healthy brain functioning and leads to children gaining the DLS.

3. Explain why, when programs are developmentally appropriate for all, they become encouraging early learning communities.

4. Describe how encouraging early learning communities provide the joyful environment needed for children to function as civil adults.

In Chapter 1 we saw that the DLS emerged from the dual motivations for safety and growth conceptualized by Abraham Maslow. We also explored the interface of the DLS and progressive education. Building on this foundation, Chapter 2

> Explores brain development from the context of environments adverse and conducive to children gaining the DLS

> Examines how guidance, empowered by DAP, is the community management system needed for children to gain and use the DLS

> Explains how a program that is developmentally appropriate for all constitutes an encouraging early learning community

> Shows how communities conducive to learning the skills contribute to a civil society

To maintain the deep but scholarly decorum of Chapter 2, I suggest that readers don their mortarboards and robes, if you can locate them.

In the 1960s, Maslow was joined by Erik Erikson in theorizing that dualistic psychological forces are ever-present in individuals' lives. In his construct of eight stages of psychosocial development, infancy through the senior years, Erikson posed a separate psychosocial challenge that individuals face at each stage. An individual's mental health, he wrote, derives from how well they manage the life challenge at each stage. During the four stages Erikson assigned to childhood, children need the support and guidance of significant adults to meet the life challenges they face. For instance, in infancy, the very first life challenge is basic trust versus mistrust. Success in the life stages of adulthood depends largely on how the young are able to handle the challenges of childhood with the help of significant others (Erikson [1963] 1993).

The genius of this dual-motivation theory from the twentieth century is that it has been supported by twenty-first-century neuroscience (Benarroch 2020; Masten & Barnes 2018). Maslow and Erikson were more than 50 years ahead of their time in recognizing that there are separate and often conflicting motivational dynamics operating within everyone. How can seemingly contradictory forces coexist in mental functioning? The answer is that it involves the *brain,* the most complex of organic entities, the bestower of consciousness and conscience in our daily lives.

Neuroscience is still in the early stages of learning how the brain works, let alone being able to address the "unanswerable" question of why. But we have learned a lot about motivation and brain functioning that explains behavior in relation to the two basic needs for safety and growth.

On the surface, a reader might think that the dual forces in the brain are for "good" and "evil." maslow's gift is the understanding that the one dynamic is a need for psychological security and the other is a need for psychologically growing. The latter is dependent on the attainment of safety and security, and on the mental health that this *homeostatic* (harmony-tending) mental state affords.

Survival and the Stress Response

Basic-needs theory holds that the drive for safety is strong, especially in children. Since Maslow's and Erikson's time, the neuroscience now provides a reason; it has to do with the amygdala and hypothalamus, structures in the limbic system of the brain (Benarroch 2020).

Survival is the paramount need of the young. Already functioning at birth, the amygdala is extremely sensitive to danger in the young child's world. When the amygdala system senses threat, the system instantaneously conveys the danger to the hypothalamus (Harvard Medical School 2020). With similar blazing speed, the hypothalamus sets in motion the combination of physiological and physical reactions necessary to help the individual survive.

Here's more on the survival-related **stress response** and the potentially harmful side effects the response can have on individuals:

This combination of reactions to stress is also known as the "fight-or-flight" response because it evolved as a survival mechanism, enabling people and other mammals to react quickly to life-threatening situations. . . . Unfortunately, the body can also overreact to stressors that are not life-threatening, such as traffic jams, work pressure, and family difficulties.

Over the years, researchers have learned not only how and why these reactions occur, but have also gained insight into the long-term effects chronic stress has on physical and psychological health. . . . Research suggests that chronic stress contributes to high blood pressure, promotes the formation of artery-clogging deposits, and causes brain changes that may contribute to anxiety, depression, and addiction. (Harvard Medical School 2020)

In the book, the term *stress response* identifies the physiological fight-freeze-flee survival reactions by a child to a perceived threat. As mentioned, the **amygdala- and hypothalamus-driven stress response** is already functioning at birth. So, a baby's crying at any time of day or night is an act of "innocent aggression." In its way, the cry in infancy is an amazingly cogent assertion of will (the fighting response): "I am hungry, and I need the appropriate attention so I can be fed. Please do so with haste! I am in discomfort here!" All this in a nonverbal sound!

As the Harvard piece suggests, because they are months old, young children are particularly sensitive to perceiving situations as threatening. Some years ago, a 47-month-old in northern Minnesota became distraught when the family drove past a local golf course. The reason (which the family figured out and responded to) was that the child was hearing "gulf coast" instead of "golf course." At the time, a war was raging over Kuwait on the Gulf of Bahrain, and the child's brother was a soldier there.

Young children, especially, sometimes react to perceived threats that aren't existential. If for the child the threat is real, then we should treat it that way, realizing that the child is having an *adverse experience* and is at risk for unmanageable stress and mistaken survival behavior.

All too often, a child's perceived **adverse experience** is indeed real. Jamie, a 50-month-old, comes into his learning setting and swipes a pitcher of juice onto the floor. Just as that hungry bawling infant was not "bad," neither is the preschooler. Arriving at the program, Jamie is in no way able to articulate his experience of his mother and father fighting the night before. The child acts out due to unmanageable stress and the consequent flow of stress hormones. Jamie is showing stress-induced **reactive aggression** and might be experiencing childhood trauma.

Outside of the early childhood setting, **survival behaviors** sometimes are necessary and might serve the intended purpose. Within the setting, though, such behaviors—especially aggression—might cause a child to be disciplined, making matters worse. Jamie showed challenging behavior because he was challenged. The aggressive acting out here is *mistaken survival behavior.* Again, harking back to Chapter 1, when we view conflicts including aggression as mistaken behaviors, and not as misbehaviors, we understand children in relation to the DLS. The concept of mistaken behavior is discussed in Chapter 4 and applied in Chapters 5–8.

Adverse Experiences, Childhood Trauma, and PTSD

The Center for Child Trauma Assessment, Services and Interventions (CCTASI) at Northwestern University provides this definition of *child trauma:*

> **"Child trauma"** refers to a scary, dangerous, violent, or life threatening event that happens to a child (0–18 years of age). . . . When these types of experiences happen, your child may become very overwhelmed, upset, and/or feel helpless. . . .
>
> An event can be traumatic when we face or witness an immediate threat to ourselves or to a loved one, and it is often followed by serious injury or harm. . . . When this happens, it can cause emotions such as fear, loss, or distress. Sometimes people experience these types of strong negative emotions in reaction to the experience or because the person may not have the ability to protect or stop the event from happening. Reactions to a traumatic event can also have lasting effects on the individual's daily functioning including possible changes in a child's mental, physical, social, emotional, and/or spiritual health. (CCTASI, n.d.)

Not all childhood adverse experiences reach the level of trauma. In a similar sense, what is an adverse experience for one child may not be for another. Children interpret their experiences differently (CCTASI, n.d.). Children who experience adverse experiences might or might not show a degree of *post-traumatic stress* in the classroom. Almost by definition, children who experience trauma do, and sometimes the full **post-traumatic stress disorder** (PTSD) syndrome may develop (CCTASI, n.d.).

From the Stanford Medicine Children's Health comes an article about PTSD in children. The following excerpt adds to our discussion:

> Posttraumatic stress disorder (PTSD) . . . can affect people of all ages including children. . . . The symptoms of PTSD may start soon after a stressful event. Or they may not happen for 6 months or longer. Some children with PTSD have long-term effects. They may feel emotionally numb for a very long time. PTSD in children often becomes a long-term (chronic) problem.
>
> What are the symptoms of PTSD in a child?
>
> ❯ Have problems sleeping
>
> ❯ Feel depressed or grouchy
>
> ❯ Feel nervous, jittery, or alert and watchful (on guard)
>
> ❯ Lose interest in things they used to enjoy. They may seem detached or numb and are not responsive.
>
> ❯ Have trouble feeling affectionate
>
> ❯ Be more aggressive than before, even violent
>
> ❯ Stay away from certain places or situations that bring back memories
>
> ❯ Have flashbacks. These can be images, sounds, smells, or feelings. The child may believe the event is happening again.
>
> ❯ Lose touch with reality
>
> ❯ Reenact an event for seconds or hours or, in rare cases, days
>
> ❯ Have problems in school
>
> ❯ Have trouble focusing
>
> ❯ Worry about dying at a young age
>
> ❯ Act younger than their age, such as thumb-sucking or bedwetting
>
> ❯ Have physical symptoms, such as headaches or stomachaches (Stanford Medicine Children's Health, n.d.)

If TTs observe signs of adverse experience, trauma, and/or PTSD in a child, they should recognize that the child is struggling with DLS 1. They conference among themselves and with program administrators and/or professional support staff. Recognizing the benchmark that the family seems to be at (see Chapter 4), the TT and program staff meet with the family. They initiate an individual guidance plan (IGP) and use **comprehensive guidance** with the child. (See further Chapters 4 and 5.) Working with the family to build a trust relationship, they recommend a mental health or other assessment for the child. If the family declines, the staff continue work to build relations with them. Especially if the child does not respond over time, in my view the staff are right to insist on the family's cooperation in seeking further help as a condition of the child remaining in the program. Throughout, staff rely on the Code of Ethical Conduct and Statement of Commitment (NAEYC 2011) as they work with both the child and the family.

Stress-Conflict-Punishment Syndrome

When the impact of adverse experiences becomes chronic, young children are at risk for falling into a state of hyper-amygdalae functioning (Dye 2018). Unless caring adults nudge these children toward resilience via secure relationships, guidance, solid family-teacher connections, and an encouraging early learning community, children may develop a long-term, harmful syndrome that entails

❯ Sensing threat

❯ Feeling high stress

❯ Reacting with survival behaviors (often aggression)

❯ Being disciplined (punished) for causing the conflict

❯ Experiencing continued unmanageable stress

Works by several researchers (e.g., Dye 2018; Gunnar, Herrera, & Hostinar 2009; Lupien et al. 2018; Shonkoff et al. 2012; Shonkoff & Phillips 2000) provide insight into the long-term harmful impact of an *unmanageable stress-conflict-punishment-unmanageable stress syndrome,* which Shonkoff termed *toxic stress response.* In this book the toxic stress response and the unmanageable stress-conflict-punishment-unmanageable stress syndrome refer to the same phenomenon. The latter term is shortened to **stress-conflict-punishment syndrome.**

One subtle but horrific effect of the stress-conflict-punishment syndrome is that these children are more likely to suffer from a deficit in foundational cognitive gains, due to the all-consuming attention their brains give to survival (Dye 2018; Lupien et al. 2018; Shonkoff et al. 2012). Yet, while knocked off course, the child is still thinking and learning. Through repeated experiences of the stress-conflict-punishment sequence, children channel their developing thought into survival. Frequently, the child learns strategies to manipulate and control conflicts (and perhaps escape detection) as ways to temper the stress of adverse experiences—what we call **instrumental aggression.** Caroline, in an anecdote in Chapter 1, showed similar instrumental aggression to Audy, here:

> In a private preschool program, Audy (62 months) began showing a pattern of dominating situations and objecting loudly when teachers intervened. Audy really liked outdoor play and many days would rebel when it was time to go in. Because of the child's objections and physical evasion at the end of outdoor play, the adults first threatened to keep Audy in, and then did. The child was furious.
>
> When Audy was allowed back on the playground, a coach who was observing staff-child dynamics recorded this note: "When it was time to go in, Audy got three children to hide behind the outdoor playhouse. Teacher Louise saw them and went around the front of the playhouse to round them up. Audy snuck around the back of the structure and got in line. As Louise brought the other children, she praised Audy for getting in line on their own. The look on Audy's face was almost scary."
>
> Following this incident, and a serious meeting with the coach, the TT took a different approach with Audy. Although Louise had to contend with negative thoughts about the child, she and coteacher Betty began spending individual time each day with Audy *outside of conflict situations.* They got to know Audy, including their likes, such as the kinds of active play they engaged in outdoors. Audy learned about Betty's baby and Louise's pet dog. Louise and Betty appealed to Audy's "seniority" by asking Audy to help with tasks around the center. They also coached Audy on techniques for getting along. Gradually, Audy grew in trust toward Louise and Betty. The child came to rely less on instrumental aggression and the need to manipulate others, and showed the beginnings of prosocial childhood leadership (as Caroline did in the earlier anecdote).

The developmental research (cited above) indicates that as they develop, children caught up in a long-term stress-conflict-punishment syndrome become at higher risk for

› Ill health

› Addiction

› Discriminatory in-group/out-group behaviors

› Abuse and neglect in relationships

› Hostility toward those in positions of power

› Callousness when in positions of power

› Crime and prison

› Self-harm and suicide

A child only months old should not be condemned to such a life. Supporting young children who struggle with Skills 1 and 2, therefore, is critical (Masten & Barnes 2018). Teachers need to be positively persistent in building secure relationships and using affirming communication practices with these children and their families (Wright 2022).

Resilience in young children is the result of psychosocial buffers that protect the child from the effects of adverse experiences (Lupien et al. 2018). In early childhood education, secure relationships between a teacher and the child are at the heart of the effort to support and nudge (Masten & Barnes 2018). The next section discusses the main objective of the buffering process—to empower young children to gain the safety-needs skills so that they can shift focus and work on the growing-needs skills. For reasons that will be more clear later in the chapter, I call this guiding process in the encouraging early learning community *liberation teaching.*

Psychological Growing: Executive Function

The psychological dynamic counter to the stress response is **executive function.** To cite NAEYC's (2022) definition, executive function is

> The network of abilities that allow children to manage their thoughts, emotions, and behavior as they pursue their goals. These include attention, working memory, self-regulation, reasoning, problem solving, and approaches to learning. (318)

Beginning to form in early infancy and growing dramatically from ages 3 to 5, executive function develops in the frontal cortex of the brain. The Center on the Developing Child at Harvard University provides useful context for our look at executive function. The online piece also directs readers to other related pieces. Here is an excerpt:

> As essential as they are, we aren't born with the skills that enable us to control impulses, make plans, and stay focused. We are born with the potential to develop these capacities—or not—depending on our experiences during infancy, throughout childhood, and into adolescence. Our genes provide the blueprint, but the early environments in which children live leave a lasting signature on those genes.
>
> This signature influences how or whether that genetic potential is expressed in the brain circuits that underlie the executive function capacities children will rely on throughout their lives. These skills develop through practice and are strengthened by the experiences through which they are applied and honed. Providing the support that children need to build these skills at home, in child care and preschool programs, and in other settings they experience regularly is one of society's most important responsibilities.
>
> Being able to focus, hold, and work with information in mind, filter distractions, and switch gears is like having an air traffic control system at a busy airport to manage the arrivals and departures of dozens of planes on multiple runways. In the brain, this air traffic control mechanism is called executive function. (Harvard University, n.d.)

Notably, executive function does not operate with maturity until individuals are in their 20s (Benarroch 2020; Harvard University, n.d.). This point of maturation accounts for the relatively sound judgment we attribute to young adults as opposed to teenagers. Samuel Clemens is said to have remarked on the adolescent to adulthood transition more or less this way: "When I was a teen, I thought my parents knew nothing. When I was a young adult, I was amazed at how much they'd learned in just a few years!" On a serious note, this is why teenagers should not buy or own guns—along with alcohol and cigarettes—until they are 21.

A useful way to look at executive function is that it happens well when children are supported in building the skills that underlie it and can keep unhealthy stress in check. In these settings, to a high degree, *healthy* stress is manifest in intrigue, engagement, discovery, and earned gratification. The mechanism propelling children to active pursuit of their growing-needs skills is **mastery motivation**—the universal, intrinsic need to grow through ongoing learning experiences.

Over time, developmental psychologists have distinguished between "good stress" necessary for learning and "bad stress," the unmanageable psychological reaction to trauma and threat. Every child experiences stress differently (Dye 2018). So, I tend to write about *unmanageable* or *high stress* to indicate various levels of the unhealthy kind, and *intrigue* as the healthy stress that enables learners to engage positively with new experiences. Intrigue is the healthy reaction to cognitive dissonance, the engaging perception that something is missing and can be fixed, improved, or built upon.

Illustration. To a young child often teased or chastised for "scribbling," a blank piece of paper and washable markers might cause high stress. To a child who has every picture on a refrigerator and most on a school bulletin board, a blank piece of paper and washable markers are likely intriguing—an opportunity to engage mastery motivation in the resolution of cognitive dissonance and to use and develop executive function.

There is an anecdotal way to determine whether healthy executive function is a widespread dynamic in learning settings. Children take it upon themselves to initiate learning activities, often exceed teachers' expectations in creations, and want to communicate about their experiences. Children's busy, creative juices are flowing because teachers have built secure relationships and created encouraging early learning communities for all in the group. Fully engaged in developmentally appropriate activities, children's attention spans often exceed adults'! (How many times have you had to read *See the Cat: Three Stories About a Dog* or *Goodnight Moon?*)

In contrast to intrinsic mastery motivation, fragile but universal in children, there is **extrinsic motivation.** For centuries, adults have used extrinsic rewards and punishments to elicit set, desired learning behaviors from children. Though now more nuanced, practices of extrinsic motivation are ubiquitous in schooling today. The more distant learning experiences are from developmentally appropriate practice, the more adults must rely on extrinsic motivation. In settings where adults heavily rely on extrinsic motivation, mastery motivation might survive, but it cannot flourish. For many children, the use of reward and punishment systems to instill knowledge and skills not developmentally appropriate for them often leads to high "bad" stress and burnout.

Naturally, conflicts over materials, between children working together, and between children and teachers are a part of the encouraging early learning community. But resolving these conflicts cooperatively is a defining feature of healthy executive function. If not overly stressed, children as well as TTs work to resolve disputes quickly; they have better things to do. As leaders, teachers proactively mediate between the logical curriculum and each psychological child to kindle mastery motivation and foster executive function. Note that forming encouraging early childhood learning communities begins within the minds of teachers—and building the emotional-social foundations for these communities is the focus of chapters to come.

The following illustration of emergent curriculum in a kindergarten offers a peek of a TT using developmental guidance to promote the manifestation of intrigue, mastery motivation, and practice with executive function:

Roddie, 66 months, found a dead robin and brought it to kindergarten in his pocket. He showed the bird around. It had been dead for a while and looked it. The TT had to think quickly about what to do. The unit on living and dead things was not scheduled for another month, but this was a teachable moment. Lead teacher Ms. Emmy found the most decorative small box she could. She sat down with Roddie to explain that when things die, the community cares for the dead. Roddie agreed that they should put the robin in the box.

Assistant teacher Ms. Marla found a tattered copy of Margaret Wise Brown's *The Dead Bird* in a closet. Relieved, Ms. Marla read the book to the children during group time. But to set the scene, Roddie told about the robin and how he thought he saw it pulling worms from the garden where they were supposed to be helping the soil. So, he was calling the robin "Robber." The box sat prominently near the group.

Encouraged by the TT, many in the class made **story pictures** about Roddie and Robber—and about family members and pets who had died. (The paper for story pictures was blank on the top with lines on the bottom. The children did combinations of open-ended art and developmental writing that told their stories.) At recess, most in the class went with Roddie and the TT to the edge of the playground where they buried Robber. After school, the TT made a book of the story pictures for the reading center and planned how to skip to the living and dead things unit the next day.

Reflection. Roddie was a child who often blended in and did not have many friends in the class. Ms. Emmy said she had never heard Roddie say so much at one time—and in front of the group! The TT also appreciated how many children shared their own experiences about death through their story pictures. With more than one child, the TT sat in the reading area and talked with them about their individual tributes and recollections in the story picture book. The bird—which was definitely "bug ready"—could have been summarily dispatched by the TT, whatever the effect on Roddie. Instead, the TT mediated between the curriculum and their totally engaged kindergarten class.

Beyond Discipline to Guidance

At this point, the status of early childhood professionals as the most important teachers in a child's life should be known as my position. The question turns to how educators teach effectively for children to gain the Democratic Life Skills. How do they teach well enough to empower children's resilience and healthy personal development? We respond to these questions in the discussion of developmental and intervention guidance, to follow. But first, let's look at the need to move beyond **conventional discipline**, still used in way too many K–12 classrooms and prekindergarten settings.

Discarding Conventional Discipline

Conventional discipline too easily slides into punishment. To discipline a child is to punish. From the neuroscience, we long have known that punishment heightens, not diminishes, unmanageable stress. For some children, early childhood programs begin a pattern of institution-caused adverse experiences, which directly contributes to the stress-conflict-punishment syndrome.

A most common punishment in conventional discipline is *embarrassment*. Embarrassment is used "to shame children into being good" and to make an example of a child so that other children feel compelled to stay in line (Gartrell 2020). Common measures of punitive embarrassment include calling out certain children, usually in front of others, and placing them on time-out chairs (which is temporary expulsion). From kindergarten on, some teachers write children's names on boards (a pretty lousy way for classmates to learn your name), remove children from the group, or give them detention. (Removal from the group at any level is temporary expulsion—not something we want children to get used to!)

Lacking sufficient mindfulness, the adult who relies on conventional discipline causes children to internalize social rejection and negative self-messages. The educator is making the task of learning foundational emotional-social skills (DLS 1 and 2) more difficult. Out of a need for psychological safety, children who have these teachers must push mastery motivation into the shadows and fend for themselves in terms of executive function. Whether children are victims of, or witnesses to, acts of conventional discipline, the joy of learning is suppressed for them.

Schooling for Some Is an Adverse Experience

For the many children who fit in and meet the expectations of early learning programs, decades of research show that early childhood education provides ample lasting benefits (Bustamante et al. 2021; Feldman 2018). But since the beginnings of American education, students who did not adapt to the top-down, basically authoritarian structure of public schooling have been pushed out the door. In previous times, the large population of young people without a high school diploma could find jobs with livable wages; today, not so much—a grave social problem.

Conventional discipline long has been the tool of schooling to make students walk the line or move out of the system. A report of the Crime and Justice Research Alliance (2019) documents the situation. In more than 15 states, corporal punishment is still legal. In 2013–14, about 2.6 million public school students (5.3 percent) received one or more out-of-school suspensions. Figures are not really kept on the number of incidents of in-school suspensions each year. Indications are that in 2020–23, COVID-19 disruptions have aggravated children's stress levels, contributing to a higher percentage of students acting out in classrooms than in 2013–14 (CDC 2022).

So, what do you think? Maybe children experience 12–15 million incidents each year of removal from the group either within the classroom or school—including detention—or as out-of-school suspension? What percentages of these students are of color or low income? "Punishment by exclusion," leading in too many cases to dropping out (psychologically if not physically), and expulsion (including in preschool) are indicators of the continuing repressive socialization undercurrents rocking education's unstable bow. To repeat a statement made earlier, temporary expulsion is not a phenomenon we should want children to get used to.

With relative certainty we can say that children who have a history of receiving conventional discipline through the elementary grades into high school

During the last century, Maria Montessori, Jean Piaget, and Lev Vygotsky wrote about what developing executive function looks like in young children. They didn't know the brain science term, of course, but they carefully described the developmental process of healthy executive function as they saw it.

Montessori saw progress in children's thinking as they moved through a sequence of materials and occupations in her "prepared environment" and her stages of learning. Directresses (teachers) guided children through the intentional use of the sequenced materials to give them the opportunity to develop self-discipline (Montessori [1949] 2007)—a key ingredient in executive functioning.

Piaget identified four stages across childhood, with children's thinking and learning developing through open-ended exploration in distinct ways depending on the stage they are in (Piaget & Inhelder 1969). Given that children's development progresses at different rates across different areas, it may be useful to think in terms of waves of development rather than stages (NAEYC 2022). But there is no denying that the thinking and world view of a 50-month-old is qualitatively different from that of a 100-month-old. My thinking is that every once in a while, there must be a "super wave" of development.

Vygotsky ([1935] 1978) constructed a concept of developing language as the trigger for learning and development. He described *scaffolding*, whereby more experienced others note a level of learning the child is at and guide so that the child progresses through a personal *zone of proximal development* to attain a new level of understanding.

These archetype psychologists recognized and accommodated general patterns in young children's progression of thought: from concrete to abstract; simple to complex; few to many; similar to different; and present to past, present, and future. Still, because of the charm young children show in their thinking, others overlooked then (and still overlook) the significance of early learning that children accomplish, including through play and even informal conversations.

> **Felicia (39 months):** Look at that big birdy.
>
> **Teacher Jon:** That crow is really flying fast. I wonder where the crow is going?
>
> **Felicia:** The crow is going to our house, of course, 'cause my dad says my mom got crow's feet. [Can't resist: And mom says dad's beard is a crow's nest!]
>
> **Teacher Jon:** That crow is really flying. (*Has difficulty hiding laugh; knows Miles and Samantha, Felicia's parents.*)
>
> Jon is glad he decided to teach early childhood rather than high school math.

Felicia's thinking shows the charming egocentrism of a 39-month-old that adds to why many of us, like Jon, are drawn to preschool education. Worth noting in the anecdote, though, is that via this one conversation Felicia likely progressed from class to species in her recognition of birds. (It probably will be a while before she grasps the cosmetic meaning of crow's feet!) Young children progress in their own ways through unique zones of proximal development, and not necessarily through a set zone that the adult might have anticipated. Again, curriculum is logical, and children are psychological. Good teaching is prosocial, friendly mediating between the two—different for every child and for any child on any given day.

have had their share of institution-caused adverse experiences. They likely have fallen into the stress-conflict-punishment syndrome. These young folks tend to externalize their cumulative negative self-messages to adults and institutions in the form of two conditions:

1. **Authority aversion:** A common effect in the young who are subject to the stress-conflict-punishment syndrome, who lose trust in significant adults and develop oppositional attitudes toward them and the institutions they represent.

2. **Establishment aversion:** Also a consequence of a child's falling into a long-term stress-conflict-punishment syndrome. An attitude toward society generalized beyond an aversion to schooling. A significant contributing factor is when educators did not or could not help children to alleviate unmanageable stress and mistaken survival behavior.

Preschool Push-Out

Though not necessarily with this term in mind, early childhood professionals have been using guidance rather than conventional discipline in their settings for over 200 years (Froebel [1826] 1887). Many current professionals in the field use guidance practices, but society still has a widespread problem in its preschool programs. For years, children have been expelled from preschools at much higher rates than from K–12 classrooms—boys more than girls and Black boys more than anyone (Meek & Gilliam 2016).

So, what pushes so many preschool children out the door? In my view, it is adults' habitual reliance on traditional programs and conventional discipline, what they grew up with and are used to. The blinders of conventional discipline used to maintain traditional programming, from my perspective, makes it difficult for these educators to know what else to do in the face of a child showing serious mistaken behaviors. Persistent biases against certain groups of children—such as Black boys—aggravate the practice of conventional discipline, too often leading to **preschool push-out**. Bias-influenced punishment and the eventual expulsion, even if temporary, of children whose behavior challenges their teachers have become ill-conceived, too-common solutions (Meek & Gilliam 2016).

Toward Guidance

Let's look at the present via the past though a seminal quote from my cultural guide John Dewey—to remind us about the sea change from discipline to guidance.

> If you have the end in view of forty or fifty children learning certain set lessons, to be recited to a teacher, your discipline must be devoted to securing that result. But if the end in view is the development of a spirit of social cooperation and community life, discipline must grow out of and be relative to this. . . . There is a certain disorder in any busy workshop; there is not silence; persons are not engaged in maintaining certain fixed physical postures; their arms are not folded; they are not holding their books thus and so. They are doing a variety of things, and there is the confusion, the bustle, that results from activity. But out of occupation, out of doing things that are to produce results, and out of doing these in a social and cooperative way, there is born a discipline of its own kind and type. Our whole conception of school discipline changes when we get this point of view. (Dewey [1900] 1969, 16–17)

Guidance has two functions. An everyday definition of guidance in relation to its most known, *intervention function,* is

> Teaching children to solve their problems rather than punishing them for having problems they cannot solve; teaching children to learn from their mistakes rather than punishing them for the mistakes they make.

A more encompassing definition that addresses the *developmental* as well as the intervention function of guidance is

> Managing the resources of the encouraging early learning community—including partnerships with parents—to teach for healthy personal development and social cooperation.

When TTs use both functions effectively, they are fully teaching for the five DLS.

Both developmental and intervention functions of guidance require dedication, hard work, and cooperation with others—hence the book's emphasis on TTs. Teachers start and sustain both functions through supportive relationships with every child and family in the encouraging early childhood learning community. The more difficult it is for teachers to understand or like a particular child or family, the harder they try. As teacher Louise illustrated by her initial negative thoughts about Audy, for TT members to use guidance well, they must learn even as they teach.

· ·

Contrary to a common myth, TT members do not have to love every member of the community. But, to use guidance well, they do need to build a secure relationship with every member, and believe in the other's worth and ability to learn.

· ·

In the guidance approach, young children are best thought of as months old and not as years old. A 2½-year-old has just 30 months of on-the-ground experience. A just-4-year-old has only 48 months. Even an 8-year-old has but 96 months, one-tenth of many lifespans today. Yet, we expect young children to quickly learn complex life skills that many adults haven't mastered. In learning difficult skills, young children, with only months of brain development and experience, make mistakes in their behavior. Children who are still working on DLS 1 and 2, especially, will show sometimes spectacular mistaken behaviors.

Using Guidance

There are several behavior/classroom management programs out there whose names include terms like *cooperative discipline, positive discipline,* and *democratic discipline.* So long as the adjectives mean that the punitive practices in conventional discipline have been discarded and replaced by humane teaching, I am fine with these programs. Still, for me the term *guidance* identifies the clean paradigm shift necessary for teachers to make—in their minds and actions—to replace discipline with friendly and firm but flexible teaching for healthy personal development.

Since the 1970s, I have been writing and speaking about the need for early childhood educators to use guidance. From 2005 to 2015, my column Guidance Matters appeared in issues of the NAEYC journal *Young Children.* I write about guidance as an educational approach rather than as a commercialized program. (The approach I write about is out there for anyone to use without financial burden.) Many of us early childhood professionals must work continuously to consistently use guidance in practice. Some teachers, consistently at DLS 5 themselves, have internalized the principles and use them organically, like Head Start teacher Terry (see the note below).

· ·

Terry, for decades a wonderful Head Start teacher and team leader in Blackduck, Minnesota, once told me it took three years of intentional practice for her guidance responses to become automatic. We began placing student teachers with Terry in her first years of being lead teacher. During those early years, apparently Terry was one of those smooth swimming ducks whose legs were paddling like crazy below the surface. But I never knew, even in Minnesota's mostly clear waters.

· ·

Instant mastery of guidance practices is not what the approach (or the book) is about. Moving toward guidance does require a big leap, but then "early childhood steps." The good news is that if well intended, guidance practices do not have to be done perfectly to make a positive difference. Remember, Terry mentioned that it took her three years for guidance responses to become automatic. In an earlier anecdote, despite her feelings about Audy's behavior, Louise figured out a way to relate to the child. Over my many years of early childhood teacher education, few students in practica used guidance practices perfectly, but almost all used them well enough for everyday success.

Principles and Practices of Guidance

Under its two functions, developmental and intervention, guidance is best considered as a set of principles that early childhood educators might aspire to, and a collection of practices that operationalize the principles.

Developmental Guidance Principles

Developmental guidance entails (1) managing learning communities that are encouraging, inclusive, and developmentally appropriate, and (2) interacting with all members in supportive, mutually beneficial ways.

Principle 1: Use democratic leadership to create an encouraging early childhood learning community for every member of the group. TTs practice DAP for all. They build positive group spirit with all community members, big and small. TTs incorporate joyful learning through play to nurture mastery motivation and maximize interactions with and among children. Small groups (ongoing formal and situational) give children active experience with relationships and cooperative learning.

Teachers use large group circle times selectively; often they are music and movement activities held to encourage participation by all. TTs also hold regular *large group meetings*—sometimes called class meetings or Morning Meetings—that function to provide experience with talking and listening publicly, resolve problems within the group, and build a sense of democratic ownership toward the encouraging early learning community. *Perhaps no other guidance practice models and teaches for the DLS as much as group meetings.* More on large group meetings is found in Chapter 4.

Principle 2: Emphasize emotional and social learning through a whole child/personal development perspective, within the context of developmentally appropriate practice.
TTs use developmentally appropriate curriculum models that provide for intentional planning and teaching in all developmental domains. Featured is emergent curriculum, incorporating the interests, experiences, and cultural practices (not stereotypes) of the children and families served. Questions and topics for investigation in emergent curriculum often originate with respectful group meetings. Emergent curriculum can also arise from mistaken behaviors shown by individuals and group of children. For example, a child leaves a group walk to follow an ant, which leads to learning more about ants through projects, books, story pictures, and songs. These are examples of the versatility of group meetings and emergent curriculum in fulfilling both developmental and intervention functions of guidance.

Quieter activities involving books, puzzles, hands-on materials, and group meetings are of course part of the early childhood curriculum. But to accommodate the active nature of young human mammals, the overall milieu of the program is one of activity, teaching and learning through body motion. TTs emphasize big body movement each day and provide an array of large and small motor activities during choice time. The intentional emphasis on physical development is, at least partially, to start children on the way toward—especially in these times—a not-so-sedentary, potentially healthier lifestyle.

> TTs can adapt even small rooms to enhance physical activity. One TT moved furniture in from the wall to make a walking track around it with duct tape. Another team set up a small fitness center in a corner of the room that included a mini-trampoline and a salvaged weight table. Kids lifted a weight bar that was a sawed-off broom handle and two half-gallon milk containers partially filled with wax. A third TT kept a four-sided climber in the room with a two-sided sign that said "Open for Climbing" and "Closed to Climbing." In all three settings, the TTs held large group meetings to agree on—and to reinforce—guidelines for the group's active play.

Principle 3: Foster mastery motivation and the expression and healthy development of executive function. TTs create programs, activities, and experiences that encourage ongoing mastery motivation and healthy executive functioning. They avoid preset products, including outlines of figures to be colored in, models illustrated on boxes to be followed, and teacher-made projects to be copied. Instead, teachers provide a plethora of materials that are open ended and can be used flexibly—like art materials and *blank* paper, blocks, playdough, and carpentry (engineering) benches. For materials such as puzzles that are self-correcting, teachers provide a variety of levels of complexity.

Teachers use culturally and linguistically appropriate **authentic assessment,** including samples of each child's efforts and creations (like story pictures) that they regularly collect as written and photo/video records, to note progress in children's learning. Cooperative family-teacher conferences using the progress assessments start early in the program and happen periodically.

Sample Story Pictures Over Time

Florida winter samples by Bernie:

At 35 months: a controlled blue, circular scribble of "My dad swimmin' in the bay"

At 55 months: two people in a kayak, with *m n frnt n r kyk* written on the lines; she comments to the teacher, "My dad's in back paddlin.'"

Minnesota winter samples by Ayesha:

At 35 months: broad white chalk scribbles on blue paper of a "big bizzard"

At 55 months: *Mm pln sn*, written below an elaborate red rig with plow, and Mom smiling from the driver's window

Principle 4: Practice mutually beneficial communication techniques with both children and adults. These eight techniques, or practices, are simple but profound:

> Smile and nod.

> Acknowledge and pause.

> Make contact talks happen.

> Use friendly humor.

> Use appropriate, friendly touch.

> Utilize compliment sandwiches.

> Give encouragement: privately to individuals, publicly to the group.

> Remember names, contact talks, and promises.

We discuss each practice in Chapter 4. Like group meetings and emergent curriculum, the communication practices can be used in both developmental and intervention guidance and with both children and adults. The following anecdote highlights two key practices: *acknowledge and pause* and *contact talks*.

Teacher Basma did not know Terrence, age 68 months, very well. She decided to have a contact talk with the kindergartner during choice time to get to know him better. She watched Terrence draw what looked like a dog, lying down with a red tongue hanging out of its mouth. Next to the dog was a person with big blue tears falling. Basma commented, "Your picture looks sad, Terrence." After a long pause, Terrence said, "My dog Rowlf died. He was old, and we took him to the vet. The vet put him to sleep. She gave me some of his fur in a baggie." Basma said, "I bet Rowlf's fur is special to you." Terrence replied, "Yeah. I keep it on my pillow." Basma put her arm around Terrence, who settled in and shed a few tears. The teacher had no idea how important the talk might have been for the child on this day, at that time.

Intervention Guidance Principles

The second function of guidance, **intervention guidance,** is the kind we often think about first—calming and teaching when there are conflicts. The following three principles (with related practices) apply particularly to the function of intervention guidance.

Principle 5: Use a general guidance plan for social problem solving in the community. The plan I advocate is the five finger formula.

> Thumb: Calm everyone down—yourself, too. Set the scene for the mediation.

> Pointer: Guide the children to accept how each person sees the conflict. (Individual perspectives might not be what others thought happened. Understanding this is key to conflict resolution.)

> Tall guy: Brainstorm possible solutions. (Provide suggestions for children who are dual language learners or who have limited oral language. Respect nonverbal signs of agreement or disagreement.)

> Ringer: Agree to one solution and try it. (The solution may not be what you had in mind, but if it makes sense and all are okay with it, go with this solution.) Sometimes steps 3 and 4 naturally merge.

> Pinky: Monitor the solution and positively acknowledge cooperative efforts and acts of reconciliation. Hold guidance talks with individuals as needed. Discuss what children can do next time instead.

TTs use the five finger formula more formally in conflict mediation. They use the formula less formally in guidance talks and group meetings. And, when they need them, TT members have their fingers to count off the steps with.

Principle 6: Respond to conflicts using a collection of guidance practices that affirm and teach. These five key intervention guidance practices are further discussed in Chapter 4 and featured in Chapters 6 and 7.

> **Calming methods.** Few adults, and certainly not children, can resolve conflicts cooperatively when they are upset. The skills of calming all down (including oneself) are important for TTs to gain.

> **Guidance talks.** Not talking *at* children, but *with* them, teachers discuss how the child saw the conflict, how the other person might have felt, what the child can do to make things better (different from a forced apology), and what they could do differently next time.

> **Conflict mediation.** To resolve a conflict with two or a few children, TTs formally use the five finger formula. TT members follow the steps to model and teach them. Sometimes, they use "peace props" like talking sticks and talk-and-listen chairs to reinforce the importance of taking turns listening and talking (discussed more in Chapter 4). As children gain experience and confidence, over time TTs move from coaching to facilitating to observing children negotiate for themselves.

> **Intervention large group meetings.** When conflicts become public in the community, affecting more than just a few, TTs hold intervention large group meetings. They informally follow the five finger formula to guide children to identify the problem, discuss how individuals feel about it, decide on a reconciling course of action, and then with the children manage putting the solution into action. TTs and children hold the meetings mindfully, respecting each other's views, and teachers protect the identities of involved group members. The community sets up meeting guidelines in developmental meetings early in the year.

> **Comprehensive guidance** used on behalf of a child by the family-staff team. This practice has its own principle (below). But a point made earlier bears reinforcing: TT members do not have to love every big or small member of the community, but they do need to maintain secure relationships with them and believe in their ability to learn and grow. Together with parents, teachers can accomplish what they cannot alone.

Principle 7: With children experiencing frequent and severe conflicts: Collaborate with a team, including staff and parents, in the use of comprehensive guidance. The need for comprehensive guidance means that the child is struggling to meet DLS 1 and 2. In comprehensive guidance, the TT informally or formally uses an *individual guidance plan* and leads through what I call **liberation teaching** (see the sidebar at on page 33). Liberation teaching involves working within and, if necessary, gently bending the system to get needed assistance to a child. Asking the child to leave a program is a very last resort. If a program change proves necessary, TTs collaborate with community resources to find a program that has specialized resources for the child and family. Dedicated TTs never give up on any child. Earlier in the chapter, we examined the devastating long-term effects for children who fall into the stress-conflict-punishment syndrome. *Liberation teaching, in the guidance sense, refers to the active leadership that TT members use to prevent children from the devastations of becoming victims of this syndrome.* The intentional use of comprehensive guidance signifies that liberation teaching is at work—for me, this is the highest form of guidance practice.

I have been using the term *liberation teaching* and writing about it since 1994. The common definition of the term *liberation* refers to populations of oppressed people becoming free. Within the context of my writing in early childhood education, I use the word *liberation* in conjunction with *teaching* to explain the concept of guiding a child to gain DLS 1 and 2 and to engage with attaining DLS 3, 4, and 5.

My concept is related to, but not synonymous with, *liberation pedagogy,* a term originated by Brazilian educator and social philosopher Paulo Freire (1970). Rather than pertaining to liberating oppressed populations via education in general, liberation teaching focuses on a specific guidance practice. In the guidance context, the term refers to the will and consequent leadership of the teacher to (1) assist a child to make unmanageable stress manageable, and (2) nudge the child toward healthy personal development. In the language of the book, liberation teaching refers to guiding the child to gain DLS 1 and 2 and willingly engage with attaining DLS 3, 4, and 5. In everyday language, it refers to never giving up on a child.

Developmentally Appropriate Practice and the Democratic Life Skills

In this section we take a fresh look at DAP, in relation to the five DLS. We do so by first sharing the definition of DAP and then discussing how the three core considerations of DAP are congruent with the Democratic Life Skills. We relate the basics of teaching for the DLS to each core consideration, thereby demonstrating compatibility between the DLS and DAP—a connection readers probably have already surmised.

Let's begin with guiding statements from the fourth edition of *Developmentally Appropriate Practice in Early Childhood Programs Serving Children from Birth Through Age Eight* (2022). NAEYC states that "developmentally appropriate practice is a position statement, a book, and an approach to teaching" (xxi). NAEYC defines developmentally appropriate practice as

> Methods that promote each child's optimal development and learning through a strengths-based, play-based approach to joyful, engaged learning. Educators implement developmentally appropriate practice by recognizing the multiple assets all young children bring to the early learning program as unique individuals and as members of families and communities. (xxx)

The progressive educational position of NAEYC regarding DAP is this:

> Each and every child, birth through age 8, has the right to equitable learning opportunities—in centers, family child care homes, or schools—that fully support their optimal development and learning across all domains and content areas. Children are born eager to learn; they take delight in exploring their world and making connections. The degree to which early learning programs support children's delight and wonder in their learning reflects the quality of that setting. Educators who engage in developmentally appropriate practice foster young children's joyful learning and maximize the opportunities for each child to achieve their full potential. (xxx)

In support of citizens in countries across the world committing themselves to democracy—often at awful costs—nowhere but in a democracy can NAEYC's positions hold.

Three Core Considerations of Developmentally Appropriate Practice

The DAP book identifies three core considerations, nine principles, and six guidelines for practice. The principles and guidelines are supported by numerous references. Almost 100 vignettes illustrate facets of DAP in action. Example illustrations of DAP with infants and toddlers, preschoolers, kindergartners, and primary-age children fill the book. In chapters to come on each DLS, we provide more context and further document ways in which DAP and the DLS are compatible.

In the pursuit of DAP, teachers use the three core considerations: commonality, individuality, and context (NAEYC 2020) to inform every aspect of their decision making. For each of the core considerations, I highlight the compatibility of teaching for the five DLS with the use of DAP.

Additional corroborating language for the compatibility of DAP and the DLS is found especially in these chapters of the DAP book: Chapter 2, "The Principles in Practice: Understanding Child Development and Learning in Context"; Chapter 6, "Creating a Caring, Equitable Community of Learners"; and Chapter 9, "Teaching to Enhance Each Child's Development and Learning."

Commonality

Commonality—current research and understandings of processes of child development and learning that apply to all children, including the understanding that all development and learning occur within specific social, cultural, linguistic, and historical contexts (NAEYC 2020, 6).

All children come to early education programs with universal basic needs for safety and for growing. They know only the emotional, social, cultural, linguistic, and historical contexts of their families and communities; this is their world. As a part of the human package for safety and growing, all children arrive with an intrinsic dynamic for development and learning. However, as we saw previously in this chapter, adverse experiences can cause unmanageable stress for some children and lead to the hormone-driven need for survival behavior. When this happens, it becomes more difficult for the child to engage in meaningful, joyful learning experiences, actualize their intrinsic motivation for learning, and undertake healthy executive function development.

By working hard with these very young youngsters and their families, early childhood educators guide children to learn that they have a place of belonging in their expanded new environments and that they are worthy and capable of learning.

In the encouraging early learning community, most children can then manage stress and gain DLS 1 and 2 to the degree that they can turn their attention to *joyful learning* (working on DLS 3, 4, and 5). With all children, the DLS construct asks teachers to *respond to both sets of skills at all times*—to support and guide so that children can gain the safety-needs skills and to support, nudge, and teach as children engage with each DLS. TTs work with young children and their families throughout to help children gain resilience.

Individuality

Individuality—the characteristics and experiences unique to each child, within the context of their family and community, that have implications for how best to support their development and learning (NAEYC 2020, 7).

In 2015, the US Census Bureau reported over 350 languages spoken in the United States, including 150 or more Native American languages. There are innumerable shades of skin color among its people. Every family has their own heritage and their own racial, historical, ethnic, religious, linguistic, and social identities, which impact each family member uniquely.

It is hard to miss the emphasis on joyful learning in the 2020 DAP position statement and the fourth edition of the DAP book. There are many references not just to "joyful and engaged learning" in the DAP definition, but to "play," "playfulness," "meaningful, joyful learning experiences" and so on throughout the book. (Chapter 5 is titled "The Power of Playful Learning in the Early Childhood Setting.") For graduates to identify with and stand up for the values and knowledge of their education, they need to have *liked* their schooling (see more on page 37). What better way to make education lovable than to fill learning settings with "meaningful, joyful learning experiences"? (Via joyful learning experiences, friendly humor triumphs again!)

Moreover, children are born with their own special genetic characteristics, potentials, abilities and disabilities, temperaments, and personal preferences. Given the incredibly complex mix of environmental, genetic, and personality factors that impact the months-old beings who enter our programs, yup, it is safe to say that every child is unique.

The early childhood educator's job is to make the program welcoming and encouraging for every child and family, and in this effort to develop secure relationships with each. Teachers who work for building the five DLS recognize that the early childhood program is likely a first socializing experience outside of the family, that each child is only months old, and that children react to sources of support and stress differently. For those children who face unmanageable stress upon entering this new, challenging extension of their world, the TT works hard to relate positively to that child and to use guidance practices in individually attentive ways to empower the child to grow toward resilience.

For these children, as well as those who have not faced tumultuous experiences in their young lives, TTs sustain an encouraging learning community. The team works actively to prevent institution-caused unmanageable stress and mistaken behavior by managing programs that are developmentally appropriate not just for most in the group, but for each child.

Context

Context—everything discernible about the social and cultural contexts for each child, each educator, and the program as a whole (NAEYC 2020, 7).

The encouraging early learning community is inclusive of the social and cultural contexts of the children and families in the program. If members of the TTs are from the local communities they serve, these teachers act as leader-models, embracing the cultures they represent, with full faith in the potentials of the youngest community members to make progress with the DLS.

If teachers are from outside the program's home community, they maximize coteaching possibilities with adults from within the community. These teachers use democratic leadership so that all in the setting recognize that staff members are a close, cooperative team.

As well, teachers from outside the community become students of the program's home community and acculturate themselves via the children, families, staff, and community experts. As much as they can, they aim to be **culturally responsive** and lead for cultural responsiveness in community members. Diverse languages provide an example. Learning at least some words in the languages spoken in the children's homes shows respect for those you work with—although children will look at you funny until you get words right. After all these years, I still remember the Red Lake Ojibwe words for rabbit (*wabooz*), skunk (*zhigaag*), and coffee (*makade-mashkikiwaabo*—"black medicine water").

We illustrate context and the DLS further through a classroom story that reflects a rural Minnesota community's high interest in fishing and especially the "fishing opener." (Minnesota is among the top five states per capita in populations that fish.) This TT (with Terry as lead), in Blackduck, Minnesota, provides a whopper (in the big fish sense) of an example of germane emergent curriculum.

> In materials, equipment, activities, and daily program, TTs incorporate tangible elements of the home community. In Blackduck, Minnesota, where the opening of fishing season is a big deal, the Head Start initiated an extended fishing theme. Books about fish and fishing were plentiful in the library. Children's wax paper "lake art" hung from the ceiling; a fishing "camp" was set up in the dramatic play area (complete with tent, rubber raft with plastic paddles, and hookless fishing gear); live minnows were put in the water table to be netted and quickly placed in one of three assorted "fish tanks." (As a life lesson, when minnows died, the class put them in their garden as fertilizer.)

Cheyenne, a 46-month-old struggling with DLS 2, reveled in being a "fishing guide," like his older brother, in the fishing camp. The staff marveled at Cheyenne's level of involvement as he guided trips in the raft to where "the big ones are." Another child, Greta, went out by herself on the rubber raft. The 58-month-old softly told a teacher she and her family did not fish. The staff pivoted for Greta to make the theme "fish and lakes" rather than fishing; they were pleased to help the child have a happy "Lake Week." The children all had special journals to write and draw in. Greta made several pictures, including an underwater picture that showed smiling fish ignoring dangling hooks!

Weeks after the theme, at lunchtime the class enjoyed the early peas from the class garden (fertilized by the buried minnows from the year before), even some kids who didn't think they liked peas. (Teacher: "Just try these three.") The lunch was also a fish fry with Minnesota's favorite gourmet state fish, walleye pike. (With permission of her parents, even Greta tried a walleye filet. She ate the whole thing.)

Through the theme, the TT engaged the entire group around an intriguing, culturally responsive theme. They were able to assist Cheyenne, who struggled with strong emotions, become engaged at a level they had not seen before. They made sure that Greta,

who might have been stressed by a theme she did not relate to, had a learning experience of personal meaning. And, significantly, the Head Start center implemented all three of the core considerations.

Why Is It Important for Democracy that Graduates Love Their Schooling?

Every act of learning has an emotional (affective) dimension as well as a cognitive dimension. If the learning is a positive experience, the brain hums along smoothly, and executive function motivates one to engage in further learning experiences. Examples are a child who wants you to read a book again and again or a sixth-grade class that sits listening, enthralled, to the teacher read *Charlotte's Web*. We can say that the child at such moments has engaged in a developmentally appropriate experience. Adults know such experiences when they occur because children's attention spans usually are longer than theirs! (Like when an adult pushes a child on a swing.) The children are completely tuned in.

Through kindling resilience (a found willingness to actualize the growing-needs DLS), individuals gain in the ability to engage in **significant learning**. Identified by Carl Rogers in 1961, positive significant learning is integral to the education experience of needs-secure individuals. This is the kind of learning that stands the learner in good stead over time.

Such learning includes the gratification of a personal connection with one's classroom community where that learning occurred (Pallas 2000). Zooming in, an early childhood education program that a child loves offers lasting benefits in all domains of development. Graduates of such programs have the ultimate gift in terms of **readiness**: not a collection of assorted bits of concrete knowledge, but a willingness and a capability to engage with the new—in Dewey's thinking, an openness to continued and ongoing experiencing.

Mary, a veteran Head Start teacher in Badger, Minnesota, once shared this experience. She was walking down the main street (the only street) when a former student came up to her. That student, Nancy, introduced herself. She told Mary that ever since she'd had Mary as a teacher, Nancy had wanted to be a teacher too. Nancy shared she now was majoring in early childhood education at the University of North Dakota. The two talked for a bit, hugged, and parted. Mary was deeply touched. As she got in her car, Mary suddenly remembered Nancy and exclaimed, "That kid?!" Mary's comment to me was, "That kid drove me bonkers every day she was in my class." My comment to Mary and to you is, "But Nancy never knew."

The early childhood learning experience had lasting value for Nancy. Often, an individual associates warm experiences at learning with an adult. What was your favorite project when you were in school, your favorite subject? Can you connect a teacher you still feel warmly about with that experience? And, in your decision to become a teacher, can you think of a favorite teacher who influenced your career direction?

We feel long-lasting identity with individuals and institutions that afforded us significant learning (and helped us progress through the five DLS). As graduates, most of us would stand up for those individuals and institutions if assailed by others. As citizens, we would stand firm for the disciplines, heritage, and universal truths those institutions embody. I believe that learned truths about climate change, threatened democratic processes, population displacements, racism, and widespread world hunger would not be ignored or denied, but met with mindfulness and proactive civil support. From that significant learning in those hallowed classrooms with those beloved teachers, I believe we gain the abilities to contribute to civil democracy.

DISCUSSION QUESTIONS

1. Identify three key concepts (listed below and in the glossary). If you are a visual learner, write each out with its definition from the glossary. Then, referring to the section of the chapter where the key concept originated, reflect on what the concept means to you now that you have read the chapter.

2. Various anecdotes in the chapter illustrate TT members working with children to progress with the DLS. Identify one anecdote that has meaning for you. Reflect on how the anecdote enhanced and/or changed your possible response to a similar situation.

3. Consider the three core considerations of DAP. Discuss how you would connect each to DLS theory.

4. The book is about education for democracy. Identify a new or newly reinforced idea for you from the chapter. Discuss how that idea contributes to your own approach toward teaching for democracy.

5. How have the thoughts and ideas shared in this chapter impacted your thinking about being a professional working with young children?

Key Concepts

adverse experience

amygdala- and hypothalamus-driven stress response

authentic assessment

authority aversion

child trauma

comprehensive guidance

conventional discipline

culturally responsive

developmental guidance

establishment aversion

executive function

extrinsic motivation

instrumental aggression

intervention guidance

post-traumatic stress disorder (PTSD)

preschool push-out

reactive aggression

readiness

significant learning

story pictures

stress-conflict-punishment syndrome

stress response

survival behaviors

CHAPTER 3

The Community of Relationships

Unmanageable Stress and the Centrality of Secure Relationships

---

SUGGESTED GOALS FOR READERS

1. Recognize physiological, environmental, and developmental sources of unmanageable stress in children, and the multitude of stressors that modern families face.

2. Gain an understanding of how secure relationships, including with early childhood professionals, assist children to manage stress and show resilience.

3. Understand the basics of attachment theory and implications of secure and insecure attachment patterns for children's development.

4. Identify a supporting or nudging action arising from a secure teacher-child relationship as children work at each DLS in the encouraging early learning community.

Sources of Unmanageable Stress

This is a time in the world of war, natural disasters, climate devastation, pandemic, and famine. In a period of immediate existential threat for so many, the perceived threats faced by young children in unassailed areas might seem like "just part of life that they have to adjust to." But at a time when brains are most sensitive to threat, discomfort, and pain, adverse experiences have the potential to inject unmanageable stress into young children's lives (Nelson et al. 2020). In Chapters 1 and 2 we discussed how adverse experiences and the resulting amygdala- and hypothalamus-driven stress response can drive young children to feel they are without group acceptance and personal worth. In the first part of this chapter, we look at three sources of potentially unmanageable stress for children and families.

Physiological Stressors

Physiological stressors—differences in brain functioning and development due to conditions like autism spectrum disorder (ASD), attention-deficit/hyperactivity disorder (ADHD), childhood mental illness, and extreme temperaments—can cause children's brains to become overloaded by what others consider "ordinary" situations (Nelson et al. 2020).

Raising a child with a disabling physiological condition poses accentuated challenges to families, with parenting already being complicated in these complex times. A lack of adequate resources heightens the challenge, but well-resourced families too can be overwhelmed by young children with disabilities. Perhaps society doesn't as readily notice parenting difficulties in affluent families. There is so little preparation and accessible support available to new parents of any income level. Initiatives like early childhood special education, community education parenting classes, and Head Start parenting programs are a start. Home visiting by family professionals is key, a service that should be better recognized and funded. Whatever the family resources, parenting can suffer when physiological stressors are present, causing additional **environmental stressors** for the family.

Environmental Stressors and Families

Some families face more life challenges than others, and parents show different degrees of resilience in relation to the challenges they face. But only for very few is parenting without obstacles and potholes. Parenting is difficult, whether children develop as hoped or otherwise.

So, due to the multitude of stressors in modern life, parents, just as their children, are vulnerable to **unmanageable stress.** Unless they have the means to mitigate high stress, survival behaviors in many manifestations can creep into parenting (Nelson et al. 2020). To one degree or another, modern parents are subject to the effects of the nearly 50 stressors listed in the sidebar on page 41. This "rogues' gallery" was generated by me, pulled from my professional experience and scholarly endeavors.

For reasons of unmanageable stress, to one extent or another the survival behaviors of fleeing, freezing, and fighting too easily invade parenting efforts. In reaction to the responsibilities of childrearing under adverse circumstances, some parents flee the scene literally or psychologically; grow passive, defensive, or erratic; and/or strike out physically or emotionally. Survival behavior that seeps into parenting is a prominent source of unmanageable stress and survival behavior in children (Dye 2018).

Environmental Stressors and Children—Home and School

Family struggles affect children differently, depending a great deal on the relationship between the parenting adult(s) and child (Purnell 2010). Sometimes in the face of adverse experiences for families, significant others are able to sustain secure relationships with the young. Children then receive the blessed gifts of buffers that help keep trauma at bay and of resilience, the capacity to gain DLS 1 and 2. But sadly, this is not the case for too many children whose families are affected by high stress.

For many kids, adverse experiences don't even have to be due to outright abuse or neglect (CCTASI, n.d.). Parents might habitually frustrate children by ignoring their attempted efforts to try to make contact. Children may suffer in self-esteem when

A Rogues' Gallery of Stressors Facing Families

The short and long-term effects of

> Natural and human-made disasters

> Diseases, individual and contagious, including pandemic

Societal shortcomings and failings in

> Education systems

> Infrastructure systems

> Law enforcement systems

> Medical systems

> Political/governmental systems

> Religious systems

Discrimination by others toward families due to

> Institutional racism/racial factors

> Prejudiced and inadequate policing

> Marginalization of culturally diverse factors, including home language

> Immigrant/noncitizen status

> Socioeconomic vulnerabilities

> Diverse religious beliefs and practices

> Diverse family structures

> Gender identities of family members

> Strongly held political or ideological views of members

> Behavior patterns that do not fit community norms

Manifold stressors on families

These conditions are exacerbated, if not root caused, by racism and discrimination within society. A related, concausal factor is living in poverty.

> Job and livable wage insecurity

> Parents working long hours/multiple jobs

> Food insecurity

> Housing insecurity

> Neighborhood insecurity

> Farming/rural residence insecurity

> Challenges of single parenting

> Challenges of parents who are separated

> Challenges faced by surrogate parents and guardians

> Discord between parenting partners

> Marriage/partnership dissolution

> Violence within family

> Alcohol and chemical dependency

> Violence/crime that touches family

> Death of a family member

> Incarceration of a family member

> Mental health issues in family members, including PTSD

> Family members who need much support

> One or more in family disabled

> Conflicting generational values

> Strong political conflicts within family

> Nonacceptance of family members' gender identities

> Workplace frustrations and tensions

> Illness/health services insecurity

> Technological access issues

> Isolation of family from close others

> School expenses/student loans

> Difficulties of members with schooling

> Problems relating with educators

> Problems relating with other officials

the family spotlight shines on siblings who are more assertive or "cute"—children cannot live up to parental expectations—or shines on no child in the family at all. When parents are out of the home, substitute care providers may be less caring. Being only months old, young kids are sensitive to such stressors.

Then, the very young come into the new environment of their early childhood program, filled with an active roomful of unknown peers and unfamiliar adults. Whatever their home circumstances, young children are susceptible to unmanageable stress at school as well. Throughout childhood, unhealthy stress experienced in the classroom compounds the stress children might feel in home surroundings.

Some potential *school-related* sources of unmanageable stress for children include

> Settings that are unwelcoming or chaotic

> Cultural expectations that differ from those at home

> Curricula that are rigid and unresponsive to diverse learning needs

> Teachers who are biased, impersonal, judgmental, and/or overwhelmed

> Behavior management procedures that are nonexistent or punitive

Children's acting out due to classroom-caused stress is what I call **institution-caused mistaken behavior**. When vulnerable young children feel discord and stress within the early childhood program, they are more likely to begin a stress-conflict-punishment pattern. Institution-caused mistaken behavior then can become a debilitating factor, potentially for all the years the young remain in school and thereafter (Nelson et al. 2020).

Developmental Stressors: "Life Among the Giants"

Even for young children who are relatively free of physiological and environmental stressors, progressing to DLS 3, 4, and 5 is not necessarily an easy endeavor. The **developmental egocentrism** factor, necessary for evolutionary survival, increases the likelihood of ongoing conflicts with home and school caregivers. The young child does not

understand why eating marshmallows before lunch is not a good idea—or that rest after lunch is. Being a months-old small person in a big person's world means that young children mostly live in a state of dependency on others—good for their ultimate survival, but not necessarily for progressing to a state of resilience and personal flourishing. Enter **developmental stressors.**

Adults make so many decisions for children each day, from when to get up to what to eat and wear to where the day will be spent to whether electronic screen use will be allowed at certain times, anytime, or at all. Ginott ([1972] 1993) argues that the self-message of imposed dependency on all humans, especially children, is inadequacy, resulting in feelings of resentment. (You make decisions for me; therefore, I must be inadequate. I feel resentment about this.)

••

The nature of ongoing conflict resolutions between adults and children—hopefully more like dancing than wrestling—follows the child into learning experiences to come. Here's an illustration. Dancing: "Eat five peas and then you are done . . . okay, three peas." Wrestling: "You will stay at the table until you eat all of your peas." (Children have more taste buds, and more sensitive taste buds, than adults.) Which child is more likely to eat peas—or new foods in general—as an adult?)

As the child grows, the dependence-independence dynamic remains largely the same; it is just that the child has additional adults to contend with, adjust to, and hopefully work with. Who leads in the many dances of childhood? Since Dr. Benjamin Spock ([1946] 2018), the ultimate pro-democracy child psychologist, adults have been wrestling with themselves and their partners over this question. Spock may have made parenting more complicated, but for our children and democracy, I think better.

By the way, the phrase "life among the giants" in the heading on this page comes from the writing of Leontine Young (1966).

••

Because we want children to feel capable, so they can learn and grow, most adults provide ongoing opportunities for them to participate in reasonable decision making. This means that the child does not decide whether to go to the program, but which of two tops to wear; not whether to eat breakfast, but which of two breakfast cereals to choose; not whether to use their screens whenever, but not at all or for 30 minutes after (dinner, homework, or housekeeping chores). At school, encouraging independence means not being made to copy a teacher-made model of Frosty, but instead being invited to create one's own picture of "outside in the winter." It also means not hearing "You did it wrong" (however the adult says it) but "Yes, you sure made a blizzard with that white chalk!"

Temperaments in children have a lot to do with how they manage their internal dynamic for learning. But, learning always involves a degree of independence, the ability to be free of constraints others tend to put on them. Children fall into or cause conflicts with adults around this large-looming dependence-independence issue all the time. The relationships that significant adults build with children largely determine whether the very young come out of expressed disagreements feeling unhealthy stress or gaining in significant learning.

Attachment Patterns and Children's Personal Development

The developmental data about the impact of early caregiver-child attachments on behavior and development owes much to the landmark studies of attachment patterns by psychoanalyst John Bowlby and field psychologist Mary Ainsworth. Taking a clinical approach, Bowlby (1969) demonstrated a firm connection between a positive, predictable caregiver-child attachment in the first years of life and the growing young child's confidence, competence, and sociability in new situations (Bowlby 1988; see also Stern, Barbarin, & Cassidy 2022). Purnell (2010) phrased it this way:

Appropriately responsive caregiving to attachment needs is likely to provide what Bowlby called a "secure base," namely a point of contact with someone who will provide the reassurance, comfort and safety that will make an individual feel sufficiently secure to interact with and explore the outside world. (1)

After working with Bowlby in Britain, Mary Ainsworth studied mothers and infants in Uganda, looking at how infant attachment behavior emerged and what maternal behaviors might be linked to attachment styles. Significantly during this time, Ainsworth originated the term *attunement* to refer to the responsive state of mind of mothers able to build secure attachments with their infants. Ainsworth identified three attachment styles: secure, ambivalent, and avoidant (Ainsworth et al. 1978). (Later, other researchers added a fourth attachment pattern, disorganized—or "chaotic.") From her cross-cultural studies, Ainsworth also found that children securely attached to a parent are less anxious and aggressive and more empathetic than children experiencing attachments marked by ambivalence, avoidance, or gross inconsistency by the adult (Ainsworth et al. 1978).

There is concern that **attachment theory** is **culture bound**—and inappropriately generalized beyond the specific Western White milieu in which the theory was developed. Ainsworth's study in Uganda provides cross-cultural validation for her conclusion that caregiver **attunement** to the infant might be the universal ingredient in secure attachments. In their analysis of studies of attachment in more than 18 countries in Africa, Latin America, and East Asia, Mesman, van IJzendoorn, and Sagi-Schwartz (2016, 870) suggest that there is a "balance between universal trends and contextual determinants." Specific behaviors through which parents express sensitivity will vary with cultural context; different behaviors may have the same function. Nevertheless, after considering the evidence from many studies, these researchers conclude that

The available cross-cultural studies have not refuted the bold conjectures of attachment theory about the universality of attachment, the normativity of secure attachment, the link between sensitive caregiving and attachment security, and the competent child outcomes of secure attachment. Taken as a whole, the studies are remarkably consistent with the theory. (871)

Trauma and Attachment Theory

The gist of the significance of attachment theory, as noted by Atwool (2006) and supported by Stupica et al. (2017), is that children's resilience in the presence of trauma is linked to secure relationships with significant others. Purnell (2010) states:

> Historically neglectful, unpredictable, or dangerous behaviour by caregivers is inherently traumatising, and leaves a child less able to deal with its longer-term traumatising effect and with no adequately secure base to turn to for safety when danger threatens. (4)

Summarizing studies by other authors, Purnell frames the interface of trauma and attachment patterns in this statement:

> Generally speaking, the more exposure to danger there has been through neglectful or abusive caregiving, the more distortion there will be in the attachment response. Trauma in itself does not inevitably lead to anxious attachment. It is possible for children to experience trauma and other hardships, but because their caregivers are adequately protective in response to the dangers, they will have secure or relatively secure attachment strategies. (4)

A general agreement among scholars (Masten & Barnes 2018; National Scientific Council on the Developing Child 2004) is that caregivers in addition to immediate family can and do form secure attachments—called **secure relationships** in early childhood education. Secure relationships center on acceptance of the other as a worthy individual, which is "sealed" by the teacher's ongoing effort to maintain mutual trust through attunement to the child. Key is that the relationship is unique to the adult and the child and grows from unique talking and listening (even when children have limited speech) between the two. They have frequent contact talks. As the child expands in ability to form bonds with others in the encouraging early learning community, those relationships too help the child to feel belonging and personal worthiness—to feel secure in the community.

Bowlby and Ainsworth increased our understanding of why children are overcome by, or can rise above, the drive to meet safety needs. Children who are deprived of a sense of trust and belonging in adult-child relationships may experience unmanageable stress and a preoccupation with meeting basic safety needs. In contrast, children in secure relationships with significant others have safety needs that are being fulfilled; they tend to view the world as relatively nonthreatening and inviting of exploration.

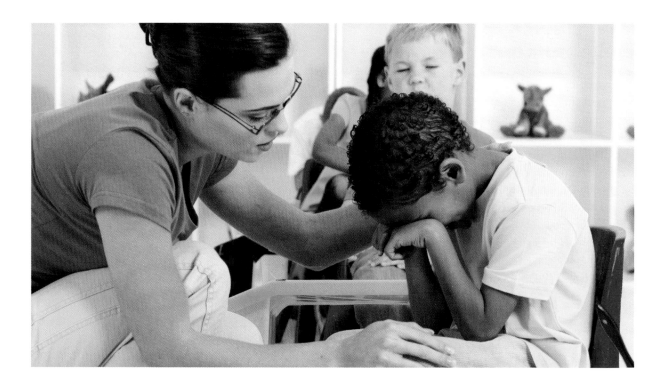

Secure Relationships and the Democratic Life Skills

From its beginnings in 2003, the National Scientific Council on the Developing Child, centered at Harvard, has emphasized the centrality of secure relationships for children's mental health and healthy development. Presenting only research-affirmed policy, the council's first working paper, "Young Children Develop in an Environment of Relationships" (National Scientific Council on the Developing Child 2004), is still featured on its website today. We begin this section by sharing this excerpt from the document:

> Healthy development depends on the quality and reliability of a young child's relationships with the important people in his or her life, both within and outside the family. Even the development of a child's brain architecture depends on the establishment of these relationships. . . .
>
> Young children experience their world as an environment of relationships, and these relationships affect virtually all aspects of their development—intellectual, social, emotional, physical, behavioral, and moral. The quality and stability of a child's human relationships in the early years lay the foundation for a wide range of later developmental outcomes that matter—self-confidence and sound mental health, motivation to learn, achievement in school and later in life, the ability to control aggressive impulses and resolve conflicts in non-violent ways, knowing the difference between right and wrong, having the capacity to develop and sustain casual friendships and intimate relationships, and ultimately to be a successful parent oneself. . . .
>
> The warmth and support of the caregiver in a child care setting also influence the development of important capabilities in children, including greater social competence, fewer behavior problems, and enhanced thinking and reasoning skills at school age. Young children benefit in these ways because of the secure relationships they develop in such settings, and because of how the caregivers provide cognitively stimulating activities and support for developing positive relationships with other children. (1–2)

This working paper speaks to the heart of early childhood education. In encouraging early learning settings, teachers are caregivers who impact both children and their families. Secure relationships within the setting empower children to gain safety-needs skills and work on growing-needs skills. Building and maintaining positive relationships with families accomplish what neither party, teacher nor parent, can accomplish on their own. Building and sustaining supportive relationships provide the foundation for guiding children to gain the DLS.

TTs build secure relationships to assist children at building skills in relation to both sources of universal motivation, for safety and for growth. In three words, we can say that early childhood professionals **support and nudge.** (Even for DLS 1, support alone is not enough.) For each DLS that follows, we explore how teachers *support* children in their work on the skill and *nudge* them toward further progress.

Safety-Needs Skills

DLS 1: Finding acceptance as a member of the group and as a worthy individual

DLS 2: Expressing strong emotions in nonhurting ways

Growing-Needs Skills

DLS 3: Solving problems creatively—independently and in cooperation with others

DLS 4: Accepting unique human qualities in others

DLS 5: Thinking intelligently and ethically

Supporting and Nudging for Skill 1

Children who work on this skill lack secure relationships to the extent that the world seems untrustworthy and threatening. As these children form stable, caring relationships in the encouraging early learning community, TTs help them figure out how to find a place of acceptance and to gain a sense of self-worth. For children not yet at Skill 1, forming a secure relationship with at least one member of the TT is everything.

Still, due to the dual nature of children's needs, early childhood teachers do not just provide support, important as that is. As well, teachers nudge children toward working to attain the skill. As the relationship builds, teachers blend *nudging* with the support, gently easing the child into situations where the child has a good opportunity to experience significant learning. It is difficult for me to write about the DLS without using illustrative anecdotes. Here as in chapters to come, anecdotes provide a focus for the discussion of each skill.

> **Support:** Because of the conflicts that seemed to often occur around Garner, 44 months, the Little Angels child care staff actually felt relieved when he was not scheduled to be there. New lead teacher, Velma, decided to have *contact talks* (one-on-one quality times) with Garner right away on days he attended. As soon as Garner arrived, Velma greeted the child, and they did things together—like read and talk together about their favorite book. Velma began to have dreams about *The Grouchy Ladybug,* but she realized the contact talks she and Garner were having around the book were helping the child. Although this meant that the other TT members had more jobs to do during the greeting times, they gradually understood that these times eased Garner into the day and reduced conflicts for Garner and everyone else.

> **Nudging:** Responding to the cues of Garner over time, Velma fit in another child or two in the regular book reading. She kept Garner on her lap, but included the others, working hard to make the experience for all cozy and warm. Other TT members sometimes read to children in "lap groups" at the same time, but Velma kept the timeless *Ladybug* on reserve for Garner and the regulars that he learned to share the book with. The TT noticed Garner begin to play first with one and then another of his reading mates.

Supporting and Nudging for Skill 2

With children struggling to gain DLS 2, the teacher works to keep secure relationships stable, come tempest or teapot. A child working on DLS 2 has progressed enough with DLS 1 to venture out into the group and try new experiences. TT members guide the child into situations that have a high success probability—activities like playdough and water play, organized to prevent competition over space and materials. (Teachers do this by having lots of interest centers and materials for the group to choose from and doing planning with the group beforehand to limit numbers at key centers.)

Naturally, teachers cannot and should not eliminate all challenges and frustrations for kids working on Skill 2. But children can grow only when the conflicts they face do not heighten unmanageable stress, so teachers support and nudge kids so they can learn the skills to manage it. Guidance talks and conflict mediation, discussed in the next chapter, always begin with calming children down—and kids struggling with Skill 2 often need lots of calming. To sustain good relations, adults check in with these children after conflicts have been resolved.

> **Support:** Teacher Sienna knew Darius, 45 months, needed sensory experiences like water play and helped him get signed up for the activity. (A guideline in the community was that if kids signed up for an interest area, they could stay there as long as they wanted for that playtime block.) Another teacher wondered if Darius might get aggressive in water play, but Sienna explained that the sensory experience would relax him. This happened as Sienna expected, and she helped by reminding other children of the guideline when they wanted to use the water table (and helping them find other activities while they waited).

> **Nudging:** Artema, 54 months, tried to take table blocks and figures from Darius. Darius yelled no and, with both arms holding the blocks, tried to bite Artema's arm. Teacher Sienna quickly got between the two children, told them she would help take care of the problem, and modeled deep breaths to help them calm down. She used conflict mediation (more in the next chapter) to show that it was Darius's turn to use the blocks and figures, and that Artema needed to ask to use them or wait until Darius was done. Darius finished his turn quickly and Artema had a turn, but not before Sienna had a guidance talk with each child. She thanked Darius for saying no—using his words—and got him to agree that also calling "Teacher!" instead of biting would be a good idea. "I will help you, so no one needs to get hurt," she assured him. Darius nodded and they exchanged fist bumps.

Supporting and Nudging for Skill 3

The two processes of supporting and nudging often merge with children who struggle with Skill 3. Many young children who don't have a lot of problems with Skill 2 are reluctant to plunge into the independent activity—exploring, engaging, creating, problem solving, discovering—that we associate with Skill 3. From family members or older children, many of these children have learned that they cannot yet meet the expectation that products must look like "reality" to be worth anything. If their early efforts at tasks go unappreciated, are criticized, or are made fun of, young children feel distress and can become challenged by open-ended and complicated cognitively oriented activities.

> **Support and nudge:** After a warm spring weekend, teacher Chris said this in the morning class meeting: "Today in the art center, we are wondering if you could make pictures of what you like to do outside in the sun. You know what we say, 'All of your pictures are going to be different, because you are all different. All your pictures are going to be special, because you are all special.' Teacher Ellie will be at the art center to help you get started."
>
> **Iris:** I don't know what to make, Ellie.
>
> **Ellie:** Well, what do you like to do outside in the sun?
>
> **Iris:** I don't know. Swing. Would you make the swing for me?
>
> **Ellie:** However you make your picture, it will be delightful. We all love your pictures, Iris.
>
> **Iris:** I don't know how to.
>
> **Ellie:** (*Goes into definite nudge mode.*) I need to go to the sink to clean these brushes. When you are ready, just get started.
>
> Ellie collects some brushes that may or may not need cleaning and walks over to the sink, leaving Iris. After a few minutes she returns to the table. Iris has made a start on her picture and is busy.
>
> **Iris:** Is it good?
>
> **Ellie:** Your pictures always make us teachers smile, Iris.

> **Iris:** (*Repeats insistently.*) But it is good?
>
> **Ellie:** When you finish your picture, you tell me what you think. Then we will put it up on the "Today's Art" board. Your mother will be so proud.
>
> **Iris:** (*Briefly frowns at not getting the answer she wanted, then resumes working.*)

With many children, encouragement at the initial stages of an activity is important. Then, as the child gets into it, the TT can back away and allow the motivation of the activity itself to carry the child along. Sometimes, leaving a child is a helpful nonverbal nudge. Just remember to check back later. (And, avoid parallel creation, where you are making something alongside the children. Children will stop what they are making and try to duplicate your project. Even if you do it "sloppy," they can't duplicate yours and will be frustrated.)

Peer Play and Skill 3

Playing with peers reduces the social pressures individual children feel toward compliance with adult expectations in activities. Social play is the natural realm of creativity for young children. To see them fully engage in it often means that the TT can suspend efforts at both support and nudging. The children are providing these helps for each other. The following illustration happened after a mixed-age early childhood special education class went on a picnic.

> The children, ages 30 months to 6 years, got especially busy at their play after breakfast. Two had found the full-sized checkered tablecloth used at the picnic outing. "Let's have a picnic," Chantelle (57 months) said. "Yeah," said Eduardo (just turned 5). The two spread out the tablecloth on the carpet, got *all* the plates and other items from the dramatic play area, and few by few the other 10 children, including 34-month-old Cecily, who used a wheelchair, came to the picnic. All 12 children, some barely verbal, some with complex disabilities, "picnicked" for the next 30 minutes! The playtime had been scheduled to end after 15 minutes (too short for me).

The TT couldn't believe what they were seeing. Children were expressing themselves through cooperative activity in ways that the teachers had never seen before! The teachers sat back, drank coffee, and enjoyed watching the picnic as much as the children enjoyed having it! They decided to go on another picnic the next week.

Supporting and Nudging for Skill 4

Along with the many steps to ensure anti-bias, equitable programming to support children's understanding and acceptance of differing human qualities, TTs need to use both support and nudging as they teach for DLS 4. The reason is that due to sensitive triggering of the amygdala-hypothalamus response, young children are quick to see threat in what is new and unfamiliar. Nonetheless, members of the community—usually the TT but sometimes even other children—can step in to make situations less stress producing and more conducive to intrigue and significant learning.

Support: A firefighter came into the classroom with all the gear on. Most children were alarmed, even the child whose mom was wearing the gear. The staff realized they should have had Harriet arrive in street clothes, explain the equipment, and then put it on piece by piece. So, while one teacher got the children settled and into the large group area, the other teacher spoke to Harriet, and asked the firefighter to take off the gear and start the experience in street clothes. Harriet was happy to, with daughter Mathis sitting beside her. The teachers and Mathis introduced Mom, who explained each piece of gear and then put it on. At first wary, the kids became interested and stayed attentive to everything that Mom the firefighter said and did. The TT took photos of the firefighter and the children together and put them on a low bulletin board in the reading area. Mathis, especially, liked going into the area to look at the photos.

Nudging (by child): A new child, Xavier (just 4), was going to join the early childhood community the next day. Xavier had just begun to get around by using braces and a wheelchair. At a class meeting, TT member Alex showed the children a couple of different crutches and a child-sized wheelchair (with wheels locked), which were then put in the dramatic

play area for the children to explore. The next day when Xavier arrived, the children were friendly. Hilo, 60 months, took Xavier under his wing, showing him around the classroom.

Six weeks later, Xavier advanced to a new leg brace with which he could walk more easily. In a large group meeting, he showed how he made the brace work. The next day a visitor came to observe. Hilo approached the visitor and explained, "Xavier's got a new leg brace. It squeaks a little, but he gets around on it really good." The TT thanked Hilo for thinking about his mate and helping to orient the guest.

Supporting and Nudging for Skill 5

Hilo was showing Skill 5 behavior and Skill 4. Young children show these skills together when the expression of Skill 4 is proactive, rather than relatively passive such as by accepting diverse children into a play group. We can teach for Skill 4 more directly than for Skill 5. Children emerge to show Skill 5 on their own, although this ability commonly happens when children have had sensitive support and nudging with the other four skills.

Still, since they are just months old, children working on Skill 5 can experience mistaken behavior. Because they understand a lot, these kids might assume a role of being an "assistant teacher" and alienate themselves from peers. They might try to settle conflicts between two mates who aren't having it, and the young mediator gets caught up in the conflict—as you'll see with Jolie in the wand conflict in Chapter 6 (pages 92–93). Another teacher might have chastised Hilo for talking to an adult visitor about another child in a program. ("That's my job, not yours. You have your own job.") Instead, the team acknowledged Hilo's friendly and civil efforts.

In this scenario, the TT did not nudge Hilo to look after Xavier at all. In relation to Skill 5, TTs sometimes must be wary of pushing children too much rather than too little. Like Ruby Rossi, whose parents and brother are deaf, in the Oscar-winning film *CODA*, it is easy to view children who are driven to show Skill 5 for what they can do, and not for who they are. Children can give too much of themselves in their interactions with others—until they hit a breaking point. All kids need to be kids.

Support and reverse nudging: The mother of Margo (just 5) and Rocky (just 3) enrolled the children in a preschool program for the summer. Just before she left after dropping them off on the first day, Mom instructed Margo to look after Rocky and make sure he was all right. Margo had probably heard these instructions before, and she kept an eye on her younger brother. She sat next to him at snack and made sure he found activities to do. When another child accidentally knocked Rocky down outside, Margo jumped into action, glaring at the other child and comforting her sibling. After a few days, Rocky showed signs of wanting to be free of his sister's well-intended efforts.

Teacher Noori spoke to Mom at pickup and gently explained the situation. Mom promised to talk with Margo. The next day, Noori spent individual time with Margo. She explained to Margo that preschool was for her too, and it was just fine for her to do things for herself and let the TT take care of Rocky. Noori explained that she had talked with Mom, and Mom said this was okay.

Margo at first seemed hesitant—she took her role seriously—but with nudging gradually did more things that she herself enjoyed. She sat with her own mates at snack, as did Rocky. Both young children seemed happier, to the relief of Noori and her TT.

The Complexity of Skill 5

Teachers should be especially supportive when a child tries to be at Skill 5 in a complex situation—like when a few children, and not just one or two, are embroiled in a conflict, or when the one other child is a sibling. In interactions with children trying to be good citizens, we might at times need to do "reverse nudging," reminding the child that we can take care of things and they don't have to worry about them. This was the case with Margo. Whenever kids try to act intelligently and ethically, our first message to them should be "Thank you for caring" and not "Mind your own business." The compliment models the supportive and nudging nature of relations in the encouraging early learning community.

In the guidance approach it is both a hope and a goal of early childhood educators that their graduates have supportive, meaningful experiences with efforts to show DLS 5. Children learning to act intelligently and ethically are our best hope in the future for a "more perfect" democratic society.

DISCUSSION QUESTIONS

1. Identify three key concepts (listed below and in the glossary). If you are a visual learner, write each out with its definition from the glossary. Then, referring to the section of the chapter where the key concept originated, reflect on what the concept means to you now that you have read the chapter.

2. Various anecdotes in the chapter illustrate TT members working with children to progress with the DLS. Identify one anecdote that has meaning for you. Reflect on how the anecdote enhanced and/or changed your possible response to a similar situation.

3. Consider the many stressors faced by families and children noted in the chapter. Based on your own experiences, personal and/or professional, how might sources of stress affect the learning of young children? What measures might an early childhood professional take to help a young child meet their safety needs in such situations?

4. Reflect on your current understanding of attachment theory in relation to the personal development of children. In what ways might both secure and insecure attachment patterns affect how children see the world and respond to others?

5. The book is about education for democracy. Identify a new or newly reinforced idea for you from the chapter. Discuss how that idea contributes to your own approach toward teaching for democracy.

6. How have the thoughts and ideas shared in this chapter impacted your thinking about being a professional working with young children?

Key Concepts

attachment theory

attunement

culture bound

developmental stressors

environmental stressors

institution-caused mistaken behavior

physiological stressors

secure relationship

support and nudge

unmanageable stress

The Substance Chapter

A Guide to Studying
the Democratic Life
Skills in Practice

SUGGESTED GOALS FOR READERS

1. Become familiar with the 10 headings that serve as points of analysis for each of the DLS (in the five chapters to follow).

2. Increase understanding about key practices in developmental and intervention guidance.

3. Establish a context for intervention guidance through study of three levels of mistaken behavior.

4. Form a working understanding of benchmarks of engagement in building cooperative relations with families.

5. Explore two key aspects of developmentally appropriate practice that are central to teaching for the five DLS.

6. Increase understanding of how teaching for the DLS contributes to civil living in a democracy.

DLS 1	DLS 2	DLS 3	DLS 4	DLS 5
Finding Acceptance as a Member of the Group and as a Worthy Individual	**Expressing Strong Emotions in Nonhurting Ways**	**Solving Problems Creatively— Independently and in Cooperation with Others**	**Accepting Unique Human Qualities in Others**	**Thinking Intelligently and Ethically**

Chapter 4 introduces 10 points of analysis that together explain elements of DLS theory. The elements are dynamic because they interact with and reinforce each other. The 10 points of analysis, which serve as headings in the chapters on the DLS, are

1. Starter Notes
2. Anecdotes and Reflections
3. Eight Communication Practices for Building Relationships
4. Three Levels of Mistaken Behavior
5. Developmental Guidance: Major Practices
6. Key Intervention Guidance Practices
7. Working for Family Engagement
8. Ensuring an Encouraging Learning Community for All
9. Education for Living in a Democracy
10. Summary Grid

Various combinations of the 10 headings are used in the chapters on DLS 1–4. What about Skill 5? Children achieve Skill 5 as an expression of mastery of Skills 1–4. Skill 5 is aspirational for young children. That is, we can't as directly teach children to achieve it, but we can and should support children in their beginning efforts to use the skill. So, Chapter 9 on DLS 5 more loosely follows the 10-heading format and provides (hopefully refreshing) narrative.

Orienting readers to the 10 headings makes Chapter 4 the longest in the book. This substance chapter is a numbers stew, but don't worry about the numbers; just enjoy the ideas.

Introductions to headings 1 and 2 in this chapter contain an illustration and an explanation; these headings stand on their own, and the headings are discussed relatively briefly. Information under headings 3–8 is more involved, as these sections introduce concepts in teaching for the DLS that might be new. Explanation of headings 9 and 10 is brief.

1. Starter Notes

The starter notes set the place of each skill in the broader context of the DLS. These sections offer an insight into the skill by spotlighting a selected aspect of it. An example of what a starter note looks like in a particular chapter follows; it is a hypothetical lead-in to the discussion of Skill 3. DLS 3 describes most closely the skills of learning that early childhood professionals guide children to gain. Skill 3 has manifold permutations that can be divided into many cognitive/academic "rooms." The intent in this sample set of starter notes is to highlight one consummate activity for cognitive and personal development that, to my mind, is central to DLS 3: story pictures.

Illustration of Starter Notes, DLS 3

Remember that most of the art that children see in the classroom is in books that tell stories—not to mention the glut of "moving pictures" that most children view at home on screens. Contrary to the long-standing view that children's art is an outlet for nonverbal expression, for the most part young children associate pictures—including the ones that they create—with telling stories.

When the materials are provided (hopefully every day), story pictures let even very young children depict in their own ways experiences of joy, grief, anger, hope, discovery, and relations with significant others. (In this sense, story pictures are a young child's journal.) Story pictures are cognitive because children must problem-solve what to create and how to represent the idea visually and physically on paper. They are creative because the picture on the blank top of the paper is unique and empowers growing representation abilities. They are emerging literacy experiences, because children practice developmental writing (and reading) on the lined part of the bottom half of the paper.

If TT members make these experiences into contact talks, children also build vocabularies, spoken language skills, general communication abilities, and secure relationships. Staple together story pictures of individual children, and you have personal or scientific journals. Staple together story pictures of many children, and you have class books.

But wait, there's more! In story pictures, TTs have ready material available for authentic assessment over time. A 34-month-old might make brown circular scribbles for a picture and linear scribbles on the lines (or vice versa). To a teacher who says, "You are really working hard on that story picture" and pauses, the senior toddler says, "Yep. My dog's runnin'. She can run fast!" Then she points to a linear scribble and says, "My name." From this academic activity—because it is—what might the child be learning? And what might the adult be learning about the child and the child's developing skills? Perhaps the teacher saves a dated photo record of the child's story picture. What might the teacher find if the child, with daily practice, made a similar story picture in a year, in two years?

And (for those who believe children's art should remain nonverbal self-expression), what if a kid replies, "Teacher, this is not a story to tell. It is a picture to look at"? With a smile, the teacher who had this happen said, "Cool."

2. Anecdotes and Reflections

Almost all the anecdotes in the book *are not* invented to demonstrate predetermined points. Instead, the classroom stories start with one or more actual events in early childhood settings— toddler through primary grades. Some anecdotes are from observations of single events. Examples are those transcribed from videotaped clips in pre-K and kindergarten classrooms in metro and rural Minnesota. The videos from which these anecdotes were taken were part of a NAEYC project by two colleagues and me.

Other anecdotes are composites of two or more, dating from recently to way back in my history. Some classroom stories are mine, the byproducts of years of my teaching and observing in early childhood settings. A very few anecdotes came only from my head, "unencumbered" by actual events. These few help move the text along, and I felt them necessary to include. (If readers want to guess which, let me know and I will fess up if you are right.)

Most anecdotes, though, were shared with me in the form of classroom stories by former students and teacher colleagues. Several that were shared before 2000 appeared in my book *What the Kids Said Today: Using Classroom Conversations to Become a Better Teacher* (Gartrell 2000). (See my note about this book on page 6.) Reflections by me follow most anecdotes. The reflections relate the classroom stories to ideas in the immediate discussion of a skill. Names of children and most teachers have been changed.

In the chapters that follow, anecdotes and reflections are not limited to this first part of the chapter, but are sprinkled throughout to best support the various points of analysis.

3. Eight Communication Practices for Building Relationships

The eight communication practices first appeared in Gartrell (2020). An emphasis in that book and in this is that the communication practices can be used with adults—colleagues and family members—as well as children.

> Smile and nod.

> Acknowledge and pause.

> Make contact talks happen.

> Use friendly humor.

> Use appropriate, friendly touch.

> Utilize compliment sandwiches.

> Give encouragement: private to individuals, public to the group.

> Remember names, contact talks, and promises.

Smile and Nod

This practice is simple—and simply foundational for the other practices. In group situations and when talking with an individual, nothing conveys you are listening and understanding like smiling and nodding. (I am not talking bobblehead here; you know how to keep it natural.) The nonverbal affirmations tell the other person they are worthy enough for you to pay attention to, and that what they are saying to you is not off-putting. (If the content is close to off-putting, cut back on the smiles, but keep up the occasional nod to show you are listening.)

These nonverbal responses serve as a reminder to you that the person's words are important to them and deserve your respect, even if you see things a different way. Nodding and smiling can make it easier to frame your response in a way that does not seem alienating to the other person. Sometimes an intentional self-reference is helpful to make a subtle suggestion. (Examples appear in chapters to come.)

Acknowledge and Pause

Acknowledge and pause is the official team sponsor of the guidance approach. It is the bread and butter, chips and beer, kale and arugula of techniques to build relationships. Like smile and nod, acknowledge and pause is simple: compliment a detail in the other person's effort, then pause and wait for the other's response. Like smile and nod, acknowledge and pause shows that you care enough to pay attention. It is a personalized message, and so much more authentic than adults' conventional mental-shortcut replies like "Good job." (I once heard an exasperated kindergarten child reply to this phrase with "Teacher, you say that to all the kids.")

Acknowledge and pause is helpful when an adult wants to recognize someone's efforts but isn't sure what to say. Before the pause, compliment the effort and/or the details you see.

A handy starter phrase is "You are really . . ." and then identify what you see:

> "Painting that picture"

> "Working hard on that"

> "Playing together"

> "Looking upset"

As intended encouragement, some teachers immediately say is, "Tell me about what you are making [or doing]." For a first comment, though, using acknowledge and pause seems to me a bit less intrusive. For children to respond freely, they need to feel unpressured.

Especially when acknowledging feelings, some educators use the term *reflective listening* as another label for acknowledge and pause. Leaders use acknowledge and pause to recognize actions, thoughts, and feelings of fellow staff as well as children. Here's an illustration:

> **Lead teacher Allison to staff member:** Maya, you look pretty tired; baby have a hard night? (*Gives staff member a concerned smile and pauses.*)
>
> **Maya:** Yeah, she did, and Roger was up with an earache, so guess I need an extra coffee this morning.
>
> **Allison:** Maybe we can get you a break later in the staff room.
>
> **Maya:** I don't take many of those, but maybe today.

Acknowledge and pause can also aid communication with those for whom a first or second language is emerging. This kind of acknowledgment takes reading the other's face during the pause and putting into words your guess about the other half of the contact talk. Smiling at parent Lula and gesturing toward her son, teacher Rory says, "Nito had a good time today. He made a new friend." During the pause, Lula nods and smiles, seeing her child is still playing with the friend. Rory and Lula exchange thumbs-ups! Warm words (and gestures) with others are never wasted.

Acknowledge and pause, of course, is essential with infants: while changing a nappy and smiling, teacher Jordan says, "Margareth, your digestive system is working A-OK today!" Jordan looks into the infant's eyes and smiles and nods. Margareth gives some fun echolalic babbling while looking at Jordan, who again smiles. "I couldn't have said it better myself. Now, let's go have some mat time, shall we?"

....

Ever have a conversation with a baby like Jordan did, but when the very little one's attention span was longer than yours? I admit I did with a grandbaby once—I was ready to take a nap, but lying on my chest, Thomas wasn't! Jordan was building an attachment, a secure relationship, with Margareth. Now an adult, Thomas and I still get along pretty well too—though his attention span for some things is still way longer than mine!

....

If TTs take the time, acknowledge and pause easily evolves into contact talks—the heart of building relationships.

Make Contact Talks Happen

Life is full of **task talk** because there are so many tasks to be done—everything from "Get your shoes on and we will tie them together" to "Our teaching team needs to meet at rest time." In contrast, **contact talks** are for the purpose of spending a few moments of quality time with a child or family member, sharing experiences and getting to know one another. Contact talks don't have to be long, but they do need to happen often, every day with every child, or more!

Teacher Shawn: Mornin', Alphonso. Sherry told me all about how she can run really fast in her new sneakers. She showed me too!

Dad Alphonso: (*Grins.*) Yeah, she likes them so much she never wants to take them off. Last night they were dirty, and she got all worried. We washed and dried them, and this morning they were ready to go.

Shawn grins. Alphonso and Shawn exchange "Have a good day's," and the brief contact talk ends.

It didn't take much to reinforce this relationship. Talking positively about parents' kids always works.

Contact Talks During Play

Play is a natural time to have contact talks with children. In my view, it is usually best if the adult is a responsive observer rather than a coparticipant. (In activities other than dramatic play—like restaurant or car repair—adults who play "cooperatively" with children tend to influence their minds away from directing their own play to following the adult's lead.) Stay near to the child to show that you are paying attention. Then comment on the child's efforts in a way that builds on what the child is doing. Very often, you will get a response. If not, wait a bit and offer another compliment. If still no response, just enjoy the child's steadfast creating silently with them—and maybe do a bit more assessing to learn more about the child!

Teacher: You are really working hard on that tower. (*Pauses.*)

Helena (mid-4): Not a tower, a Hogwarts. There's Hermione. (*Puts a figure on top.*) (Pre-Harry Potter, not many 52-month-olds would name a figure "Hermione"!)

Teacher: She's there on the Hogwarts tower. (*Pauses.*)

Helena: Yeah, Harry is still in the box. Out you go, Harry. They're waiting for Ron.

Teacher: You must like Harry Potter.

Helena: Yeah, we got wands! My sister reads the books.

Teacher: My kids still do too.

Helena: You got kids, teacher?

Use Friendly Humor

Friendly humor means finding humor *with* another person, not at their expense. Friendly humor helps an early childhood professional build relationships, diffuse tense situations, and make it through the occasional craziness present in any work setting. Friendly humor puts people at ease. For some of us, the humor comes naturally. Others have to work hard to get another to smile. The good news is jokes don't have to be great, just well intended. A bit of self-deprecation often adds, like when another person forgets something important—says the author who forgot to shave before a presentation and brought the wrong adapter for his Mac.

Illustration. An early childhood professional said to a parent, "Gloria, I am still smiling. During that cloudburst today, I told the kids it was raining cats and dogs out there. They all looked outside. Your Andrea said, 'And elephants even!' She said it better than I did!" Finding friendly humor in what children say is a perk for all in the profession. Example: Erin had been riding a Hot Wheels hard on a hot afternoon. Teacher Cleo asked Erin about getting a drink of water. Erin replied: "Yeah, I need a drink, and my shadow does too!" The two smiled at each other.

When we frequently encourage friendly humor in young children, I really think that as they grow, they keep and share this gift.

....

After a couple of beverages of my choice, I once had a "warm" discussion with an English professor about my contention that J.K. Rowling is as important to British literature as William Shakespeare. Rowling changed the whole world for children and books. An 8-year-old in any of 250 countries reads a book as thick as an encyclopedia—and this is only Volume 1! What a gift to worldwide literacy. Yes, Rowling deserves criticism—about her attitudes and some of her post-Potter books. While I don't begrudge the criticisms at all, I think we have to give Rowling's *Harry Potter* series its amazing due.

....

Use Appropriate, Friendly Touch

Appropriate, friendly touch does what words cannot (Carlson 2006). Sitting on a lap or sharing a hug, a pat on the shoulder, or at least high fives and fist bumps are organically reassuring to children. Along with nodding and smiling, friendly touch is vital in the caregiver's nonverbal vocabulary. We all know this, but in our age of vigilant awareness, programs need to be transparent regarding policies and practices regarding friendly touch.

As to policies, I suggest a "Welcome to Our Program" guidebook, given to and gone over with new families and staff members, and referenced as needed at other times. The guidebook addresses important matters like your mission statement, education philosophy (including on equity), guidance approach, **family engagement** invitation, and your program's policy on appropriate, friendly touch. I probably don't have to mention this, but I came across it once: please have the same touch policy for both men and women early childhood professionals!

As to practices, staff members who work together know how they each use touch in the daily program. They know and follow the policies in the guidebook. They understand that friendly touch is vital in caring for children. If a family member expresses a concern about touch, TTs show respect for the family member's concerns and work closely with administrators—but they stand up for their policies, practices, and each other.

Yes, when conflicts happen, touch calms most children in ways that words alone cannot. Teachers use touch when they sense that the physical contact will calm and refocus children so that problems can be cooperatively resolved (Carlson 2006). Most children with whom teachers have taken the time to build relationships accept touch as a part of the teacher's calming efforts, and afterward as an indicator of renewed good relations. Still, teachers have a sense of how to use touch and when, based on their knowledge of the child. They are sensitive about the limits of touch with some children who show aversion to physical closeness—but do their best to figure out why. Cultural reasons? Temperament reasons? Sensitivity to sensory stimuli? Reasons involving aggravated strong unmet needs? In these situations, teachers find other ways to respond that the child is more comfortable with.

Used naturally but with sensitivity, appropriate, friendly touch guides children through tough times even while it helps to build relationships. Give me a high five or a fist bump here, readers—or at least a smile and nod.

Utilize Compliment Sandwiches

The **compliment sandwich** is a self-check on how to respond to others in situations that might be problematic. It is a specific request with at least the initial and closing interactions being positive and encouraging. The purpose is to let the other know you are on the same team, working together, and not working against them. Here are a couple of examples:

With staff member: "Marlo, the seven assessments are complete and written very objectively. Yay! Just need to finish the other five. I said by today, but Monday morning would be fine if that would help out? I always look forward to reading your reports."

With children: "You have the blocks all put back on the shelves. That must have taken some muscles. Just need to get the trucks in the box, and we are ready to go outside! You all are really working hard."

Compliment sandwiches are versatile. You can use them in an initial exchange or as a follow-up. It is best to use three or four pieces of bread—compliments—for each layer of liver with pickled-cabbage-and-pesto. Like acknowledge and pause, compliment sandwiches don't have to merge into long conversation. Sometimes the other person wants them short, especially when they know that you know the whole story.

Compliment sandwiches are a practical and helpful tool. When people feel that the compliments are authentic, they are more likely to listen to suggestions for change. It helps, though, to have a relationship with the other person. And for most of us, the sandwiches take practice.

Give Encouragement: Private to Individuals, Public to the Group

First, let's reiterate an idea key in developmental guidance. If you want a compliment to mean something real to the other person, cut down on short-cut generalities like "Nice work" or "Good job." I refer to such well-intended general judgments as *praise*. Instead, use **encouragement**. Compliment details in children's efforts: "You are working hard to make that breakfast." After a pause, you might hear, "Yep. Mom says not too much bacon, but lots of eggs."

Encouragement, in contrast, is specific, positive acknowledgment, the feedback we should want to give while an effort is being made at least as much as after a project is completed. With individuals and small groups, we give private (at least quiet)

encouragement. Then, the individuals know that we mean the encouragement just for them, which affirms their sense of belonging and blooming creativity.

Folks generally know about giving specific encouragement to individuals. Less well known is the importance of giving a different kind of positive feedback, *public encouragement*, to the group. To sustain an encouraging, inclusive setting, teachers avoid singling out individuals when they give public encouragement. In other words, not this: "Sonny and Brooke are busy putting things away," but this: "You all are really putting everything away!" In the first example, the reaction of the others is going to be, "I am putting things away too, Teacher." What is unspoken in the reaction of the children is, "I am putting things away too! You didn't say my name. You must like Sonny and Brooke better."

••

I have tried this "experiment" of singling out individuals when I present to adults, and they have the same reactions kids do! After getting the names of two in the audience, I say, "I really like how Lilley and Linda are paying such close attention." Immediately others say, "What about me, I was listening too" and "me too"—much to the chagrin of my two "favorites." I then apologize to them all, including the two, and tell the group I appreciate how attentive they all are.

••

Public comments that single children out set up winner and loser patterns in the group. The teacher may think they are motivating the group to do something, but the social psychology of this act tends to indicate a different effect. Singling out individuals in public tends to divide the group rather than bring it together, and it might make classroom life more difficult for the identified children. Better to compliment all by either calling out every name or making a comment that affirms the efforts of everyone.

But what of the few kids who are not helping to put things away? We speak to them individually and quietly. No sense going public with individual mistaken behaviors. TTs try to avoid embarrassing individuals in front of groups for any reason. If the group has a general problem with putting things away, TTs hold a group meeting—without using individual names—to resolve the issue. (This would be a use of a large group meeting that is *intervention guidance* in orientation.)

Remember Names, Contact Talks, and Promises

Remembering names is a gift that some folks are born with. If the skill is not a natural one, intentionally cultivate it. One teacher for whom remembering names was not a gift used an attendance activity to match name tags to children, which they wore until she no longer needed them. Most kids stopped using them when the teacher gave them the choice.

Remembering previous contact talks means a lot to people, more than one might think. When teachers can refer to them, it is a sign of respect for the other person. Almost always, the other will remember the gist of the first talk and continue the conversation as if there were no interruption. Let's return to the example of teacher Shawn and parent Alphonso:

> **Shawn:** Well, Alphonso, Sherry is still running around in those sneakers! Cool that they light up with every step!
>
> **Alphonso:** Yeah, they may be the first pair that she wears out before they get too small. We had to get the other two shoes like hers. We turned off all the lights and watched the kids dance around. It was fun.
>
> **Shawn:** (*Gives a big grin and a thumbs-up.*)

4. Three Levels of Mistaken Behavior

The *three levels of mistaken behavior* is a construct to explain the mistaken behaviors that young children fall into during conflicts. I inherited the roots of the concept from Professor Steven Harlow, my mentor during doctoral work at the University of North Dakota. Harlow and a colleague developed a concept of "three levels of social relations" (Harlow 1975), from which the three levels of mistaken behavior are derived. A value of the levels of mistaken behavior concept is that it assists the TT to focus on the reasons for the mistaken behavior rather than dwell on the morality of the act.

An overview of the levels of mistaken behavior follows. The ordering of the levels—three, two, one—is intentional.

Level Three Strong Unmet-Needs Mistaken Behavior

This level of mistaken behavior is the most disruptive that TTs encounter. While anyone can have a one-time meltdown (a "Level Three day"), Level Three mistaken behavior shown on a regular basis means children are struggling with DLS 1—finding acceptance as a member of the group and as a worthy individual. Level Three mistaken behavior is survival behavior, generated by the amygdala and hypothalamus in the brain in reaction to perceived threat. Until children have a grasp of DLS 2, they will show Level Three mistaken behavior. As kids gain a foothold with DLS 1, their unmet needs gradually change from being *existential* to *experiential* (explained more in the chapter to follow). After children gain DLS 1, their Level Three mistaken behavior tends to be less tumultuous, but it still can be disruptive.

Aggression shown at Level Three is the survival behavior of acting out to defend oneself. The aggression might be *reactive*—an impulsive emotional reaction to feeling threatened—or *instrumental*—aggressive or oppressive behaviors done intentionally. Yes, even conflicts begun "on purpose" are mistaken behaviors. Unmet needs and mistaken efforts to meet the needs are still behind intentional conflicts, a challenging situation for any TT. In the next two chapters, readers encounter five impressive examples of Level Three strong unmet-needs mistaken behaviors, and impressive teacher responses.

It is important to note that Level Three strong unmet-needs mistaken behavior also can be self-isolating, not just aggressive. Depression in children is a common reactive behavior to adverse experiences. Watch for this potential manifestation of mistaken survival behavior and not just the aggressive kind—more on this in the next chapter.

Level Two Socially Influenced Mistaken Behavior

When young children emulate the words and deeds of significant others during conflicts, they show Level Two mistaken behavior. The influencer might be a significant other, often but not always from *outside* of the group setting. Children also might be socially influenced by peers *in* the setting, often falling into group "catchy" mistaken behavior.

Illustrations. If they get too much glue on their paper, an individual child might use a choice term, like "shit," learned in the home or neighborhood. As to "catchy" Level Two mistaken behavior, within the early learning setting a child might get caught up in the contagious mistaken behavior of a group calling each other "poopy butt" or "butthead." (Timeless terms.)

Level One Experimentation Mistaken Behavior

Children who have largely gained the safety-need skills make mistakes in their behavior as they progress with the growing-needs skills. Being new to the world but ready to engage with it, the problem solving of early childhood takes the form of life experiments, both controlled and uncontrolled. *Uncontrolled experiments* are situations that go in a direction the child did not expect. An example is a child who puts chairs in a row as "the bus to Head Start." The child who set up the chairs is expecting to be the driver, but as that child goes off to find a steering wheel, another child takes the first seat. Instead of calling for mediation, the child physically tries to take back the driver's chair.

A controlled experiment is when a child tests limits to see what will happen. A kid looks at you and, with a grin, engages in a self-initiated word recognition activity: "Shit, teacher." The lack of intense, lasting negative effect behind the mistaken behavior tells the teacher it is likely Level One or Level Two, but not Level Three. The kid is experimenting to find out more about this powerful word—and what you are going to do about it!

Children who are working on DLS 5 provide an interesting lesson in Level One mistaken behavior. Connie (62 months) tells you, "Carlos called Melvyn a bad name." Do you tell Connie in one way or another to mind her own business, or instead say, "Thank you for caring, Connie," and check it out with the two children? Suppose the name were a racial epithet? If it is only tattling, we can talk with Connie, and if tattling becomes contagious, discuss in a group meeting the difference between tattling and reporting. (See "Tattling: It Drives Teachers Bonkers" [Gartrell 2007], a *Young Children* piece. Oldy but goody.)

In a Minnesota winter a driver has forgotten their cell phone and their car slides into a ditch. That person wants someone to stop and check on them. Besides thinking "There is no way I am ever driving in Minnesota in the winter again" (at least without a cell phone), wouldn't you want someone to stop if it were you? As the good old Department of Homeland Security says, more or less, if you see something amiss, say or do something. To report a serious concern is a DLS 5 skill. We call it being "Minnesota nice," but really it is any human being nice. Being kind.

Why TTs Should Work for Children to Show Level One Mistaken Behavior

The level of mistaken behavior mirrors the mental health of the child. Children showing Level Three are struggling with the attainment of the safety-needs skills. Level Two mistaken behavior means that kids haven't fully gained DLS 2. Level 1 mistaken behavior indicates so much healthy personal development that the months-old child is willing to risk mistakes and engage with new experiences. Let's talk more about the dynamics of Level Two mistaken behavior.

Some adults might like the attentive dependency of a "good" child who hangs on their every word. These adults should realize that as this child grows, their needed source of influence is likely to shift to other (perhaps less scrupulous) adults and to peers, some who are wild and crazy. For me, the long-term pitfall for children who do not grow out of Level Two mistaken behavior is this: unless individuals develop the personal resources to see matters as they are for themselves, they are in danger of falling into a pattern of uncritically following significant others long term. They come to need the personal security of going along to get along.

Believing conspiratorial views on the internet because influential peers do—despite what the evidence says—seems to me to be an example of a long-term manifestation of the effects of people being stuck at Level Two. A need to blindly conform to pressures from esteemed authority sources, whoever they are, tends not be healthy for the long-term continuation of democracy. Democracy needs people who think for themselves and are persuaded by cooperative discourse, not by the power of influential others. (Some of us, including my mentors Adler, Maslow, Erikson, Katz, and Rogers, think this is also the path for a most full and rewarding individual life.)

We should want teachers in their work to nudge and guide toward ethical independent thinking—even in young children. Early childhood educators should understand that emerging, ethical long-term independence comes with occasional Level One mistaken behavior.

Encouraging independence in children is sometimes viewed as a culture-bound idea, pertaining particularly to the United States. Training the young to be rugged individualists—me against the world—is not what this discussion is about. It is about empowering individuals who shoulder an injured fellow racer and the two crossing the finish line together or who stop for a stranded motorist and lend that person a cell phone. Ethical independence embraces cooperative activity. It means a person who makes their own decisions based on the facts *and* cares about others. In efforts to be intelligent and ethical, all of us occasionally make mistakes, especially little humans who are only months old. But to gain this skill is to contribute to modern democracy.

5. Developmental Guidance: Major Practices

TTs use guidance in two circumstances: in nonconflict situations, which I call **developmental** (no longer "preventive" or "proactive") **guidance**; and when conflicts occur, which is **intervention guidance**. The eight communication practices introduced on pages 53–58, which build and sustain relationships, are helpful both in developmental and intervention guidance. So are large group meetings. **Large group meetings** epitomize democratic living in the encouraging early learning community, and so provide direct practice for adult community life. The meetings are a cornerstone of early childhood education as progressive education in and for modern democratic society. Intentionally developing curriculum that builds on children's interests—often termed **emergent curriculum**—is also a practice of developmental guidance.

Developmental Large Group Meetings with Young Children

Circle gatherings long have been used by Native Americans and other cultures for matters of group deliberation in a spirit of equality. The circle suggests the worth of each individual and lends itself to building of community spirit. Circle times in the classroom go back 200 years to Friedrich Froebel's first kindergartens in Germany. Traditional circle times long have included fingerplays, songs, stories, movement activities, weather, calendar, and show and tell (Gartrell 2014). While these rituals might provide the predictability that young children need, my experience is that teachers need to take attention spans into account when leading circle time.

On occasion, circle times flow into class meetings, but each has a different focus. Large group meetings (also called *class* or *community meetings*) transcend daily routines to deal with life in the classroom. The large group meeting is designed for the active involvement of each child. Its purpose is to encourage listening, thinking, and sharing by children and teachers about their experiences, needs, problems, concerns, and triumphs (Vance 2014). Class meetings enable children to be contributing citizens of a learning community, work together to attain a sense of belonging, develop individual responsibility, and cooperatively solve problems (Vance 2014). Group meetings not only help children practice social problem solving but also empower individual children to build communication and social skills.

· ·

A go-to resource for me for information on large group meetings has been the book Class Meetings: Young Children Solving Problems Together, revised edition, by Emily Vance (2014). Unfortunately, it is now out of print. In "The Beauty of Class Meetings" (Gartrell 2006), I discuss why I believe class meetings are the single most important institutional function in the encouraging early learning community. They teach for the DLS as no other single activity can.

· ·

Holding Large Group Meetings

Group meetings provide opportunities for the teacher and children together to set guidelines for the class; plan for and decide on events, issues, and procedures; and solve problems. As community leaders, TTs often hold special meetings with the group at the beginning of the year to develop a few overall guidelines (Gartrell 2014). Typical guidelines for the meetings are these:

> Anyone can talk.

> Take turns and listen carefully.

> Be careful about using children's names.

> Be kind.

How TTs lead the meetings is crucial. The teacher uses direct teaching about the meeting process and gives ongoing verbal and nonverbal support to make sure the meetings stay focused on positive problem solving. Vance (2014) offers helpful advice for teachers ready to try class meetings:

> If you are just beginning to use class meetings and are weighing the benefits, make a commitment to hold them for at least three months before judging the results. It may take that long for children to incorporate their new social skills, begin to use

them regularly, and learn to trust one another. The change in the classroom's social climate will be noticeable. (29)

To sum up, large group meetings

> Boost individuals' confidence at using civil words to solve social problems

> Provide children experience in balancing the needs and viewpoints of others with their own

> Offer supportive opportunities to learn to speak in public (a prevalent phobia in the United States)

> Build group spirit and inclusiveness in the early learning community

> Give children practice with using the DLS

Each time a meeting occurs, children are reminded that the classroom is a community that includes all. The meetings contribute to building a new generation with potentially years of experience in the democratic functioning of groups, well prepared to face and respond proactively to society's problems. Illustrations of large group meetings appear in Chapters 6 and 7.

Emergent Curriculum

Emergent curriculum stands on its own as an education approach, often associated with the Reggio Emilia approach. The idea of emergent curriculum is that early childhood educators pick up on the interests and experiences of young children and with them build creative, multisensory thematic investigations that incorporate interdisciplinary content (Masterson 2022). TTs observe group and individual activities during these times, noting possible topics that could lead to a next thematic wave.

As developmental guidance, emergent curriculum can start from regularly scheduled large group meetings, intervention group meetings, or even children's experiences and mistaken behaviors. (Individuals may be kept anonymous.) An illustration of emergent curriculum via a group experience is the discovery by an urban kindergarten class of wind-strewn flyers across the playground. The TT brought the litter to the attention of the class in an afternoon group meeting and asked the group what they could do. The kindergarten kids, of course, said they could pick it up. Together, they made a plan for the next day.

The TT went into action. One member contacted families through a class website to have their children bring in paper shopping bags (recyclable). The other got hold of a large box of extra-small nonlatex gloves. During outdoor time the next day, the children and teachers bagged the remaining flyers and other litter and brought it in. The children stored their gloves in their cubbies for possible reuse. Using glue and tape in two groups, they made two large litter collages. The teachers wrote on the collages the captions that the two groups decided on: "Don't litter. Keep the playground clean" and "Put the stuff in the cans."

With the principal's permission, the TTs and class hung the collages in the central hallway and by recycling and trash receptacles in a sheltered area by the front door. Both the principal and janitor visited the class to thank them. Being a Mr. Rogers fan, one teacher retrieved an episode of his on littering. The group watched and discussed it, then loaned it out to other teachers to show. Some of the students in the upper grades told their former kindergarten teacher that they were impressed that the "kindygartners" could do all that.

Seems like a great project for building good neighbors. As developmental guidance, emergent curriculum flows naturally into teaching for the DLS.

6. Key Intervention Guidance Practices

The purpose of intervention guidance is to bring *mindfulness* to the matter of resolving conflicts in the encouraging early learning community—regarding both adults and young children. Mindfulness for children means helping them identify their strong feelings, learn to manage feelings during conflicts, and gain the awareness that conflicts can be solved cooperatively. Striving for mindfulness, TTs bring the nonjudgmental concepts of mistaken behavior and teaching for healthy emotional-social development into conflict situations. In an encouraging early learning community, all members feel physically and emotionally safe, and no one is to be harmed.

Mindfulness:

1: the quality or state of being mindful

2: the practice of maintaining a nonjudgmental state of heightened or complete awareness of one's thoughts, emotions, or experiences on a moment-to-moment basis. (*Merriam-Webster.com Dictionary*, s.v. "mindfulness" (n), www.merriam-webster.com/dictionary/mindfulness)

Earlier in my career, after researching problem-solving models to maximize mindfulness, I came up with a **five finger formula** that teachers might use when resolving conflicts that involve strong feelings. The five finger formula is designed to assist all to get calm and work through the conflict in a mindful manner, considerate of all. The formula serves teachers well as an overall strategy for resolving problems in the encouraging early childhood learning community. Steps in the five finger formula are as follows:

1. Thumb: Calm everyone down—yourself, too. Set the scene for the mediation.

2. Pointer: Guide the children to accept how each person sees the conflict. (Individual perspectives might not be what others thought happened. Understanding this is key to conflict resolution.)

3. Tall guy: Brainstorm possible solutions. (Provide suggestions for children with limited language or who are dual language learners. Respect nonverbal signs of agreement or disagreement.)

4. Ringer: Agree to one solution and try it. (The solution may not be what you had in mind, but if it makes sense and all are okay with it, go with this solution.) Sometimes steps 3 and 4 might naturally merge.

5. Pinky: Monitor the solution and positively acknowledge effort. Hold guidance talks with individuals if needed. Discuss what children can do next time instead.

Referring to the intervention guidance practices listed below, TTs use the five finger formula more formally during conflict mediation and less formally in guidance talks, intervention large group meetings, and comprehensive guidance (both with adults and children). Calming, after triaging for injury, is always the first guidance step. Five key guidance practices are

1. Calming methods
2. Guidance talks
3. Conflict mediation
4. Intervention large group meetings
5. Comprehensive guidance

Use Calming Methods

I use the word *calming* because it is more calming than *de-escalation*. When a conflict occurs, teachers understandably want to get the situation back under control as soon as possible. But in a guidance approach, the teacher responds to the conflict more like a first responder and mediator, and less like a police officer and judge. So, after making sure no one is injured, calm everyone down, starting with yourself if necessary. Folks—especially children—find it impossible to resolve conflicts when stress levels are high. The goal is to help everyone cool down so they can talk about what happened. Some suggestions from former students for cooling down are these:

> Use deep breaths. Model the deep breathing if this helps (you or the child).

> Ask the children to sit like a pretzel, close their eyes, and think of their favorite thing.

> Have the children choose their own calming technique—deep breaths, counting slowly, just sitting quietly, jumping up and down 10 times. Support the children's choices.

> Use reflective listening: "I can see those tears on your cheeks. You are really upset."

> Provide hugs and laps. (As kids get calm, they often lean into you.)

> Help children leave the conflict situation; provide the separate space and time they need to cool down. Provide a cooling-down time.

Please note that a cooling-down time is different from a time-out. Time-out, or temporary expulsion for something a child has done, is punishment. A cooling-down time is to help the child regain composure so you can talk about what happened. In deciding whether to have a child move away from the conflict, it helps to remind yourself of this difference.

To emphasize that children are not being punished, staying with them for a few minutes is sometimes effective. Use your knowledge of the child to determine whether to stay. Some children, in particular some boys (Gartrell 2014), need more than a few minutes to get calm. Give it to them. Explain that after everyone is calm you will talk about the situation and "fix this problem." (This is where you depend on the relationships you have been building with children outside of conflict situations. If your effort is firm, friendly, and flexible—even if not perfect—it *will* make things better.)

Use Guidance Talks with Individuals

Teachers use **guidance talks** when individual children show mistaken behavior at any level and need to learn an alternative behavior. A guidance talk is not a contact talk. Unlike a contact talk, a guidance talk is task oriented; it is specific teaching for expected learning. A guidance talk also is *not* a lecture, giving a child a "talking to." During a guidance talk, the teacher speaks individually with (not to) the child. TT members use the five finger formula, although the steps are more informally used than in conflict mediation (discussed in the next section), to guide both the child and adult to resolve the conflict.

Guidance talks are important because there is a consequence for a child who causes a conflict: make amends and learn a better way to handle the situation. *As well, there is a consequence for the adult:* teach the child for progress with DLS 1 and 2. Through using the guidance talk, the teacher scaffolds from the mistaken behavior toward a less hurtful conflict response. The following illustrates a guidance talk, reported by Francisca with Roland, who had just turned 5. A word about the code in the conflict resolution vignette: *FFF* stands for five finger formula; *FFF 1* means the first step (calm all down). Here is Francisca's account:

> Roland was having a tough day. Nothing was going right. He spilled his milk during breakfast. Two children got on a teacher's lap first for reading a story. Other children took all the slots at the playdough table so he couldn't do his favorite activity during choice time. While he was building with the unit blocks,

another child accidentally knocked over part of his tower. At this point, Roland lost it. He kicked at the child as she walked by, threw a block at the wall, sat down, and cried.

I went over and sat by him and put my arm around his shoulders (FFF 1). After a minute, he snuggled against my side, and we sat there. I said, "Things don't seem to be going your way today" (FFF 2). He shook his head and sniffled a bit but stopped crying. I asked, "When things bother you, I wonder what you can do to help you feel better?" (FFF 3). I paused and waited.

Roland said, "Tell you." I said that I thought that was a good idea (FFF 4). I said he could either call for me or come over to get me. I told him he could count on me or Lisa (the other teacher) to help. We talked about how a child could get hurt if kids threw blocks. He listened, looked down, and gave a nod. I reminded him that Carla (the other child) maybe felt bad about what happened. I asked Roland how he could help her feel better.

"Tell her sorry," he said. I asked Roland if he would like me to go with him or if he could do it by himself. He said he could do it, and he did. Roland worked some more on his tower, knocked it over himself, and put the blocks away. I later complimented him by saying, "You talked with Carla, and it looks like you had fun again with the blocks" (FFF 5). Not looking at me but slightly smiling, Roland said, "Yep, I did."

Every guidance talk is different. This one worked because Francisca had been building a relationship with Roland for two months when this conflict occurred. She knew he was dealing with a lot at home and at this point didn't play with other children much. Roland had begun to trust Francisca for help, but this day was just too tough for him. Notice that Francisca did not force an issue by saying "Now you go tell Carla you're sorry." She asked Roland what he could do to help her feel better. This freedom lets the child own the act of reconciliation, an important aspect of mastering Skill 2. And if a child says no? "That's okay, maybe you can think of a way later." And watch, the child probably will.

Guidance talks require us to be mindful. Perhaps the one thing harder than learning the DLS yourself is teaching them to others—although the task is

perhaps easier in early childhood than in middle and high school! A goal in guidance talks is to reaffirm the relationship with the child despite the mistaken behavior. This is why the teacher needs to be firm, keeping the goal in sight, but also friendly and flexible. Is there a danger of Roland becoming too dependent on Francisca? This risk is why we guide for both growing-needs and safety-needs skills. As Roland gained in a sense of belonging and self-worth, Francisca nudged him toward relationships with others in the community. On another day, Roland would be more ready to join with others, manage his emotions, and cope.

Use Conflict Mediation

TTs adapt conflict **mediation** to the particular DLS that the children are working on. When working with one or both children on the safety-needs DLS, teachers use *high-level mediation* (active coaching). As children make gains with Skills 1 and 2 and begin to pivot to the growing-needs skills, teachers move to *low-level mediation* (facilitating). With practice in the mediation process, children making gains with Skills 3, 4, and 4 become capable of *child negotiation*—even before kindergarten (Gartrell 2014).

In the following illustration of high-level mediation, Jenner, an experienced student teacher, clearly uses the steps of the five finger formula.

One morning two kindergarten boys were arguing over some LEGO wheels. Their faces were getting really intense, and their voices were getting louder.

Dylan: Hey, those are my wheels. You took my wheels. (*Whining loudly.*)

Austin: (*Yelling.*) No, I had them first.

Dylan grabbed at the wheels. Austin pulled them away. Dylan looked like he was deciding whether to "pounce."

Jenner pulled up a chair between the two boys and put a hand on each child's shoulder.

Jenner: Boys, I can see you are upset. Please sit with me for a minute. I will hold the wheels just for now.

The boys reluctantly gave up the wheels.

Jenner: (FFF 1) Thank you. First, let's all take a couple of deep breaths and then we will see how we can fix this. Ready, 1 . . . 2 . . . 3 . . . Okay, now let's talk about what happened. Dylan, you can start and then I will ask Austin next. (TTs often start with the younger, smaller, or more bereaved child.)

Dylan: (FFF 2) He took my wheels that I was using yesterday and was gonna use today.

Jenner: Anything else? . . . Thank you, Dylan. Austin, now you tell me what happened.

Austin: He wasn't here yet, so I used the wheels. It was my turn.

Jenner: It sounds to me like we are having trouble figuring out who should use the wheels. That right?

Boys: Yeah.

Jenner: (FFF3) Okay, let's see if we can't come up with a way to fix this problem. Do either of you have an idea?

Dylan: He should give them back to me.

Jenner: Austin, do you think that is a fair idea?

Austin: No, he had them yesterday. When do I get to play with them?

Jenner: Can you think of another idea, so you both will have a chance to use the wheels?

Dylan: (*Tiring of the palavering.*) He can keep using them today and then next time I will get to use them.

Jenner: (FFF 4) Austin, what do you think of that idea?

Austin: (*Nodding.*) Okay.

Jenner: Great, but next time this happens you need to use your words and not get mad right away. Then if there is a problem, come and get me or Mrs. Garney. How does that sound to you?

Boys: Good.

Jenner: Okay, you have 10 more minutes to play!

(FFF 5). The boys played together with the LEGOs. Jenner stayed and monitored for a few minutes. Austin used the wheels. Dylan found an older, broken-down set but made them work. The next day at playtime, the two boys were back with the LEGOs. Jenner remembered to be close by and watched as Austin and Dylan peaceably negotiated the wheels.

Reflection. (1) So, what is accomplished if a child grows tired of mediation and wants to leave? The teachers make known they would like the children to continue. But, if a kid clearly wants out, the adults make sure the one opting out knows that the other child will gain the disputed privilege. Even in that instance, the situation has been de-escalated and the children have been able to use words to participate in the resolution. Perhaps through an intervention guidance group meeting, TT members discuss with the group that conflicts will happen. The consequence is that we need to get calm to resolve them together.

(2) What if the teacher does not have time to mediate? First, developmentally appropriate programs by design have lots of "self-selected, self-directed autonomous learning activities" (play—the principal activity during **choice times**.) During play, teachers can and should circulate, interact, encourage, facilitate, and mediate if problems come up.

Second, it pays to make the time. Teaching children to put strong feelings into nonhurting words and to accommodate words from others are readiness skills for school and life skills for life. When the group sees you modeling and teaching these skills to others, they gain as well—call it skills in language arts, social studies, and often practical math. *Leaders who teach for the DLS regard the resolving of conflicts not as diversions from the education program, but central to it.*

Still, in an emergency it may not be possible to complete all five steps of the five finger formula. But do FFF 1. After all, kids in conflict constitutes an emergency. By calming and setting up a future mediation, the teacher lets the children know that they and their conflict are important. Just remember to do the follow-up! The children probably will have moved beyond the conflict, which is fine, but then use guidance talks to reinforce the importance of reconciliation efforts and to teach for nonhurting alternatives next time.

Typically, in a successful low-level mediation, after the teacher calms all down and gets the mediation started, the children take over the process and resolve the problem themselves. The following anecdote was written by Camille, a prekindergarten student teacher. At the time of this conflict Camille and the two children, both about 55 months, were already accustomed to working out conflicts through mediation.

> Dana and Chante were in the classroom store. Dana was using the cash register, and Chante was talking on the telephone. Dana picked up another telephone and started talking to her. Chante turned to him and yelled, "Shut up!"
>
> Dana looked very sad. I knelt down and asked if he could tell Chante how that made him feel. He turned to her and said, "I felt really, really sad when you yelled at me."
>
> Chante responded, "I'm sorry, Dana. I didn't mean that, I guess. I was talking to a cust'mer."
>
> I said, "Chante, I think Dana wants to talk on the telephone with you." Chante said, "Yeah, but he's not a cust'mer."
>
> I suggested, "I wonder if Dana could take the telephone to the house and be a customer?"
>
> "I could call you from the house," Dana said.
>
> "Yeah, you need lots of stuff," said Chante, getting into it. "Go over and tell me what you need."
>
> Dana, smiling, "phoned" from the house. Chante had the "stuff" ready for him when he came to pick it up. He gave her some make-believe money, and she even gave him change! (Gartrell 2014, 359)

Reflection. Camille's journal reflection indicated how "pleased and amazed" she was that the children solved the problem. She stated, "These kinds of instances just prove to me that these children will solve their own problems. Sometimes all they need is a little guidance."

Child negotiation happens when conflict mediation skills are woven into the encouraging early childhood community and children show behaviors that reflect the growing-needs DLS. One or both children in a conflict choose not to escalate or retaliate, but to negotiate. Progress with DLS 3, 4, and 5 are clear when a child or children act with this maturity.

The following illustration of child negotiation features two children late in their preschool years. Notice how one child does not retaliate but calls for the two to negotiate. Notice also how a *peace prop*, in this case a sock puppet known as Peace Sock, aids the children as they learn the turn-taking needed in social problem solving. Again, this anecdote was written up by a student teacher.

> Nakisha and Suel Lin were caring for a variety of dolls in the kindergarten housekeeping area. They both reached for the last doll to be fed, bathed, and put to bed. They started yelling that they each had it first, and Suel Lin took Nakisha's arm and started squeezing it.
>
> "Stop, that hurts," exclaimed Nakisha. "Use your words!" "I don't know them," yelled Suel Lin.
>
> "Then we get Peace Sock," Nakisha demanded. Both girls, still holding part of the doll, walked over and got Peace Sock. "I will wear him, Suel Lin, and you tell Sock."
>
> Suel Lin said to Sock, "Baby needs a bath, but we both want to do it."
>
> "Both do it," said Sock in a deep Nakisha voice.
>
> The two girls put back Peace Sock and returned to the housekeeping area, both holding the doll. One girl washed the top half, the other the bottom half. Then Suel Lin fed the doll while Nakisha read a story to the other dolls already in bed. Suel Lin said, "Do you want to read another story?"
>
> "Yeah," said Nakisha, who read another story while Suel Lin rubbed the babies' backs as they lay in their beds. (Gartrell 2014, 360)

Reflection. When children choose to use a peace prop without teacher guidance, as Nakisha and Suel Lin did, they are using child negotiation, and gaining real practice at using DLS 3, 4, and 5. Nakisha's decision not to retaliate but to negotiate epitomizes DLS 5. In her journal, the student teacher who recorded the anecdote reflected, "I couldn't believe how Nakisha and Suel Lin solved the problem. I didn't have to do anything!" This was thanks to Nakisha's mature response when Suel Lin squeezed her arm. The student teacher was right to go home and drink a celebratory beverage of her choice.

For young children, peace props (like puppets here) can be magical. *Talk-and-listen chairs* are another prop that can be used for this purpose—children exchange chairs as they alternately talk to explain their side of a conflict and listen to the other's viewpoint. A third prop is a *talking stick*—a decorated stick held at each end by the child whose turn it is to speak, while the other child listens. For older folks, the props may not be magical, but they are a concrete reminder to take turns talking and listening.

Preventing Bullying

A strength of conflict mediation is that it allows children who are at a power imbalance during a conflict to move to a balanced power status. Conflict mediation works against a bully-victim pattern taking hold in the classroom (reinforced when a teacher comforts the "victim" and punishes the "bully") (Gartrell 2014). This is a benefit for all in the learning community. In fact, to me this outcome alone makes conflict mediation worth the effort to learn and use. Zooming back from the immediate parties in mediation, the entire group benefits from seeing democratic civility modeled as well as taught. The clear, even dramatic benefits of conflict mediation make this intervention the go-to practice when two children, or a small group of children, experience conflict.

Use Large Group Meetings as Intervention Guidance

Previously we looked at using large group meetings as a developmental guidance practice, to set guidelines for the community, formulate plans, review activities, and host guests. A second use of class meetings is to solve problems that involve the whole group. If one child calls another "butthead," that is not enough to hold a class meeting—the teacher deals with it privately. But if that term or a similar one has caught on with other children—a Level Two catchy mistaken behavior—then a class meeting can address the issue with all.

Class meetings are the guidance alternative to an outmoded practice of conventional discipline, the *group punishment*. A group punishment occurs when *some* children in the group engage in mistaken behavior. The teacher, not knowing who was involved, imposes a punishment on the whole group. Remember this experience from your years at school? Unfortunately, group punishments set teacher and students, and students and students, against each other (Gartrell 2014). By using a class meeting to address an issue together, TTs prevent the negative group dynamics caused by group punishment. Rather than the emotional message "The teacher thinks we're untrustworthy," the message children receive from group meetings is more like, "Okay, we have a problem. We can solve this together."

Two illustrations of group meetings—in a second grade and a prekindergarten classroom—show the problem-solving intervention function of class meetings.

Second grade class meeting: In a suburban classroom, some members of Ms. V.'s class were leaving the restrooms (both!) a mess. Ms. V. wasn't sure who was responsible, so she held a class meeting, reminding the children of the meeting guidelines they had set up. She passed around a talking stick so that individual children could take turns discussing the problem, identifying possible solutions, and agreeing on a course of action. Used to the meetings, class members handled the "delicate" nature of the meeting well. Ms. V. helped the group identify and list some guidelines, which she reminded them of for the next few days. It worked—the janitor reported an improvement, which Ms. V. relayed to the class.

Prekindergarten class meeting: In a Head Start class, children were having problems when playing on a new climber that had been set up in the room to promote physical activity. During an intervention class meeting, the TT used the FFF social problem-solving steps with the children.

1. The TT identified the problem and set the scene for the meeting.

2. They had the children share specific issues, such as pushing and crowding on the ladder and slide.

3. They brainstormed solutions with the group.

4. Together, they decided on three guidelines for use of the climber.

5. The TT posted the written guidelines by the climber, which the teachers and children monitored.

The guidelines they decided on were these:

1. Give kids room when climbing up the ladder.

2. Give kids room on top of the climber.

3. We go down the slide except on Fridays.

The teachers loved the third guideline—a wonderful, child-devised solution to the common problem of children trying to climb up the slide when others are coming down. This solution provided a functional calendar experience *and* allowed for (often neglected) upper-body exercise. Children come up with solutions adults would never think of. If these solutions have a chance, try to make them work.

Use Comprehensive Guidance

Anyone is entitled to a Level Three day, such as the day Roland experienced. Children who show unusual, extreme behaviors over more than a day or two, though, have problems that are getting the best of them and that they need help to overcome. In these situations, when children are clearly struggling with DLS 1 and 2, TTs use **comprehensive guidance.**

Comprehensive guidance might involve all the intervention practices. It certainly involves reliance on the relationship the teacher is building with the child. When encountering sustained Level Three mistaken behavior by a child, TTs can develop a formal or informal **individual guidance plan (IGP)**, a coordinated strategy of intervention and assistance (Gartrell 2014). (You can download an IGP form at dangartrell.net; click "Presentation Handouts.") When using an IGP, one TT member is the designated lead. This teacher serves as contact person as the team often must work to secure additional assistance: an administrator (or, in a larger program, specialized staff), as well as consultants and professionals from outside the program. The more serious a child's mistaken behaviors, the more people, time, and energy the TT must engage in working for a solution.

Always, though, comprehensive guidance includes partnerships with families that the TT has been building since day one. The full-out use of comprehensive guidance to guide children who have big problems is liberation teaching, not giving up on any child. As the lead of her TT, teacher Rena uses comprehensive guidance and liberation teaching in this anecdote, which she narrates:

Eric was 27 months old when he joined our toddler room. After a few days, Eric began to have conflicts just after arriving in the morning. He would not wash his hands or come to the breakfast table. When I tried to invite him, he worked himself into a rage, yelling the F-word (with his own particular pronunciation) and throwing things. Because his behavior distressed the other toddlers, I had to move him to a far corner of the room and hold him until he calmed down.

When Eric repeated this behavior over the following days, I asked Juanita, his young mom, if she could come 10 minutes early at pickup so we could meet. I said we enjoyed having Eric in her group and that he really liked playdough and playing outside. But, I explained to Juanita how he was having problems, especially when he arrived, and we wanted to help the boy.

Juanita responded right away. She shared that their apartment was small, and the activities of some older family members often kept Eric from settling down and getting to sleep. From their conversation, we concluded that the toddler's reactive aggression was due to lack of sleep related to conditions at home.

We worked out a strategy with Juanita and the other staff. Director Dacia sat in on the staff meeting. Together we made an informal individual guidance plan. When Eric arrived in the morning, I approached him in a low-key way and gave him the choice of getting ready for breakfast or snuggling. Eric often chose snuggling and occasionally even fell asleep. He then ate breakfast. During the day, we gave him choices between activities. Eric began making choices (often playdough) and participating more. Two assistant teachers and I sought out opportunities for one-on-one snuggling and contact talks—a few minutes of shared quality time with him—throughout each day.

Over that first month, I developed a relationship with Juanita, who disclosed more about the family's home situation. She shared that two male members of the family were particularly affected by poverty and showed mental health issues. This led me (with Juanita's permission and director Dacia's knowledge) to refer the family to Early Head Start, where they could receive family assistance. However, there was a waiting list and therefore no openings at that time.

Sometimes Eric ate breakfast. He tended to sit at the end of the table and eat little, but at least he ate with the group. In between classes, Juanita sometimes came in to eat lunch with Eric and the other toddlers. Eric loved this, although it took our team working together to help with after-lunch separations.

Gradually, Eric accepted the toddler group routine. We remained open to his need for a morning snuggle, but eventually Eric needed closeness on only some mornings. The staff realized that while they could not change Eric's home environment, they could help him feel safe and welcome in the toddler room and maintain a positive relationship with his mother (Gartrell 2012, 117–18).

Reflection. (1) Of the recommendations I give for helping children who struggle, one that has received much positive feedback is giving a child individual contact time when they first arrive. I know that this is a busy time. When teachers tell other staff they want to try this, they sometimes get hairy eyeballs (otherwise known as a disapproving expression), eyebrow raising and eye rolling, or at least some questions. This is one reason why, along with building secure relationships with children and their parents, the teacher also builds partnerships with administrators. Lead teachers need to keep administrators—in Rena's case, director Dacia—informed about the children in their group. Dacia sat in on the IGP. She backed Rena's approach. As staff realized that easing Eric into the morning schedule almost always reduced conflicts, they came to see the greeting times as an investment for all in the day.

(2) Rena's consistent affirming contact with Eric, even during conflicts, helped this very young child make progress with the safety-needs DLS. Again, guidance interventions are effective only if the teacher can form a relationship with a child

outside of conflict situations—to build trust for when conflicts occur. This relationship, along with a partnership with Eric's mom, provided the foundation for the comprehensive guidance Rena used to assist Eric to make progress first with DLS 1 and then with DLS 2.

7. Working for Family Engagement

We start this section with a recommendation of three works for further reading:

> Gonzalez-Mena, *50 Strategies for Communicating and Working with Diverse Parents*, 3rd ed. (2014)

> Koralek et al., *Families and Educators Together: Building Great Relationships that Support Young Children* (2019)

> Mancilla & Blanco, "Engaging in Reciprocal Partnerships with Families and Fostering Community Connections." In *Developmentally Appropriate Practice in Early Childhood Programs Serving Children from Birth Through Age 8,* 4th ed. (2022)

I mention these resources up front as the topic is broad, and the focus of this discussion is on one particular model early childhood educators might use to support families' engagement with their children's program. The resources above, as well as others, offer the reader additional information and perspectives.

A goal in teaching for the DLS is that educators and families have friendly partnerships. For me, the means to this end lies decidedly with program staff. Teachers initiate and sustain the actions that welcome and support families, as members come to participate with teachers in furthering the personal development and education of their children. Families are the primary teachers of their children. Teachers only help—and in turn learn from families themselves. For many families, that help is vital for partnering with program staff in furthering their children's optimal development and education. Staff actively and congenially work with family members to encourage their engagement and build a reciprocal partnership. The more diverse the family in relation to the TT, the more sensitive the team needs to be in their friendly leadership.

Four Family Engagement Benchmarks

Here we discuss four benchmarks for TTs in their leadership with families (formerly referred to as four levels of parent engagement). The benchmarks can serve as objectives for TTs as they work for engagement with individual families. Used either formally or informally, the benchmarks are indicators of progress for staff in creating partnerships with the families they serve. (The benchmarks are not meant as something that family members need to be aware of; they are intended to guide the efforts of TTs in nudging, but not pushing, families toward fuller degrees of involvement—and in informally assessing the results of their efforts for program improvement.)

1. Benchmark 1: Family members show acceptance of program and staff.

2. Benchmark 2: Family members take new interest in the learning of their child.

3. Benchmark 3: Family members become active in relation to the general program.

4. Benchmark 4: Family members progress in personal and/or professional development themselves as a result of their engagement.

The staff of any early childhood program works with all families to engage in the program at Benchmarks 1, 2, and 3, understanding that Benchmark 3, in particular, will look different for different families based on many factors. Staff of comprehensive early childhood programs—like Head Start—work intentionally to also support family members in working toward their own personal and professional aims and goals—Benchmark 4. In any program, if family members are engaging at Benchmarks 3 and 4, staff celebrate (with big beverages of their choice—could be double espresso, mocha, skinny latte, maple-flavored grandes!). An example is a parent who, over time, takes an active interest in the program, such as by talking with TTs about upcoming events (Benchmark 1); begins reading regularly to their children at home (Benchmark 2); volunteers in the classroom—perhaps at lunchtime while on break from work—and/or joins the program's advisory committee (Benchmark 3); and gains confidence to begin study at a community college (Benchmark 4).

A while back, the term for the coming together of TTs and family members for the collaborative benefit of the child was "involvement." In the last decade or two, the importance of two-way communication in this relationship—listening to families and doing "with" them rather than "to" or "for" them—has led to a recasting of involvement as "engagement." Implied in the meaning of *engagement* for the early childhood field, I'd say, are two side benefits beyond benefitting the child—family support of the program and TT support for the personal development of family members.

Benchmark 1: Family Members Show Acceptance of Program and Staff

Showing unbiased acceptance, the teacher warmly introduces family members and children to the program. Families differ in the level of participation they are ready to engage in (Koralek et al. 2019). Most families, if they feel accepted, reach Benchmark 1, at least accepting information about the program and what their child is doing and learning. Typical ways that Benchmark 1 is shown is by family members' attendance at meetings, conferences, and class events, as they can find the time.

Teachers must understand, though, that some families may want to engage in such events but, for a variety of reasons, may be hesitant or unable to. Continuing to engage with family members in ways that seem comfortable for them—and refraining from judgment—is key to building the relationship.

To encourage families in their engagement, teachers recognize the importance of both direct, friendly communication with family members *and* the impact on the family of a child who is happy at school. Families who sense that their child has positive feelings toward the TT are inclined to interact positively with the teacher.

Benchmark 2: Family Members Take New Interest in the Learning of Their Child

As families move toward Benchmark 2, they begin to positively use the information teachers share with them about their child. Often, families actively follow up on activities and projects suggested by the teachers. Perhaps even more important, families use more fully the resources in the home and community as teaching and learning opportunities with their child. Teachers help interested families access resources and reach out for additional ones to further support their children's learning (Koralek 2019).

As family members near Benchmark 2, mutual trust is growing, and parents begin to work together with teachers on behalf of their children. Important in this effort, TT members can learn more from families about their children, resulting in a more responsive, supportive program for each child. Both parties come to recognize that together they can do so much for the children whose lives they share. For example, when staff reach out with concerns about a child's psychological or physiological functioning, the family trusts the TT enough to agree to follow-up efforts such as assessments that the team suggests. And, in this collaboration, the family fills in the teaching staff about the child's functioning at home.

Children can feel when the principal adults in their lives, in this case teachers and family members, get along and cooperate. For the child, continuity then exists between home and school, and a basis for progressing in the DLS is reinforced in the child's life.

Benchmark 3: Family Members Become Active in Relation to the General Program

Families are approaching Benchmark 3 when they participate in program activities in ways that go beyond their own child. Taking an active role in benefiting the program indicates that truly reciprocal interactions are happening. Commonly—though not necessarily—this kind of engagement involves family members volunteering in the classroom. When family members first come into the classroom, teachers encourage them to participate in informal ways, like interacting with children and other adults and reading to their child and any "drop-ins." Families can also share something from their culture or a special interest with the class. Once in a case of working parents, older brother Sven brought in his tuba and played "The Farmer in the Dell" while the group sang. (No one cared about the differing octaves.)

Respecting individual preferences and needs, TT members ask family members how they might like to engage (Koralek 2019). Families confident in their engagement at a program level and with the time to do so might be willing to sit on family advisory and policy committees and even to help represent the program to the public. Sometimes out-of-class family participation can lead to a classroom visit. Working parents can sometimes build an occasional visit into their schedules—eating with a child during a lunch break is one example; taking time off from work to go on an end-of-year field trip is another.

Benchmark 4: Family Members Progress in Personal and/or Professional Development Themselves as a Result of Their Engagement

For many early childhood programs, Benchmark 2 is a reasonable benchmark for all families. Benchmark 2 marks the baseline for reciprocity in the family-teacher relationship, the two functioning as a team to help the child. In most cooperative preschools, programs have Benchmark 3 engagement as a benchmark. Comprehensive programs, again like Head Start, set Benchmark 4 as a general benchmark reached in some, but not all, families. At Benchmark 4, with successful experiences at the first three levels, family members engage in significant personal or professional development, enabled, encouraged, and inspired by their partnerships with program staff.

Examples of reaching Benchmark 4 are pursuing significant civic participation, furthering one's education, or advancing to a career. Additional schooling for a family member might mean getting a high school diploma, job training, or a two- or four-year degree. They might then become a staff member of a teaching team, enter another field, or take on substantial new activities in the home. One parent I knew began to write children's books. Another, influenced by engagement in an early childhood special education program, became an advocate and activist for her child and other children on the autism spectrum in the local school system. With support from a teacher, these parents choose to improve their life circumstances and, by their example, change the aspirations of members of their families.

In my university classes over the years, some of the most dedicated and responsive students have been family members of young children who chose teaching careers after volunteering in classrooms. In these settings, TTs welcomed them warmly, helped them get involved in activities, thanked them for volunteering, and invited them back. Finding the experience gratifying, the family members returned to the classroom and became regulars. They then made the decision and the commitment to become teachers. As a parent who was returning to college once said, "My teenage son didn't just hear me talk about it. Gerald saw Mother going to college, and now he wants to go too."

8. Ensuring an Encouraging Learning Community for All

Part of the fun for me in writing this book is the opportunity to link DAP (for all) and teaching for the DLS. The fourth edition of *Developmentally Appropriate Practice in Early Childhood Programs* (NAEYC 2022) provides the foundation for discussion of this heading. The discussion keys in on two ideas central to DAP.

1. An early childhood setting is developmentally appropriate only if the setting is developmentally appropriate for everyone.

A problem some programs face in their efforts to implement DAP is the assumption that if the program is developmentally appropriate for perhaps 80 percent of children, that is the best that can be expected, and the classroom can be considered developmentally appropriate. What of the other 20 percent of children? Due to home and/or classroom stressors, do these children fall into the stress-conflict-punishment syndrome? Are they "gently" asked to leave the program? Under this heading in the following chapters, we highlight DAP practices that ensure all and not just most children feel welcomed and encouraged. The section demonstrates the welcoming inclusivity of **equity education** that is so much a part of DAP, the encouraging early learning community, and the DLS. TTs use DAP responsibly only when all in the community feel welcomed and encouraged.

2. Children need to feel that they are accepted and valued in a setting for them to excel at learning and development in the social, physical, cognitive, and linguistic domains.

As children gain an emotional foundation, TTs use their relationships to nudge children into significant learning experiences across domains, directly with them and via social relations and interactions with peers. Curriculum, learning environment, and daily schedules that nudge children to progress from what they know to the new are critical. Under this heading in the following chapters, practices for learning and development of the whole child are cited for each DLS, particularly for DLS 3 in Chapter 7.

Explanations of headings 9 and 10 are brief, as previous chapters introduced the topics of the headings. We give full attention to the analysis points of 9 and 10 in the chapters to come.

9. Education for Living in a Democracy

Early childhood educators, of course, cannot guarantee that young children will have continued encouraging experiences as they move up the stairways of their schooling. But, at a critical time for children's brain development and personality

formation, TTs who follow the tenets of progressive education and teach for the DLS can be assured that they have done all they can for their graduates to advance in intelligent and ethical thinking and doing. This section in the next five chapters highlights the gains children make through progress with each DLS in terms of becoming productive and healthy citizens of our complex modern democracy.

10. Summary Grid

Discussion in each DLS chapter concludes with a summary grid. In a practical format, the grids give: (1) a profile of children who have not yet gained the skill; (2) typical behaviors of a child just beginning to work on the skill; (3) teacher responses that guide for progress with the skill; and (4) indicators of progress for a child in relation to the skill.

These summary grids reflect my own perspective, background, and experiences. Research is needed to discern possibly limiting cultural influences of the information in them. Every child from every culture is different. But in this duffer professor's view, every child everywhere flourishes if they can learn the safety-needs skills and make progress with DLS 3, 4, and 5.

DISCUSSION QUESTIONS

1. Identify three key concepts (listed above and in the glossary). If you are a visual learner, write each out with its definition from the glossary. Then, referring to the section of the chapter where the key concept originated, reflect on what the concept means to you now that you have read the chapter.

2. Various anecdotes in the chapter illustrate TT members working with children to progress with the DLS. Identify one anecdote (and the author reflection) that has meaning for you. Reflect on how the anecdote enhanced and/or changed your possible response to a similar situation.

3. Why would a child working on DLS 4 or 5 be less likely to show Level Three mistaken behavior than a child at DLS 1 or 2? Why would a child working on DLS 5 be less likely to show Level Two mistaken behavior than a child working on DLS 2?

4. Why would conflict mediation more likely work with a child working on DLS 2 than a child working on DLS 1? Concerning Level Two mistaken behavior, when would an early childhood educator be more likely to use a guidance talk and when a large group meeting?

5. What is the difference between encouragement and praise? When would an educator use public encouragement and when private encouragement? Why?

6. Analyze distinctions among the four benchmarks for increasing family engagement. Explain how one typical behavior of a family member would be characteristic of each benchmark.

7. The book is about education for democracy. Identify a new or newly reinforced idea for you from the chapter. Discuss how that idea contributes to your own approach toward teaching for democracy.

8. How have the thoughts and ideas shared in this chapter impacted your thinking about being a professional working with young children?

Key Concepts

acknowledge and pause

child negotiation

choice times

compliment sandwich

comprehensive guidance

contact talks

developmental guidance

emergent curriculum

encouragement

equity education

family engagement

five finger formula

guidance talks

individual guidance plan (IGP)

intervention guidance

large group meetings

mediation

task talk

CHAPTER 5

The Foundational Skill

DLS 1: Finding Acceptance
as a Member of the Group
and as a Worthy Individual

SUGGESTED GOALS FOR READERS

1. Describe how adverse experiences and stress show themselves in children's survival behaviors in the early learning setting.

2. Identify key developmental and intervention guidance practices and explain how they assist young children to gain DLS 1.

3. Examine how partnerships with others—families, fellow staff, and administrators—add to a teacher's ability to guide young children to gain DLS 1.

DLS 1	DLS 2	DLS 3	DLS 4	DLS 5
Finding Acceptance as a Member of the Group and as a Worthy Individual	**Expressing Strong Emotions in Nonhurting Ways**	**Solving Problems Creatively— Independently and in Cooperation with Others**	**Accepting Unique Human Qualities in Others**	**Thinking Intelligently and Ethically**

Concentrating on DLS 1, Chapter 5 is about how TTs assist young children who are living with varying degrees of adverse life experience. Young children are affected by adverse experiences to different extents and in different ways. Especially if they retain secure attachments through the time of trauma, many children can show resilience and gain DLS 1. Chapter 5 focuses on the guidance leadership that an early childhood educator brings to children when they are unable to find a place of acceptance in the group and feel themselves unworthy of belonging.

Chapter 4 introduced the 10 headings that organize the discussion of guiding young children to gain the DLS. In this chapter, the following headings are discussed in relation to DLS 1:

> Starter Notes

> Anecdotes and Reflections

> Communication Practices for Building Relationships

> Three Levels of Mistaken Behavior

> Key Intervention Guidance Practices

> Working for Family Engagement

> Ensuring an Encouraging Learning Community for All

> Education for Living in a Democracy

> Summary Grid

Starter Notes

The stress-conflict-punishment syndrome develops when children and adults in a program fall into this pattern:

1. A child harboring unmanageable stress acts out with a mistaken survival behavior to relieve the stress.

2. Adults interpret the resulting conflict as misbehavior on the child's part and punish to "shame the child into being good."

3. The punishment heightens stress for the child, furthers feelings of rejection, and reinforces a need to act out again to relieve the stress.

As the pattern repeats itself, young children's continuing struggles cause many to be pushed out of preschool programs. (See the sidebar on page 77.) What of these children then? If families can find other programs, these children might be enrolled in them; other family members might become full-time caregivers; parents might leave the workforce to provide care. If the children are *not* expelled, and nothing changes, some staff unfortunately count the days until these children move on to kindergarten. Works by Gunnar, Herrera, and Hostinar (2009) and Shonkoff et al. (2012) as well as the Harvard Medical School (2020) indicate that if not mitigated,

· ·

Because DLS 1 is the *foundational skill,* in this chapter we call upon all but one of the headings that were introduced in Chapter 4. In chapters that follow, I call upon a smaller number of the headings, those that best inform the DLS being discussed. While repeating the same headings in each chapter might be useful to reinforce important concepts, addressing only the most pertinent topics of inquiry for the study of DLS 2–5 will reduce repetition for readers.

· ·

the stress-conflict-punishment pattern becomes a syndrome. To amplify the point, for too many children, this repeating pattern becomes a long-term syndrome that follows the child through adolescence and into adulthood.

TTs who guide young children to gain Skill 1 do much to prevent the pattern from becoming a syndrome. They recognize that unmet-needs mistaken behaviors are not misbehaviors but misplaced *survival behaviors that control the child*. Stimulated by repeated and/or severe adverse experiences, children's powerful amygdala and hypothalamus responses hypersensitize them to threat. The resulting unmanageable stress shows itself by children's reaction tendencies of seeking to flee, withdraw and become invisible, or defend themselves through aggressive behaviors. With these vulnerable children, the TT takes special care to build trust-based, secure relationships that form the heart of the encouraging early learning community. The developmental and intervention guidance practices that caring professionals use are the focus of Chapter 5.

Understanding and Eliminating Expulsion in Early Childhood Programs

› Preschoolers are expelled at three times the rate of children in kindergarten through 12th grade.

› Preschool-aged boys are four times as likely to be expelled as girls are.

› African American children are expelled almost twice as often as Latino and white children and more than five times as often as Asian American children are.

Young children expelled from preschool are more likely to

› Lose chances to learn, socialize with other children, and interact with positive adult role models

› Miss out on chances to develop and practice the very skills they may most need, including social and emotional skills

› Develop ongoing behavior problems leading to later school difficulty

› Experience harmful effects on development, education, and health

› View themselves negatively or as not capable of learning

› Develop negative views about learning, school, teachers, and the world around them

Families who have a child who has been expelled may

› Lose access to a teacher or program that may have provided support to their child and family

› Experience increased stress, including financial challenges, as they look for alternative care. Some parents may lose their jobs when a child is expelled because there are limited alternatives for other care.

› Blame themselves or their child. This can lead to harsh and less effective parenting approaches at home.

Adapted from National Center on Early Childhood Health and Wellness, "Understanding and Eliminating Expulsion in Early Childhood Programs" (updated October 17, 2022), https://eclkc.ohs.acf.hhs.gov/publication/understanding-eliminating-expulsion-early-childhood-programs.

Anecdote and Reflection

Anecdote 1

At Campus Child Care, a former center at Bemidji State University in Minnesota, Robin was a mature, competent teacher. She had supported her husband throughout his doctoral program and had never gotten a degree herself. Robin was in the process of completing a degree in early childhood education when she recorded the following events. She qualified to be a teacher via a CDA Credential, credits earned through her university program, and experience. She relates the following about a 30-month-old and his mother:

> I met Pauley and his mother, Becky, at a Getting to Know You conference before starting our program. Pauley seemed to be a curious 30-month-old. His single mother was young and a full-time college student. I could tell immediately that Becky truly loved her son, and she appeared to be a devoted caregiver. When she told me she was all on her own with Pauley, I thought that she probably was without much support from family or friends.
>
> Two weeks into the program, Pauley began to have trouble getting along with other children. His anxiety level, beginning at drop-off time, seemed to be high. When classmates invaded his personal space, often during group activities, Pauley responded by pulling children's hair, kicking, or yelling "Shut up!" When teachers intervened, Pauley cried and kicked them. After a few weeks

of attempting to guide Pauley to use kind words and gentle touches, the director, other staff members, and I decided we needed to pursue a more comprehensive approach.

I began holding short weekly conferences with Becky to get to know her better and to offer her encouragement in her parenting. One day, shortly after our meeting I happened to look out the window and notice Becky sitting on the steps, crying. I took my break early and went out to talk with her. Becky shared her frustration over Pauley's behavior: "Why does he act this way? I am tired and don't understand. He is so naughty!"

I responded, "Pauley is a very sweet and special boy, and his behavior is the way he responds to stress. He feels threatened by many things right now, and he reacts in the only way he knows. It is mistaken behavior, and it is our job to guide him. It isn't an easy job." I reached over and gave her a hug. My friendship with Becky continued to grow and so did her trust in me.

In a late afternoon meeting with Becky, fellow staff members, and the director, we developed an individual guidance plan for Pauley. Becky suggested that we implement a reward system. We tried a sticker chart that recorded and rewarded progress. Special for me, Becky agreed to begin reading to Pauley at bedtime. Becky and I decided that Pauley and I would call her any time three serious conflicts occurred in a day. When we called, I first explained the situation to Becky and then had Pauley talk with her. Becky was firm but loving. Pauley loved talking with his mother, and we would generally see a more relaxed Pauley after these phone calls. (I kept tabs to make sure the calls didn't become a habit.)

Pauley's conflicts with other children continued. For a while, Pauley needed Morgan or me to be nearby to calm him and help direct him to more appropriate behavior. We would calm Pauley by holding and rocking him. Sometimes Morgan or I sang. After Pauley was calm, we used guidance talks, and he talked to me about what happened. These interactions encouraged bonding and a feeling of trust between us.

I also used humor. I gave Pauley options of words to use when he was upset. Yelling "Pickle!" became a favorite. I also gave Pauley a cushy ball to hold during stressful situations such as circle time and made sure that a student teacher or I sat next to him. We rubbed Pauley's back or arm or held him on our laps. The ball kept his hands busy, and the touch calmed him.

Drop-off time was difficult for Pauley and set the mood for the day. With the director's assistance, I arranged to meet him in the office or lounge to spend one-on-one time with him, playing a game or reading. The other staff noticed the difference in Pauley—and the entire group—on the days I helped ease him into the class.

Eventually Becky agreed with the staff that an outside mental health assessment was needed for Pauley's behavior. Dealing with people outside our center made Becky uncomfortable; to ease her stress, I stayed involved during the assessment process. I worked with the director and others to find resources for Becky; these included a family play therapy program and the school district's early childhood family education classes for young parents.

To keep up communication, the teaching staff that worked the later shift talked daily with Becky, and I left happygrams (complimentary notes about Pauley). Throughout this whole time, the director was a great support to me—and to Becky too.

One day, four months into working with Pauley, he was building with LEGOs when a classmate sat down next to him and took a block off Pauley's tower. Pauley's previous response would have been to pull the child's hair. This time, however, he shouted, "NO, thank you!" I told Pauley he remembered to use his words, and they worked! We were so proud of Pauley for using his words.

Our guidance plan was finally showing success. Pauley learned to say what he needed and what he didn't like. Baby steps were all we needed. Pauley grew and so did we. (Gartrell 2008, 44)

Reflection. Robin handled the situation of Pauley and Becky as competently as I have ever seen a teacher do. As sometimes happens, over the following summer the family moved 240 miles south to Minneapolis, and Robin never heard from them again. Often it is in the second year that children

helped to gain DLS 1 begin to bloom. We can only hope that Pauley and Becky had a hopeful new start that fall.

Communication Practices for Building Relationships

Robin's anecdote illustrates a practice that is central to building secure relationships with children: *contact talks.*

Contact Talks

Contact talks differ from guidance talks, which have a direct teaching purpose. Contact talks are moments of shared quality time between an adult and child, free of expectations that the child achieve something. Think of them as "rest platforms" in between scaffolding ladders from one level of the child's progress to the next. Contact talks only happen when TTs decide they will happen. Quieter children, especially those who might be showing **invisible child** survival behaviors, really need regular contact talks. TTs do well to track who they have the talks with to make sure no child is missed. Especially with children who are experiencing unmanageable stress, these talks need to happen more than once every day.

With children really struggling to gain DLS 1, one adult should be the designated contact talker. Usually this is the lead teacher, although if another member of the TT relates well to the child, it might be that person. Children build secure relationships one at a time.

Robin persuaded fellow staff that **morning greeting talks** were important. When young children working on Skill 1 arrive at programs, they are entering a room full of potential new stressors. Without sensitive greeting time that eases the child into the day, the morning transition can be particularly stressful for young children.

In having contact talks with children, it is easy to envision Robin using all the other seven communication practices:

> Smile and nod. (This fundamental practice tells the other person that you care enough to listen.)

> Acknowledge and pause. (This flows into reflective listening and often into contact talks.)

> Use friendly humor. ("You look so frowny, your eyebrows might tickle your nose.")

> Use appropriate, friendly touch. (Robin frequently held Pauley and had him sit on her lap to calm and comfort him.)

> Utilize compliment sandwiches. (Use at least triple-deckers.)

> Give encouragement: private to individuals, public to the group. ("You didn't hit or kick. You said 'Pickles!' You did it, Pauley!")

> Remember names, contact talks, and promises. (In the context of contact talks, TTs won't be forgetting children's names (!), but the teachers should remember past contact talks and promises they might have made to the child. Even though she might have been less than enthusiastic about it, Robin remembered her agreement that Pauley could call and talk with Mom.)

New teachers have told me that when they first try them, some of these practices seem contrived. With practice, as teachers discover the effectiveness of the techniques, they become more natural. (Practice, practice, practice.) We discuss the communication techniques further in the four chapters to follow.

Levels of Mistaken Behavior

> **Level Three strong unmet-needs mistaken behavior** is shown by children struggling with DLS 1 and/or 2. This level of mistaken behavior can be extreme and might show in either reactive or intentional aggression.

> **Level Two socially influenced mistaken behavior** is displayed by children who have a beginning grasp on DLS 2 and are showing beginning efforts at DLS 3. Children fall into socially influenced mistaken behavior when they are influenced by individual significant others or by others in groups.

> **Level One experimentation mistaken behavior** is shown by children who have a grasp on the safety needs and are working to attain Skills 3, 4, and 5. The experiments, either accidental (a tower that falls down) or intentional (a swear word said with a smile), sometimes go awry.

In his repeated and intense mistaken behavior, Pauley showed the effects of strong unmet safety needs. Pauley was showing what I call *existential* Level 3 mistaken behavior. By this I mean his unmet need for safety came from insecure relationships in the home compounded by traumatic experiences that made him feel threatened, as Robin related to me. He was showing the defensive survival mistaken behavior of fighting, **reactive aggression** at levels that were disruptive to all around him. Pauley's young mother was overwhelmed by the responsibilities of college study and the demands of parenting, for which she had no support. The toddler felt totally lost.

From the beginning, Robin worked hard to form a secure relationship with Pauley. With improvements in his support situation, and the hard work of his TT, Pauley gained a foundation with DLS 1 and made progress with DLS 2.

Key Intervention Guidance Practices

Chapter 4 introduced five practices for intervention guidance:

1. Calming methods

2. Guidance talks

3. Conflict mediation

4. Intervention large group meetings

5. Comprehensive guidance

Following a second anecdote, we'll look at how these practices played out in both classroom situations.

Anecdote 2

Myra was a new teacher in a mixed kindergarten-first grade class of a charter school. Myra and "Lead" Johnson (the school's alternative name for a principal) had been working as a team to assist student Monica. A staff member from the community reported that Mom and, sometimes, Dad (Chico) lived with Monica's paternal grandma, Phyllis. Mom had left suddenly for Chicago, and no one had heard from her. Monica was an only child, but Grandma Phyllis sometimes cared for two older grandchildren, who reportedly bullied Monica.

Because Monica was (perhaps understandably) showing Level Three mistaken behaviors in the classroom, Myra set up two meetings with Chico and Phyllis at their preferred time, Thursday after school. The two did not make either meeting. On this Friday, Monica's day went from bad to worse.

During writing time, Monica flipped her desk over frontward, tipped her chair over backward, and stayed on the chair until Allie approached. Then, Monica crawled under a table and would not come out. The other children were used to Monica acting out, but this was tumultuous, and they were alarmed.

According to their plan, Lead Johnson arrived and sat down next to Monica to calm her and have a guidance talk. Myra took the class into the music room, unused on Fridays. Myra held an intervention guidance group meeting with the group. Myra explained to the class that Monica had been having a hard time out of school for several days. She had a lot of mad and sad feelings inside her, and she didn't know how else to get them out.

Nino: You mean she doesn't mean to be bad?

Myra: That's what I mean, Nino. Thank you.

Jerome: I feel mad sometimes, but I don't do stuff.

Marie: Maybe you don't feel mad like Monica.

Myra: Jerome, I say this to you and to the rest of us. If you are ever feeling mad or sad, please tell me. I want to help you get those feelings out.

Jerome: My uncle's dog Bumpers got hit by a car.

Myra: Thank you, Jerome. At outdoor time would you talk to me more about Bumpers?

Jerome: (*Nodded.*)

Myra: Class, how can we help Monica feel better?

Allie: Leave her alone when she is mad.

Marie: Ask her to play, but if she says no leave her alone.

Paulene: Not laugh at her 'cause she's sad.

Myra: Those are wonderful ideas. Thank you so much. Do you think you can remember these ideas?

Class: Yeah!

Myra and the students went back to the classroom. Monica had left with Lead Johnson. Later, she came in and took her seat. She didn't focus much the rest of the afternoon. At one point, Monica slammed her papers down on her desk. But no one said a word. On Monday, student Marie offered to work with Monica, and the two got some assignments done together. (Adapted from Gartrell 2014, 281)

Reflection. As I was Myra's former student teacher supervisor, she talked with me about her experience. She said three things: (1) "That Friday I went home and had a big beverage of my choice! I needed it!" (2) "On Monday Lead Johnson told me a district special education teacher was going to do an assessment for Monica and maybe get her some services." (3) "A few in the class had been complaining about Monica, maybe taunting her. After the meeting, this stopped. The kids saw she needed space and gave it to her. The situation wasn't perfect, but it was better."

Monica did receive an assessment from special education. Her family did the minimum to allow for special education services, thanks to Myra's contacting them. But children in the charter school were not high among the special education priorities for the school district. Monica received only sporadic assistance, and the family, still without Mom, did not partner with the charter school staff to advocate for the child. Monica did finish out the year with fewer incidents of extreme mistaken behavior, and Myra was glad of this, for Monica and the other children.

Introduced in Chapter 4, the overall strategy that I write about for problem solving through guidance is the *five finger formula (FFF)*. TTs use the FFF in all intervention guidance practices, formally in mediation, and less formally in guidance talks and large group meetings. During comprehensive guidance, TTs also can use the FFF in meetings with fellow staff and families. The five steps are

1. Thumb: Calm everyone down—yourself, too. Set the scene for the mediation.

2. Pointer: Guide the children to accept how each person sees the conflict or situation.

3. Tall guy: Brainstorm possible resolutions.

4. Ringer: Agree to one solution and try it.

5. Pinky: Monitor the solution and positively acknowledge effort. Hold guidance talks with individuals if needed. Discuss what children can do next time instead.

In the large group meeting, Myra informally used the five finger formula for social problem solving:

> Thumb: Myra calmed the group by putting Monica's mistaken behavior in a context. The teacher *set the scene and introduced the problem* by talking about Monica's feeling "mad and sad" and not knowing how to get the feelings out.

> Pointer: With Myra's leadership, the children *identified the problem as they saw it*. One child shared how he felt "mad and sad" too. Another said, but "maybe not like Monica."

> Tall guy: Myra *asked the children to brainstorm a resolution.* "How can we help Monica feel better?"

> Ringer: Three children *gave (sensitive) suggestions for a resolution.* Myra got the group to agree that they would remember and try them. *They implemented the suggestions.*

> Pinky: Myra *monitored the results* and saw that the class gave Monica her space and did not bother her. On the next Monday, mate Marie offered to work with Monica. Monica accepted and the two completed some assignments together.

Calming Methods

Calming is the first and most crucial step in helping children to resolve conflicts. Let's refer to Anecdote 1 with teachers Robin and Morgan and child Pauley. When Pauley was upset, the TT would calm the toddler by holding and rocking him. Robin commented that sometimes she or Morgan would sing softly to Pauley. In Anecdote 2, Myra took the class to another room so that Lead Johnson could sit next to Monica on the floor and in a one-on-one way help her calm down. In the other room, Myra worked to calm the rest of the children at the beginning of the group meeting.

Guidance Talks

Guidance talks are not "a talking to," as in "the lecture." They involve talking *with* the child to

> Help the child get calm

> Figure out how each person perceived the conflict and decide on a way to reconcile and make amends

> Encourage the child and reaffirm your relationship with them

> Decide with the child a more cooperative solution in the future

Guidance talks can happen with individual children to resolve conflicts. In mediation between two or three children, guidance talks often happen after the conflict has been resolved, separately or with both children together. Guidance talks should always end on a note of encouragement. Though we do not know what Lead Johnson and Monica talked about in their time together, it was a guidance talk.

Guidance talks often include the teacher's positive acknowledgment of efforts and progress children might have shown since beginning in the program. In this sense, the talks are large-sized compliment sandwiches. Unlike the open-ended quality time of contact talks, guidance talks are instructive. But like contact talks, they build, reinforce, and if necessary repair relationships.

Conflict Mediation

Contrary to the notion that preschoolers are too young to work through problems together, conflict mediation even with very young children is doable. In fact, it is my view that as young children attain Skill 1, they learn the conflict mediation process more easily than older students who have not learned it as preschoolers. As illustrated in Chapter 4, in an encouraging early learning community, young children can even learn to negotiate without adult mediation.

TTs can use mediation with preschoolers who still struggle with Skill 1, but the process is difficult. Teachers need to be building mutual trust during the process, which is easier when talking with one child rather than mediating between two. There were no conflict mediation situations in the two anecdotes in this chapter. But illustrations of mediation are in anecdotes in the next, and we focus on the topic of mediation then.

Intervention Large Group Meetings

When a child shows disruptive mistaken behavior, teachers sometimes think they will distress the group more if they discuss the matter with them. Adding to this belief is the misimpression that the matter involves only the child and the teacher, that it is not the business of the rest of the group. The teacher might think that being professional means not discussing the situation with others—especially children.

When TTs work from the premise that children and adults alike are members of a community, and not just a class, they are not misled by these outdated views. A child's (or children's) severe mistaken behaviors impacts everyone. All are aware of dramatic mistaken behaviors, and the acts bother group members. Without the benefit of nonjudgmental discussion, individuals may not know how to cope with the stress from the situation or what to do in the face of similar events in the future. They can feel like victims. In encouraging early learning communities, TTs understand these dynamics. Teachers use large group meetings to problem-solve with children when a conflict has gone public and many in the group are either involved or affected.

No question, large group meetings to address Level Three behaviors by a child are difficult for all concerned. Talking publicly about public conflicts concerning an individual child is a difficult choice. The teacher must balance the child's right to the dignity of privacy with the need for other children to express their concerns about the behavior and to try to understand the child. There is no magic answer to this dilemma. It is important, though, that the teacher, other members of the TT, and administrators talk about the possibility and make the decision together. Teaming is important so that any feedback, like from parents whose children talk about the meeting at home, does not come back to a single teacher alone.

Myra conducted her class meeting admirably, and to my mind modeled an effective response in this most difficult of teaching and learning situations. The meeting helped the children understand Monica and her strong unmet-needs mistaken behavior. Myra sensed that many children were feeling distressed by witnessing Monica's severe mistaken behavior. By enlisting their help as good mates, the teacher was helping them cope and learn important emotional-social lessons from a situation that they couldn't otherwise resolve. The teacher helped the group move from feeling like victims to being participants in an effort at resolution—a good psychological place for members to be in an encouraging early learning community. Very likely because of this meeting, mate Marie showed helping behavior toward Monica—a clear use of DLS 5.

Comprehensive Guidance

TTs use comprehensive guidance when individual day-to-day developmental and intervention guidance is not successful at assisting a child to gain the safety-needs skills. The more serious the child's mistaken behavior, the more the teacher needs to collaborate with others in a coordinated effort to assist the child. Comprehensive guidance begins with an individual guidance plan (IGP). The IGP can be constructed formally in a meeting and written out on an IGP form, or informally by the TT talking together and then with administrators and the parents. (See dangartrell.net to locate and download a sample IGP form.)

Formal IGPs come out of meetings that include fellow staff and, whenever possible, administrators and families. Myra tried more than once to meet with Monica's father and grandmother, but they did not make scheduled meetings. Myra and Lead Johnson thought that with Monica's mother being absent, the child's family members might have been struggling to meet their own basic needs. The educators concluded that further efforts to include them as full partners wouldn't work at that time—a hard decision, to be sure. For as long as Monica was in her class, though, Myra worked mightily to keep communications with her grandmother going. A home visit (discussed under the next heading) was one part of this outreach effort.

Robin, though, had begun a relationship with Pauley's mother, Becky, even before Pauley's first day. Robin held an IGP meeting with Becky, Morgan and the other TT members, and director Dacia. They agreed on a course of action, with Becky even suggesting a token reward system, which they implemented. IGP efforts sometimes have formal follow-up meetings, though in this case Robin followed up more informally with Becky, the TT, and Dacia.

The first anecdote clearly shows how comprehensive guidance using an IGP that includes a family member can work. When there is minimum family engagement, TTs can still coordinate their efforts to provide planned comprehensive guidance, as shown in the second anecdote. In collaboration with others, teachers can accomplish what each TT member might not be able to on their own.

Working for Family Engagement

In Chapter 4 we considered four benchmarks TTs can use to chart their progress in building partnerships with families.

As TTs support and engage families, families may

1. Show acceptance of program and staff
2. Take new interest in the learning of their child
3. Become active in relation to the general program
4. Progress in personal and/or professional development as a result of their engagement

We focus on Benchmarks 1 and 2 in this chapter.

Family members of children who struggle with Skill 1 almost always are experiencing difficult life circumstances themselves. Certainly, this was the case with the parents in the two case studies in this chapter. Building on the close connection she had with Becky, Robin assisted the young mom to gain an understanding of Pauley's behavior and respond effectively. Becky began reading to her child every night, a keystone parent-child activity in relation to Benchmark 2. Beyond this, thanks to Robin's leadership, Becky and Pauley went to a family play therapy program, allowing Becky to continue to make progress in rising above the family's difficult circumstances.

Before she left for Chicago, Monica's mother gave permission to Lead Johnson to have a screening and Individualized Education Program (IEP) assessment done, which is a Benchmark 2 activity. But the permission was given apparently without a commitment to stand behind the child in the process, so the teachers were not able to continue building a relationship with Mom. As for Chico and Phyllis, Monica's father and grandmother, Myra made a big decision after the very public classroom conflict. Myra and a part-time family-support staff person from the school set up a visit to Monica's home. Chico was not there, but the team got acquainted with Phyllis. They began to form a grandparent-teacher relationship, indicating progress toward Benchmark 2. Myra made a point of greeting Monica warmly on the home visit. Monica seemed happy to see Myra visiting her at home. Grandma saw that the child cared about her teacher.

The Separate Roles of Teachers and Families

From the beginning, these early childhood educators served as a figures of security for the two children. They recognized that Pauley and Monica were overwhelmed by adverse experiences and needed a calming figure to make things comprehensible for them. The adults worked as caring teachers and not as "replacement parents"—the children didn't need this added complication in their lives. This is an important distinction for all early childhood professionals to remember (Katz 1977). In the following excerpt from a Michigan State University article, the authors harken back to Lilian Katz's book of essays to remind early childhood educators of differences in the roles of teachers and families:

> Many times, teachers struggle with the boundaries of the role. We find ourselves becoming emotionally attached to the children we care for and teach. . . . When we feel tempted to over-step boundaries, it is critical that every teacher remind themselves of . . . [the differences between the roles of parents and teachers] that Katz identifies. The parent's function is broad. In Katz' words, it is "diffuse and limitless." Parents are expected to function as a parent to the child for as long as they live, and provide all types of care and support, from food, shelter, and other material things to love, emotional support, guidance, direction, and counseling. The teacher's

function is narrow. The expectation for teachers is to provide learning opportunities in a supportive setting [for only as long as the child is in the group]. And at the same time, the parent's scope of responsibility is narrow. They are expected to be responsible for primarily their own children. A teacher's responsibility is broad; it extends to the entire classroom. The needs of all of the children and families are her/his task and duty. (Butcher & Pletcher 2015)

When TTs and families partner, they can merge strengths in each role and together further the well-being of the young children whose lives they share. This is why reaching out to families so they can meet at least Benchmark 2 is so important.

Ensuring an Encouraging Learning Community for All

1. An early childhood setting is developmentally appropriate only if the setting is developmentally appropriate for everyone.

The convenient path for some adults is to assume that if most children are adjusting to the program, the few who don't are outliers. In this view, the fault is not with the program; it is in the nature of the few, who for reasons of development, behavior, or even appearance are not "ready" or "a right fit" for the program.

Young children who are struggling to attain Skill 1 are the prime targets for increasingly distant relations with their teachers. When a child lacking Skill 1 begins a program, or reverts to this skill from a higher one, most teachers try their best to handle the conflicts, deal with the tears, and carry on. But without abundant personal or program resources, the pull is strong to give up on these kids, as the **preschool expulsion** rates indicate.

For some educators, understandably, the matter becomes giving up on the one so the rest in the group won't be distressed by the child. The central idea of this book is that young children benefit emotionally, even spiritually, when they see their strong TT working hard to assist a child to fit in and get along. There are lessons to be learned in terms of empathy and social skills when children learn to understand, perhaps even assist themselves, a child who has hit hard times and is struggling.

An additional complication is often parental concerns. Over the years teachers have told me often that they have "caught crap" from parents about the "misbehaviors" of a (notorious) child in the group. This is a tough problem, I know, for which there is not a ready answer. A partial antidote, though, is

building solid relations with all families from day one. And, it doesn't hurt to have a few real friends among families who are active partners in the encouraging community. The more early childhood professionals can work with others, rather than go it alone, the better the all-around chances for support and success.

It takes strong professionals with solid preparation to put in the extra time and effort to guide children who struggle with DLS 1 to find a welcoming place in the community. The importance of this challenge is that when they do, teachers make a significant positive difference in the lives of *all* the children in their care—meaning these programs truly are developmentally appropriate for all.

2. Children need to feel that they are accepted and encouraged in a setting for them to excel at learning and development in the social, physical, cognitive, and linguistic domains.

On that special day when a child initiates an action that indicates they are (finally) feeling accepted in the group, TT members do a happy dance. The signs sometime are subtle, and teachers need to watch for them:

> Pauley says "NO, thank you" when another child comes into his space.

> Monica shows less frequent and extreme mistaken behavior; she is pleased to see Myra when she makes a home visit and accepts Marie's friendly assistance with assignments.

I call these initial acts the **coming around phenomenon**. Two wonderful illustrations of children deciding a program is safe and coming around are these:

> All the first week of preschool, teacher Beatrice would invite but did not force Lucy to join in during circle time songs. In the second week, Beatrice heard Lucy singing one of the songs to herself and smiled. In the third week, Lucy sat at an angle behind Beatrice in group and sang softly. The next day she scooted herself next to Beatrice and sang, "The itsy bitsy spider . . . " Over time, she sang not softly at all!

> Casey, 50 months, did not talk in Beatrice's class. A month into the program, Beatrice was playing catch with three children, as an experienced teacher would. She bounced the ball to the first child, who would bounce it back to her, then to and from the second child, and then the third. Casey was the second child. Beatrice forgot the order and bounced the ball to the third child by mistake. "Hey, you forgot me!" Casey said. Smiling but not missing a beat, Beatrice said, "Sorry, Casey," and bounced the ball to the girl, who from that moment on talked as though she had never not spoken. (Really.)

These examples of coming around illustrate children who made the determination that "this community is safe for me." With a feeling of acceptance as members of the program, these children show the lasting gains of attaining Skill 1. For young children, all other learning flows from these moments.

Education for Living in a Democracy

Young children who are not able to gain DLS 1 are most at risk for developing the stress-conflict-punishment syndrome. They are at risk for ending their childhoods and schooling with enough negative experiences that as adults they are devastatingly encumbered when it comes to healthy relationships and social functioning (Gunnar, Herrera, & Hostinar 2009; Harvard Medical School 2020; Shonkoff et al. 2012).

The first step in assisting children to avoid a downward spiral as they grow is for them to feel accepted and loved, via secure relationships, and thus gain Skill 1, the foundational skill. The second step is empowering children to move on to Skill 2, the *pivotal skill*, of expressing strong emotions in nonhurting ways. Civil living is difficult for adults who have been unable to reach resiliency in the face of adverse experiences that undermined their ability to gain the safety-needs skills. We turn to Skill 2 in the next chapter.

Gaining Acceptance as a Member of the Group and as a Worthy Individual

Children struggling with this skill might be new to the program, feel they are in danger of being rejected, and/or deal with unmanageable stress levels due to physiological, environmental, or a combination of factors. They are particularly susceptible to life's stressors and likely to show mistaken survival behaviors in early childhood settings. Children who wrestle with Skill 1 frequently show Level Three strong unmet-needs mistaken behavior.

Typical Child Behaviors

> Observes interactions and experiences but often reluctant to join in formal groups

> Loses emotional control easily

> Experiences stress, sometimes expressed intensely, over what others regard as routine adjustments, little tasks, and small frustrations

> Resists TT's efforts to be included in class routines and activities

> Resists TT's efforts to build relationships due to general mistrust of others

> Shows lack of confidence when engaging in activities

> Reacts to adult intervention with sometimes intense emotional expressions, including aggression and/or psychological distancing

> Has difficulty regaining composure after conflicts

Teacher Responses

TTs use intentional communication practices to create relationships with children *outside* of conflict situations, sustain relationships during conflicts, build trust levels in children, and do whatever necessary to help children to find acceptance within the group and develop positive self-concept.

Progress Indicators in Gaining Skill 1

Building attachments with TT members; becoming more able to participate in activities; growing more relaxed in demeanor; showing fewer rejecting behaviors toward others; and gaining in ability to handle situations without being overcome by frustration, anger, and fear.

DISCUSSION QUESTIONS

1. Identify three key concepts (listed below and in the glossary). If you are a visual learner, write each out with its definition from the glossary. Then, referring to the section of the chapter where the key concept originated, reflect on what the concept means to you now that you have read the chapter.

2. Anecdotes in the chapter illustrate TT members working with children to progress with the DLS. Identify one anecdote (including the author reflection) that has meaning for you. Reflect on how the anecdote enhanced and/or changed your possible response to a similar situation.

3. Explain how partnerships with others—fellow staff, administrators, and families—add to a teacher's ability to guide young children to gain DLS 1.

4. Children who are not able to attain DLS 1 are most at risk for developing a cycle of stress-conflict-punishment as a long-term syndrome. Reflect on ideas acquired from Chapter 5 that would be useful in mitigating this cycle when teaching young children.

5. The book is about education for democracy. Identify a new or newly reinforced idea for you from the chapter. Discuss how that idea contributes to your own approach toward teaching for democracy.

6. How have the thoughts and ideas shared in this chapter impacted your thinking about being a professional working with young children?

Key Concepts

calming

coming around phenomenon

invisible child

Level One experimentation mistaken behavior

Level Three strong unmet-needs mistaken behavior

Level Two socially influenced mistaken behavior

morning greeting talks

preschool expulsion

reactive aggression

CHAPTER 6

The Pivotal Skill

DLS 2: Expressing Strong Emotions in Nonhurting Ways

SUGGESTED GOALS FOR READERS

1. Take an informed position about managing emotions as opposed to regulating impulses in relation to children progressing toward DLS 2.

2. Explain typical similarities and differences in the Level Three strong unmet-needs mistaken behavior shown by children struggling with DLS 1 and children making progress with DLS 2.

3. Explain how practices of developmental and intervention guidance can help prevent young children working on DLS 2 from becoming stigmatized by their mistaken behavior.

4. Form a statement regarding how start-up communication practices with families help build reciprocal family-teacher relations.

DLS 1	**DLS 2**	**DLS 3**	**DLS 4**	**DLS 5**
Finding Acceptance as a Member of the Group and as a Worthy Individual	Expressing Strong Emotions in Nonhurting Ways	Solving Problems Creatively—Independently and in Cooperation with Others	Accepting Unique Human Qualities in Others	Thinking Intelligently and Ethically

Starter Notes

Many interpretations of developmental brain research emphasize "the neuroscience of self-regulation" (Florez 2011; Galinsky 2010). **Self-regulation** refers to the ability to control thoughts, feelings, and behaviors "to appropriately respond to the environment" (Florez 2011, 46).

Among others who have researched this topic, Blair and Diamond (2008) find that "children who engage in intentional self-regulation learn more and go further in their education" (Florez 2011, 46). They cite the famous marshmallow study in which an examiner put a marshmallow in front of individual preschoolers and told them that when the tester left, they could choose to eat the one marshmallow or wait 15 minutes (!) and get two marshmallows (Blair 2002). According to their findings, the children who regulated their impulses and waited for two marshmallows did better educationally in the long term than those who did not wait (and probably had not eaten much breakfast).

Management, More Than Regulation

So why didn't I phrase DLS 2 "self-regulating strong emotions"? After all, the term has an established place in developmental science (Blair & Diamond 2008; Florez 2011) and a tradition in the emphasis on self-discipline, deep rooted in many religions for thousands of years. The developers of Tools of the Mind, a research-based early childhood curriculum, argue that a part of self-regulation parallels Vygotsky's concept of self-talk emerging into intentional thought as the child develops and is helped with emotional-social scaffolding (Bodrova

& Leong 2007). Galinsky (2010) explains how self-regulation is an essential process in developing executive function. These points are all well taken.

From the millisecond a child perceives threat, or an opportunity for personal gain, the neuropsychological response is not simply to either give in to or suppress strong impulses. In agreement with Elliot (2003), I think the term *self-regulation* is too basic to describe the instantaneous flood of perceptions, emotional interpretations, reaction formulations, response tendencies, behavioral manifestations, and resulting self-evaluative messages that happen within the mind and body of a developing child.

•••

Here goes, my one rant. Maybe because impulsiveness is a part of my temperament, I have always been uncomfortable with the marshmallow study. Young children are working hard to grow out of developmental egocentrism. What kind of an experiment manipulates preschoolers by putting them in a position where they must fight temptation? It is hard enough for us *adults* to fight the devil's favorite tool. I know just what my own reaction as a young kid would have been: ① eat the first marshmallow; ② try to convince the examiner that someone bigger than me took the first one, and since I was a victim, I deserved the other one! (Had to do something to fill in the 15 minutes! See what my nursery school teachers and family had to contend with.)

•••

To illustrate self-regulation, Florez (2011) mentions a child who sits on her hands rather than hit another child who has pinched her. In my experience, children rarely react to being harmed by sitting on their hands (and perhaps gritting their teeth). Angry children who might want to hit back, but do not, find another way to express their turmoil: they might complain loudly, cry, bury their head in their arms and yowl, bang on a box with blocks, call for the teacher to help, or show any combination of such responses. Proudly, some of us have observed older preschoolers call for negotiation: "You're not supposed to pinch; you're supposed to use your words!" In an instantaneous mental process, their brains channel the strong emotions into other actions; they *manage* the expression of the impulse—deciding what to do instead—rather than simply regulate the impulse.

For me the issue is deeper than what a child does or does not do when another grabs a favorite marker or pinches. It goes back to the legendary dispute between Freud and Alfred Adler that resulted in Adler breaking from orthodox Freudian psychology (Ansbacher & Ansbacher 1956). Freud argued that human behavior—especially in the child—is the product of an ongoing, largely subconscious struggle between the id, the strong motivation of the pleasure principle, and the superego, the moralistic mental regulator of pleasure-seeking impulses.

In contrast, Adler's thinking was that conflicts happen as the developing self of the young, with prosocial proclivities, comes into conflict with external authorities that mistakenly try to direct, control, and perhaps oppress that development. The consequence, in a term Adler originated, is the *inferiority complex* (Ansbacher & Ansbacher 1956). Adler's position was similar to Friedrich Froebel's before him: it is other people in children's lives who misinterpret their rambunctious but mostly innocent behaviors as inappropriate, and in "correcting" that behavior, convince children that they are unworthy.

In the Adlerian perspective—and later, that of psychologists like Maslow and Carl Rogers—mental health isn't about continuous self-regulation to repress internal negative impulses. Mental health is the ability to manage ever-changing thoughts and feelings to figure out what is the best thing to do, given the influences of significant others and the developmental status of one's own dynamic brain.

For most young people as they grow, no wonder that even approaching a state of mental health is difficult. Without the benefit of fully developed executive functioning, they are trying to manage feelings and thoughts in the face of increasingly complex, sometimes oppressive, social influences—which any individual at that moment can only partially understand. And yet, even young children attain DLS 2 and make progress toward DLS 3, 4, and 5. For me, this is a miracle of human life, and our hope for democracy.

As individuals mature—needing less reliance on supportive others—mental health shows in increasingly proficient intelligent and ethical decision making. For Adler and Rogers, especially, a natural expression of mental health is in being a creative, contributing citizen. Education for democracy sustains democracy.

So, in guiding for DLS 2, teachers work to assist children toward reframing hurtful impulses into more mindful courses of action, a brain process not so much focused on regulation—stifling impulses—as on **managing emotions** amid a mix of possible responses. The child is only at the beginning of this most challenging lifelong human endeavor.

In education for democracy, the matter comes down to helping children express strong emotions in ways that don't hurt others and don't harm themselves. Through relationships with a child and family, TT members understand something of the child's circumstances. They respect the young child enough to believe that they can learn not just what *not* to do, but what to do *instead*. Through being "unrelentingly positive" (a term I once heard teacher educator and author Marian Marion use), the teacher helps the child learn alternatives to stress-caused, stress-producing mistaken behavior. Management of feelings, rather than regulation of impulses, remains for me the path to civil functioning in democratic society.

Notice the phrase "in ways that don't hurt others *and don't harm themselves*" above. One common reaction in young children to perceived rejection by significant others—such as by punishment—is to internalize feelings of abandonment in the momentous self-message: "I am unworthy." This danger exists for children in the face of overt and covert rejection by teachers no less than family members. Some children externalize the resulting mix of negative feelings by acting out against others. Other children react by internalizing negative feelings, contributing to **early childhood depression** and associated mental health issues. The dynamics of fear of and resentment at perceived abandonment can play out in the internal manifestation of self-doubt and depression—hurting oneself—as well as by outward aggression.

An authoritative article (for me at least) is "Early Childhood Depression," by Joan L. Luby (2009). The author manuscript version is available through US Health and Human Services Public Access with this link on the National Institutes of Health (NIH) website: www.ncbi.nlm.nih.gov/pmc/articles/PMC3184299.

Anecdotes and Reflections

As young children gain a grasp of DLS 1, they have the emotional resources to begin to venture out in the program. In their efforts, though, they often experience conflicts, and they may react with dramatic outbursts—challenging for any early childhood professional. Again, the conflicts and reactions are due to being only months old and likely dealing with different degrees of adverse life experiences.

Anecdote 1: Reactive Aggression

This anecdote began as a video. It consists of two parts: a conflict scenario involving three children and a large group meeting addressing the topic of the conflict. These two scenes did not actually occur back to back as presented, but I have included the *intervention* large group meeting to illustrate how teachers can use a meeting to address conflicts that affect many or all the children.

In teacher Deb's Head Start class, preschoolers had been using props introduced through stories in the dramatic play area. Earlier in the week another adult had made several magic wands from cutout stars stapled with ribbons

Children's most serious conflicts are when they show Level Three strong unmet-needs mistaken behavior. Like children struggling with DLS 1, much mistaken behavior by kids working on DLS 2 is also due to strong unmet needs. Kids who have progressed to working on Skill 2, however, have gained enough of a sense of belonging and self-worth that, as mentioned, they participate more in the program. I sometimes say that a distinction between working on Skill 1 and working on Skill 2 is that the Level Three mistaken behavior of children struggling with DLS 1 is sometimes tumultuous, while the Level Three mistaken behavior of children who are tackling Skill 2 might "only" be disruptive.

Illustration. Meredith leans toward the blank far corner of an almost finished ("loaded") finger painting and is accidently bumped into the picture by another child. When struggling with DLS 1, Meredith (with paint-covered arms and hands) might have screamed and grabbed the "offending" child. When making progress toward DLS 2, Meredith might scowl at the kid, but scrunch up the paper, shove it on the floor, and yowl. A teacher who has a relationship with Meredith will view the second reaction as definite progress—given the probability of the child's earlier reaction.

on heavy-duty straws. Boys and girls had been playing with the wands, and on this day, Deb discovered that only three wands were still operational. All three were in use. Hallie joined the children with the wands and asked if she could play with one. Deb nodded and smiled sympathetically. She helped the children understand that Hallie was asking to use a wand when they were finished. They agreed, and Hallie, looking sad, sat on a bench to wait.

Anya, holding her wand, went into a special cardboard play area. Jolie, holding her own wand, looked at Hallie and followed Anya. She returned with both wands and gave one to Hallie. Anya stormed out after Jolie and said, "Hey, I wasn't done with that!"

Jolie turned to Anya and said calmly, "Well, you put it down. And when people put it down, it means they are done." Anya shot a glance at Deb, who nodded in agreement with Jolie, as this was a policy the group has decided on at an earlier developmental group meeting.

Anya dramatically held up both fists, glared at Jolie, and shouted, "I'm not playing with you ever again!" Anya lamented, "I wasn't done with that," and went back into the play area to crawl under a table.

Deb followed, knelt by the table, and said, "Anya, you sound very upset." Anya tearfully said, "Jolie took my wand and gave it to Hallie." Deb asked in a low voice, "Did you lay it down?" Anya nodded. Deb continued quietly, "When you put it down, Jolie thought you were done."

Hallie and Jolie came into the play area with their wands to see what was happening. Deb said, "Hallie and Jolie, look at Anya's face. She looks sad. She wasn't quite done with that wand. When you are done with your wand, can you give it to Anya?" Hallie and Jolie both nodded and left.

Deb turned back to Anya, who stated, "I want the gold one." Deb told her, "You'll have to wait," then added, "You know what? We can make one. We could trace a star and cut it out and find a stick to put it on."

Anya perked up: "I have an idea." She moved quickly out from under the table, past Deb, and sat down at the art table. She looked for the star stencil and yellow paper. Deb made sure Anya had the materials and watched as Anya made a new wand. Deb assisted with the ribbons and stapling.

Later Deb saw Anya and Jolie playing together and smiled. Sharing translucent pegs and deciding with very friendly exchanges where the pegs would go on the light board, the two played together for more than 20 minutes.

Observing a general problem with sharing and taking turns, the next day Deb and the TT held a large group meeting with the children. Deb reviewed the meeting guidelines the group had previously agreed to that were posted at child level (making it a functional literacy activity):

> Take turns talking and listening.

> Be kind to each other.

> Be careful about using names.

Deb: I want us to talk about playing together, but first Tilly Bear, Tommy Bear, and Frisby Frog are going to give us a play.

On a homemade stage, Shane and Loretta, two TT members, have on three sock puppets. Tommy and Tilly are playing. Frisby asks to join. The bears in unison say, "You can't play, you're too small." Frisby crumples up and looks sad.

Deb: Frisby looks sad. (*Pauses*). You know how in our group we always try to let other kids play with us. What can we tell the bears?

Anya: Let the frog play 'cause he can hop.

Carlos: The bears don't got room. They are too big.

Boone: They should get Teacher!

Deb: (*Smiles; she can often count on Boone.*) You guys have some good ideas! Let's see what Frisby does.

Frisby: I'm not too little. I can hop. (*A long sock puppet, Frisby does some amazing hops.*)

Tilly: Ho, you can really hop! (*The three cavort together on the tiny stage, then bow, and the group claps.*)

Allyn (*a true country kid*): But Teacher, bears eat frogs!

Deb: (*Smiles; replies quietly.*) You are right, Allyn, but not our bears at Head Start. (*Says with her large group voice.*) I wonder what we learned from the puppet play?

Ellie: Let kids play.

Boone: Get Teacher?

Deb: Every time or just when there is a problem?

Jolie: Just if there is a fight.

Deb: (*Thinks but doesn't say that Jolie might someday be a teacher.*) Yes! Get Shane, Loretta, or me and we will help you make the problem better, okay? (*Kids nod.*) The sock puppets and stage will be in the dramatic play area if you want to use them.

Reflection. During the conflict, Anya displayed *reactive aggression* in a way that kids making progress with Skill 2 often do. In my discussion with Deb, she mentioned that when Anya started the program, she got very upset easily and often. Deb said Anya seemed less stressed recently. In this situation, Anya's shouting, gesturing with her fists, and running under the table were understandable to the teacher. Anya felt hurt and betrayed by Jolie. Anya managed her impulse of reactive aggression in a way that did not solve the problem, but also did not physically hurt her mate. It did not help Anya's feelings when Deb chose to reinforce the group's established policy rather than to mediate in the situation. (Perhaps on that day Deb judged that reinforced guidelines and their consequences was a lesson Anya could benefit from.) So, Anya went under the table.

The bottom line in guidance is to support each child's feeling of acceptance as a member of the group and of worth as an individual. Even as TTs guide children toward progress with Skill 2 and beyond, they work to sustain the gains they have already made. Deb supported Anya's gain of DLS 1 here by looking beyond the child's outburst and recognizing the progress Anya had made with Skill 2—how hard the child was trying to balance her strong feelings with the nonhurting expression of them. Deb also recognized that Anya had a right to her feelings and understood that anyone might feel upset in a similar situation.

By acknowledging Anya's feelings and explaining them to the other girls, the teacher demonstrated acceptance of Anya. Through reinforcing the classroom policy with the child, Deb also helped Anya recognize that there was a reason behind Jolie's action, and that everyone is expected to follow class guidelines.

In the next day's large group meeting, teachers Deb, Shane, and Loretta worked as a team to encourage the children to problem-solve play conflicts. Notice that they did not single out the three children who had the conflict. The objective was to teach about cooperatively resolving play conflicts going forward, not to return to conflicts of the past. When there is a future conflict, the TT can now refer to the group meeting to remind children about the inclusive guidelines for playing and, if needed, mediate.

Anecdote 2: Instrumental Aggression

This anecdote has appeared in my writings before. It is a consolidation of a couple of observations from child care programs in urban settings.

In early childhood education, puppets are magic, and they can be helpful in teaching to resolve conflicts. With young children, the adults do the puppet role playing and guide the follow-up discussion. Young children take weeks if not months to get the hang of large group meetings (Vance 2014). Puppets can help—as long as the bears eat mostly blueberries and are friendly to the amphibians.

Kayla, 58 months, liked to shoot hoops with a favorite ball, but today Shoggie (long o, hard g), 46 months, had it. Kayla approached Shoggie with another ball, but the smaller boy wouldn't trade. Kayla told him, "That is the ball for big kids," but Shoggie shook his head no. Frustrated, Kayla knocked the ball out of Shoggie's hands. She grabbed it and started to shoot hoops. Shoggie sat and yowled. Teacher Jasper calmed Shoggie and looked at Kayla, who came over holding the ball. "Shoggie wouldn't trade," she said.

"I think we have a problem here," Jasper said. "Let's sit down, get cool, and work this out." Kayla and Shoggie both knew Jasper was going to mediate, a common practice with the group. They sat down. Shoggie followed Jasper's lead and took deep breaths with the teacher. Kayla watched and waited. Jasper put an arm around Shoggie: "Let's hear from the youngest first," Jasper said. "Shoggie?"

As Shoggie shared, Jasper guided Kayla not to interrupt. Then Jasper gave Kayla a turn to share. Jasper repeated each child's account, and the children nodded that Jasper had it right. Jasper then said, "So how can we fix this problem?" Realizing that she was not going to be punished, Kayla became less defensive. "Maybe Shoggie could get a short turn, and then it is my turn." Shoggie agreed and soon gave the ball to Kayla. Jasper stayed near and thanked Shoggie for giving over the ball. Before Kayla started shooting hoops, Jasper had a private guidance talk with her and nudged the child to use a better response for next time.

Reflection. Jasper and the TT had been teaching the use of conflict management and guidance talks from day one, starting with developmental large group meetings. Jasper had built a relationship with both children outside of conflict situations—which helped Shoggie again feel worthy as a member of the group, and Kayla to realize she would not be stigmatized by punishment.

This anecdote provides an illustration of how mediation and individual guidance talks work. As part of the process, Jasper gave clear support to the child who needed it, Shoggie. But, by not using conventional discipline—comforting the wronged child and punishing the instigating child—the teacher was also working to prevent a bully-victim dynamic between the two children. The mediation helped each child feel they were worthy members of the group who could solve problems together. When used together, the practices teach kids like Kayla that they can continue to learn to express strong feelings in nonhurting ways. By the successful mediation, Jasper sustained an encouraging early learning community for all (including the onlookers—other children in the group).

· ·

Often in older, veteran preschoolers who are between Skills 1 and 2, teachers see the type of intentional aggression that Kayla showed—imposing her will on Shoggie to get the ball. The unmet safety needs for Kayla seemed to me to be aggravated by her "senior" status in the program—perhaps also due, perhaps not, to the home environment. These veteran preschoolers know the ropes. Especially if they have been in the program for more than a year, some of these kids become accustomed to the point of being bored with the same old daily routines, materials, and activities. They need new experiences appropriate to their age and status. In my view, in particular in multiage programs, the veteran preschooler issue should be studied more. (We return to the discussion of addressing the needs of older preschoolers on page 99.)

· ·

Communication Practices for Building Relationships

Acknowledge and Pause

A common use of the technique of acknowledge and pause is to lead into a contact talk. Instead, in Anecdote 1, in a quiet way, Deb uses it to move into a guidance talk with Anya when she says, "Anya, you sound very upset." Anya tearfully says, "Jolie took my wand and gave it to Hallie." Deb again uses acknowledge and pause: "Did you lay it down?" Anya nods. Deb continues quietly, "When you put it down, Jolie thought you were done."

Give Encouragement: Private to Individuals, Public to the Group

Deb then privately encourages Anya to keep the child from having to wait: "You know what? We can make one. We could trace a star and cut it out and find a stick to put it on." Anya says, "I have an idea," and moves quickly out from under the table, past Deb. The child sits down at the art table and looks for the star stencil and yellow paper. Deb continues nonverbal encouragement by making sure Anya has the materials; she assists with the ribbons and stapling. Later, Deb smiles when she sees Anya and Jolie playing together—a gratifying act of reconciliation taken by the children themselves.

Levels of Mistaken Behavior

In this section we continue our investigation from Chapter 5 of Level Three mistaken behavior.

To reiterate a key idea regarding mistaken behavior, if during conflicts TTs focus on the level of mistaken behavior, they are less likely to be affected by moral issues in the conflict and less inclined to punish. They are in a better position to guide and teach. To illustrate in Anecdote 1, teacher Deb recognized that Anya was still showing strong unmet-needs mistaken behavior—but had made progress in how she was expressing her strong emotions. With this understanding, the teacher did not focus on the inappropriateness of Anya's outburst but on how to guide Anya toward further progress in her emotions management.

In Anecdote 2, Jasper recognized that even though Kayla showed intentional aggression toward Shoggie (taking the ball on purpose), the act was still a mistaken behavior. Jasper did not make Kayla sit out so he could "teach her a lesson"; instead the teacher helped her make the situation better and taught her about an alternative response for next time.

In the two anecdotes, Anya and Kayla had the grounding that DLS 1 provides. With children who have gained Skill 1, the expression of Level Three mistaken behavior tends to be less visceral. These children, however, are still feeling unmet needs in the form of unmanageable stress that is very real to them.

As with children who struggle to gain Skill 1, the TT responds to the child and doesn't just react to the conflict. With the trust relationship, children working on DLS 2 increase in their ability to see conflicts not as no-exit rabbit holes, but as problems that, with teachers' help, can be resolved. The consistent use of developmental guidance (as in friendly communication practices and group meetings) and of intervention guidance (as in conflict mediation and guidance talks) enables these children to progress away from Level Three mistaken behavior and toward the growing-needs DLS.

Developmental Guidance: Major Practices

Developmental Large Group Meetings

A noteworthy developmental benefit of group meetings is evident in Anecdote 1. Early on, Deb and her TT cooperatively established with the community the guideline that "If you put something down, it means you are done with it." This might not be a guideline in other early childhood settings, but it was a guideline that the group set in this one.

Setting, keeping, and teaching for **guidelines, not rules,** helps children understand that their community is reliable. Developmental group meetings introduce the social parameters by which the community can reliably function. (See further Gartrell 2012.)

Key Intervention Guidance Practices

Calming Methods

Both Deb and Jasper used calming to start the process of resolution. Deb used **reflective listening** (a form of acknowledge and pause) to convey empathy for Anya: "Anya, you sound very upset." Anya tearfully said, "Jolie took my wand and gave it to Hallie!" Deb knew Anya well enough to guess that just these few kind words would be enough for her and the child to begin resolution.

In mediating the conflict between Kayla and Shoggie, Jasper used a classic technique to cool everyone down. Jasper and Shoggie took deep breaths. Kayla, more worried about what would happen than upset, watched and waited for them to finish. This act of calming, along with an arm around the younger child's shoulders (appropriate, friendly touch), and an invitation for the younger (or more upset) child to talk first, usually works. If a child also needs time to calm down, give it to them. It is hard for anyone to settle a dispute when they are highly stressed.

Conflict Mediation

Jasper used classic five finger formula mediation. The teacher started the mediation with the first step in the five finger formula, calming (in this case, taking deep breaths) and setting the scene for the mediation. To reiterate the strategy, let's continue through the five steps of conflict resolution, beginning with FFF 2.

FFF 2: Agreeing about the problem. As Shoggie shares, Jasper guides Kayla not to interrupt. Then Jasper gives Kayla a turn to share. Jasper repeats each child's account, and the children nod that Jasper has it right.

FFF 3: Brainstorming solutions. Jasper says, "How can we fix this problem?" Realizing that she is not going to be punished, Kayla becomes less defensive. "Maybe Shoggie could have a short turn, and then it is my turn."

FFF 4: Deciding on and trying a solution. Shoggie agrees and soon gives the ball to Kayla. After successful mediation, a frequent change of turns is common. Shoggie did not have to make a point by hogging his turn. He got his point made during the mediation. Shoggie was ready to move on.

FFF 5: Monitor and follow-up. Jasper stays near and thanks Shoggie for giving over the ball. Before Kayla shoots, Jasper has a private **guidance talk** with her to nudge her to identify a better response for next time.

....

Across my 40 years of teaching college guidance courses (accompanied by all-important practica), I always gave the paper assignment to students of conducting and recording their efforts at conflict mediation in actual early childhood settings, analyzing them using textbook references, and reflecting about their learning. I gave this assignment probably 120 times, to over 1500 students—which means I read, gave compliment sandwich feedback on, and graded this many conflict mediation papers—never with notorious red ink, just blue or black.

Further, if their papers were in on time, the students could have redos to improve their grades. I probably had the highest on-time paper completion rate in the education department. (My three early childhood courses per quarter, then semester, each had three such assigned papers that required participant observation, text-referenced analysis, and personal reflection about learning. No wonder I now have cataracts!)

Few of the students' first tries at mediation were spot-on perfect, but almost all first or second attempts were successful—to the students' gratification and mine. The major causes of imperfect attempts were (1) children who weren't calmed enough to mediate, and (2) college students who decided a resolution for the children rather than guiding them to find a solution themselves.

Good intentions in mediation go a long way. Mediations tend to take less time than TTs might think. But, if necessary for you or the kids, calm everyone down now and mediate later.

....

Intervention Large Group Meetings

TTs hold intervention group meetings when mistaken behaviors become public, and most in the group are aware of, perhaps alarmed by, what is going on. The TT of Deb, Shane, and Loretta held an intervention large group meeting after the wand kerfuffle. The team decided that it was time to revisit how the community could be inclusive during social play. As with intervention group meetings generally, they informally used the five finger formula to guide the agenda, aided in this case by two bears and a frog. The meeting explored new ground for the children on how to respond when play conflicts happen. (For more on setting guidelines with the group, see Gartrell 2012 and Vance 2014.)

Working for Family Engagement

Four benchmarks that early childhood educators might use in building cooperative engagement indicate families'

1. Acceptance of program and staff
2. Taking new interest in the learning of their child
3. Becoming active in relation to the general program
4. Progressing in personal and/or professional development as a result of their engagement

Neither anecdote in Chapter 6 included interactions between teachers and families. So, let's discuss here a wellspring matter for TTs: start-up communications. Teacher Sammy related this experience to me, and I have shared it more than once.

> Mom and Dad did not make it for a *welcome conference* that the mother, Rory, and teacher Sammy had scheduled for late Friday afternoon. Grandma had picked up Dawnita, just 4, early as was planned. Knowing that family life is complicated, Sammy wondered what had happened. On Monday, Sammy greeted Rory and Dawnita with a smile and a fist bump as she always did. Rory spoke quietly with Sammy. She said that on Friday as they arrived at the school for the meeting, her husband, Joaquim, had had a panic attack. Joaquim had

experienced such an awful time as a student in school that he literally retched when he got near a school building. Because it was preschool, Joaquim thought he could make it, then couldn't. Sammy asked if it was all right with Rory if the teacher thought of something else they might try, and Rory nodded.

When Rory picked up Dawnita that Monday, Sammy asked Rory if she thought Dad might join a meeting at a local fast-food restaurant. Late that Friday, all four met. While Dawnita went climbing, Mom, Dad, and Sammy talked at a table over two diet beverages and a regular. Sammy shared samples of Dawnita's work and photos of the child playing with friends. The teacher said more than once how much they all enjoyed having Dawnita in the group. After this first time, the family and teacher continued the fast-food conferences, as conferences were a part of the program. Rory, Dawnita, and Sammy had hopes that Dad would make it to the end-of-year open house.

Perhaps the key element in communication with families is to *be friendly first*. Like Joaquim, family members might have had painful experiences with their own schooling and bring heavy baggage into encounters with teachers. Given any number of racial, social, cultural, and linguistic factors, parents might be anxious about how they and their children will be treated. They might be unsure about their own parenting and how their child will react to the challenges of the new group situation. They might have suspicions about the program, arising from their own first impressions or things others might have said. Being friendly first goes far to allay such concerns.

Here are three start-up communications ideas for building encouraging, cooperative relations with families.

1. Programs do well to give out **welcome booklets** that provide content about mission and goals of the program, the importance of family-teacher partnerships, adult-child touch policies, guidance practices, and other important matters. The welcome booklets should be available, as much as possible, in families' home languages and distributed both in hard copy and electronically. TTs go over the booklets at **greeting meetings** preferably held at more than one time and date to accommodate families' schedules. The booklets provide reference points for families as things come up. (Friendly humor at the meetings is almost always welcome: "I have a similar booklet that I go over with my family once a week." Then smile and let them know you are joking. You would be joking, right?)

2. Hold **welcome conferences** with every family before or when a child starts. TTs use as much flexibility as they can to set up these informal meetings. (As Sammy teaches us, the conferences set the tone for relations throughout the year). In addition to warm messages about having their child in your group, use the conferences to learn a bit about the family and the child. Make a point of getting the names of siblings, other persons important to the family, and pets. (A teacher might go into the meeting with a mental list of questions and take notes afterward for future contact talks with children.)

TTs usually—but not always—hold conferences at the program. One TT made a decorated partition cardboard "parent nook" in their (not large) room—with two cushioned chairs, a small table and lamp, a bulletin board, and a coat hook. They held meetings with families there, and it was a location where classroom volunteers could put their things. It was their "place" when they came into the classroom.

Of all the settings for holding conferences, many consider home visits to be the best. There is no better way to get to know a child and family than visiting them in the home. Some families, however, are uncomfortable with having a professional visit their home. If the visiting teacher is not from the local community, they might bring another staff member who is—even better if that person is known to the family. Greeting meetings in the home might be inconvenient and impossible in some programs and with some families, but they let the family know that you care about them, and they are not something that the child will soon forget. When home visits can be arranged, they are a sound investment in cooperative TT family relationships.

3. Send home **happygrams**. Learn the day-to-day communication system that families prefer: apps, texts, voice messages left on the phone, or paper notes. On a regular basis, send home or post brief written compliments. These recorded messages supplement in-person contacts, such as at pickup and drop-off. Introduce families to the happygrams through the program guidebook, greeting meetings, and welcome conferences. In the past some parents might have experienced only negative messages sent home from a school. Happygrams are a method to let parents know how much you enjoy having their children in the group. (For serious business, set up in-person meetings.)

A wrap-up thought about communications with families is this: When their children like coming to your program, families grow interested in getting to know you and in engaging with you on behalf of their child.

Ensuring an Encouraging Learning Community for All

1. An early childhood setting is developmentally appropriate only if the setting is developmentally appropriate for everyone.

In the vignette with Jasper and Shoggie, Kayla was an "old hand" preschooler. What was novel to the newer children was old hat to her. Children ready for the next level offer a particular challenge to TTs. Because life is complicated, it is easy for TTs to slide into routines that are no longer intriguing for the **veteran preschoolers** in the group. Without enough to engage them, some kids—like Kayla—tend to find other ways to assert their seniority.

Keeping close relationships with the veteran preschoolers is important. Contact talks give TTs new information about the veterans' interests. TTs can then provide emergent curriculum (developmental guidance) that picks up on those interests.

On a Friday, Jasper held a meeting with the older children who would be going to kindergarten that fall. Together, they planned for the older preschoolers, as leaders, to do special activities with the younger children during certain times the following week. (Jasper's TT prepped, coached, and supported each child leader.)

On Monday, in a regular large group meeting, the TT introduced the plan for the week and what each of the five older preschoolers would be doing. For a few days when outside, the younger children could shoot hoops with Kayla (who, with Jasper's help, would facilitate, not dominate). Also, Marie would help younger children who wanted to do colored chalk on the sidewalk. Inside during work time, Simon (popular with the younger ones) would read books with them. Catherine would do new, complicated puzzles with children who joined her. Alaine would assist those who wanted to use the computer.

The week went without too many glitches. The TT monitored when the older preschoolers got tired of "hosting" and eased them out of their "teacher" roles.

On Friday, the teacher walked with the five to visit a local kindergarten, where Jasper knew the teacher. While the kindergarten students were outside, the kindergarten teacher gave the five a tour of the room. When the kindergartners came inside, Jasper introduced the group and then took them outside to the kindergarten play area to try out the equipment. (Kayla's older sister was in the class, which pleased Kayla to no end.)

Yes, these activities took extra arrangements and special efforts by the TT. They had to decide which staff would stay at the program and which would go. Jasper had to get special permissions to visit the kindergarten. To one degree or another, the older preschool leaders needed support and coaching. TT members had to explain to the younger preschoolers that they would get a turn next year before they went to kindergarten. But the following week, the TT saw a new pride in the five. There was less mistaken behavior, especially bullying behaviors, and more helpful leading.

Like all cases in the book, the above anecdote is not a magic answer but, hopefully, the illustration highlights the importance of responding to the often-overlooked needs of veteran preschoolers.

2. Children need to feel that they are accepted and encouraged in a setting for them to excel at learning and development in the social, physical, cognitive, and linguistic domains.

Notice that in two anecdotes with Anya and Kayla, the arguments were over property—not enough wands or big-kid basketballs. The answer to property-generated mistaken behavior is not just more materials—although having resources for more materials is always appreciated. In the daily reality of more kids than popular materials, TTs work hard to help them engage meaningfully with materials every day. They do this by using fair-choice systems, like revolving **turns lists**, but even more important, by being caringly intentional in their *own* use of DLS 3, 4, and 5.

In her view, when Anya had her wand taken by her good mate and given to another, this was awful! Teacher Deb was caught between a sensitive child who felt wronged and a classroom guideline that in this case worked against the child. By remaining calm and navigating the situation competently, she helped a child who showed Level Three mistaken behavior find resilience and reestablish herself with her friend. Young children gain so much when they are assisted to move beyond the hurt of conflict toward

resolution. As this anecdote shows, young children can move from dramatic conflict to reconciliation in less than a half hour's time! A quick switch from frustration to mutual resilience like this takes empathetic guidance leadership in an encouraging early learning community.

Education for Living in a Democracy

Life is largely about managing resources, getting or trying to get more, managing and sharing what we have, and doing our best given what we don't have. These transactions, if done cooperatively, suggest a lot about the way modern civil society needs to function. The patent reality, though, is that transactions around materials and opportunities aren't always cooperative—in adults' lives or in children's lives. People with more power often use it to get what they want. People with less power often leave transactions over resources feeling victimized. Sometimes the tables get turned or a resolution is reached for the common good, but not often enough. Sometimes we all suffer, as in climate change, pandemics, and natural and human-made disasters, but even then, some people (and some countries) suffer more than others.

When we teach children to manage conflicts civilly by listening and talking together, we are hardwiring brains for cooperative communication skills. We are nudging their ongoing neuroplasticity toward respecting others' viewpoints, responding thoughtfully, and finding common ground. Hopefully, these young, hardwired brains have lots of reinforcement in the growing and learning years to come. Intelligent and ethical communication skills are the heart of education for democracy. But even if not, when we help young children use and develop communication skills, we have done *something*, and likely have made a positive difference in those children's lives.

Expressing Strong Emotions in Nonhurting Ways

Children working on this skill have progressed enough in DLS 1 to initiate interactions with peers and adults. They now feel they are at least somewhat part of the community. Conflicts occur because young children are just beginning to learn skills to prevent and resolve problems and to express strong emotions in ways that do not make conflicts worse. When frustrated, children tend to show reactive or instrumental aggression, physically or verbally. Children who wrestle with expressing their strong emotions in nonhurting ways usually show Level Three strong unmet-needs mistaken behavior.

Typical Child Behaviors

> Still working on ability to share, take turns, cooperate; has conflicts in these situations

> Shows frequent, sometimes dramatic frustration and/or aggression during conflicts

> Shows frequent reactive (impulsive) aggression (for younger preschoolers)

> Begins to show instrumental (intentional) aggression, like bullying (for older preschoolers)

> Resists TT interventions out of fear of punishment

> Usually recovers in self-esteem after guidance interventions, though it may take a while

Teacher Responses

TTs sustain secure relationships with children outside of conflict situations and build trust levels that make guidance interventions effective. They use what they have learned about what works with particular children to ease them through, and help them resolve, conflicts. Young children at DLS 2 typically experience problems involving *property*—"I had it first." Older preschoolers struggling with DLS 2 also experience conflicts regarding *territory* ("You can't play here. I am") and *privilege* ("I got here first so I sit next to Teacher"). TTs use the full range of guidance practices as needed: calming techniques (different from time-outs), guidance talks, conflict mediation, sometimes class meetings, and (with repeated conflicts) comprehensive guidance. To sustain relationships with children, teachers avoid embarrassing and shaming and teach them alternatives to hurting reactions—to others and themselves.

Progress Indicators in Gaining Skill 2

These include using verbal aggression and no longer physical; moving toward nonhurting verbal outbursts ("Teacher, help!"); de-escalating words or actions ("Let's share"); sitting down instead of confronting; self-removal from conflict situation; steering around situations that the child believes will result in conflict. (These are skills most of us adults still work on.)

DISCUSSION QUESTIONS

1. Identify three key concepts (listed below and in the glossary). If you are a visual learner, write each out with its definition from the glossary. Then, referring to the section of the chapter where the key concept originated, reflect on what the concept means to you now that you have read the chapter.

2. Consider the experiences of Anya and Kayla and the other children in the first two anecdotes in the chapter. How does each anecdote show a leader's teaching for, and a child's making progress toward, DLS 2?

3. What do you make of the matter of older preschoolers becoming bored with the routines, activities, and materials of their programs? How might you adapt ideas from the book and/or think of new ideas for positively addressing this issue?

4. Review the developmental guidance practices of group meetings and emergent curriculum (from the follow-up anecdote with Jasper and the five older preschoolers). Discuss how one of these two practices of developmental guidance might assist you to guide young children toward DLS 2.

5. Review the intervention guidance practices of calming, guidance talks, and conflict mediation. Discuss how each practice of intervention guidance might assist you to guide young children toward DLS 2.

6. Analyze one of the three start-up communication practices with families discussed in the chapter that you have used or might use in the early childhood setting. Assess how one of the communication practices that is relatively new to you might help you in building cooperative relationships with family members.

7. The book is about education for democracy. Identify a new or newly reinforced idea for you from the chapter. Discuss how that idea contributes to your own approach toward teaching for democracy.

8. How have the thoughts and ideas shared in this chapter impacted your thinking about being a professional working with young children?

Key Concepts

early childhood depression	happygrams	turns list
greeting meetings	managing emotions	welcome booklets
guidelines, not rules	reflective listening	welcome conferences
	self-regulation	veteran preschoolers

The Learning Skill

DLS 3: Solving Problems Creatively—Independently and in Cooperation with Others

---

CHAPTER 7

SUGGESTED GOALS FOR READERS

1. Show an understanding of how teaching for DLS 3 connects to developmentally appropriate practice.

2. Explain how a teacher might know when a child progressing toward DLS 3 needs support, nudging, or to work through something on their own.

3. Analyze similarities and differences in children's problem-solving process when alone and with other children.

4. Determine how a teacher can identify which phase of the problem-solving process a child is engaged with.

5. Theorize about the relationship of young children's developing communication abilities and their ability to function as adults in a democratic society.

DLS 1	DLS 2	DLS 3	DLS 4	DLS 5
Finding Acceptance as a Member of the Group and as a Worthy Individual	**Expressing Strong Emotions in Nonhurting Ways**	**Solving Problems Creatively— Independently and in Cooperation with Others**	**Accepting Unique Human Qualities in Others**	**Thinking Intelligently and Ethically**

As we address the growing-needs DLS, the chapter format follows less formally the 10 headings/analysis points introduced in Chapter 4. By now, readers have gotten acquainted with the eight communication practices, three levels of mistaken behavior, and key developmental and intervention guidance practices. So, in Chapter 7 through 9, we strike a more flexible balance between concrete mechanics and more open-ended issues regarding the growing-needs skills.

Starter Notes

Problem Solving and Learning

The psychological process of problem solving is when executive function gets to shine. Due to the comprehensive nature of the mental operation, problem solving is largely how we learn.

DLS 3 includes two dimensions, individual and social. Why not make DLS 3 two skills? As I see it, the psychological process of problem solving is similar whether the child is engaging on a task solo or with others. The application of the process in the social dimension differs in that verbal and intuitive *interaction with others* happens throughout, but the steps of problem solving are the same—though in some ways more complex, certainly more complicated, when one is engaged with others. Here is my take on three phases of problem solving, which for the most part run together intuitively in children's minds. As you think of children engaging in problem solving, consider whether the three phases have validity for you.

Intrigue phase. With DLS 1 and 2 mostly mastered, the child in the encouraging early learning community is able to ignite the intrinsic, mastery motivation to learn. Having ample time to explore

sparks and sustains the child's engagement with materials and ideas, so choice/play/work times should not be short. Here are individual and social illustrations:

> A child regards with anticipation: a puzzle to do, a book to read, a structure to build, a story picture to create, a doll to care for, a wheeled vehicle to ride, a bird feeder to study. Individual children naturally favor some of these activities over others, but the great news for them is that they have choices.

> Often with one child's leadership, a few children figure out how the play will proceed— who will do what and how they will do it together. Brian shouts, "A wildfire across the lake!" (As we saw in Chapter 1, there actually had been.) Together with Louella and Darwin, Brian decides they need to turn the play oven, refrigerator, and wardrobe into open-door fire-fighting planes. "Cause we gotta get in them, scoop up water, and put that fire out!"

Observation and engagement phase. Phase one generally merges quickly into phase two. Examples:

> With each attempted placement of a puzzle piece, a child makes mental adaptations based on whether the piece fits or not. A child using an eyedropper draws from one of three colors of water in three small jars, squirts the colored water into a bowl of clear water, and decides which color to mix in next.

> If two kids are "going up top to look out for pirates," they have to give each other room as they scamper up the climber. One gets inside the pipe cubicle on top. Finding this space too small for two, the other child perches outside. They do body-motion 360s looking for pirates.

Synthesis and follow-up phase. As the activity winds down, the child or children draw meaning from the experience. Examples:

> ❯ The child finishes with the puzzle and, depending on the outcome, decides whether to re-do it, choose another puzzle, or move on to a new activity. The child mixing colored water squirts blue and yellow into the clear water many times. Living on a farm, the child looks at the color and exclaims, "John Deere green!" (Really.)

> ❯ The children spy pirates and agree, "We gotta get outta here!" They clamber down and ride off on a Hot Wheels "Wave Runner" to escape, one peddling, one standing on the back. They live to fight another day.

The learning derived through problem solving always includes an affective as well as a cognitive dimension (and generally physical and social dimensions as well). Still, for the sake of self-esteem, early childhood educators should not necessarily want children to experience consistent success in their problem solving. Constant success—in final product terms—is not helpful preparation for realities to come. But if a child can gain an "I can do it better next time" affirmation from the experience, this is what a teacher hopes for. Positive meaning from an experience means children want to engage in similar activities (perhaps more advanced, perhaps not) again. Repeated mastery at one level builds increased meaning for the child as they get ready to move to the next level.

TT members observe a child do the same puzzles four days in a row. On the fifth day, the child chooses and works on a new, more complicated puzzle. Or, on the fifth day and all the next week, the child continues to sit down and do the same puzzles. Is a child's staying with the same activity an intuitive rehearsal for something bigger? Or, is doing the same activity every day an attempt to find security by an anxious child? With DLS 3 in particular, TTs address both motivational needs: supporting for safety and nudging for psychological growth. Striking the dynamic balance requires knowing the child.

You might have noticed that in the above illustrations, no teachers participated. In using developmentally appropriate practice to promote the problem-solving process—whether the activity is "academic" or not—we give children enough assistance, but *only* enough assistance, for them to do the rest. When teachers provide scaffolding during a child's problem solving, the teachers themselves are also solving problems creatively—hopefully in a way that is congruent with the child's aims. The most effective scaffolding takes mental and conversational attunement to the child (Dombro, Jablon, & Stetson 2020). In this effort, the teacher's playbook includes acknowledge and pause and using reflective responses, compliment sandwiches, friendly humor and touch, guiding questions, and open suggestions ("I wonder what would happen if . . ."). When TT members choose to provide active support, the satisfaction in the learning must be the child's and not just the adult's.

Here's an illustration. A child abandons a difficult puzzle and appears to be deciding what to do next. A teacher who knows the child says, "Lulu, that's a hard puzzle! You decide: We can do that one together. You can work on one of these two (carefully selected) easy-schmeasy ones. Or, you can go do something else."

If Lulu chooses the first suggestion, the two do the hard puzzle together, with lots of encouragement from the teacher. If Lulu picks an easier puzzle to do, the teacher steps back and later says something like, "You did it. You put both puzzles together!" If Lulu takes the "out-choice" and goes on to another activity, the teacher has faith that Lulu will return to puzzles another day—with new spatial knowledge and confidence in the teacher's support.

For more on successfully scaffolding children's learning, see *Powerful Interactions: How to Connect with Children to Extend Their Learning* (Dombro, Jablon, & Stetson [2020]).

Given the creative minds of the young who have attained the safety-needs skills, materials themselves provide not just the incentive but much of the guidance that children need for productive problem solving. Two centuries ago, Froebel's kindergartens featured a sequence of materials for children to learn with (which he called *gifts* and *occupations*). A century ago, Montessori based much of her approach on children's growing ability to select and problem-solve with her prepared hands-on materials. In the twenty-first century, models and approaches to early childhood education such as HighScope, The Creative Curriculum, and Reggio Emilia center their programs around children's active engagement with materials, along with responsive interaction from teachers who share and expand on the children's wonder.

In my view, education at all levels benefits when teaching and learning are less instruction centered and more experience facilitated. Children in too many classrooms still have too much sit-down-and-recite instruction. For transitioning to a better balance, plentiful hands-on materials are needed. Books and direct instruction contribute to a project, unit, or theme, but deep, rich exploration and learning come when activity—active, hands-on learning—takes center stage.

Why Is Emphasizing *How* We Learn Important?

DLS 3 is the skill most closely related to our usual concept of learning in the classroom.

But even Skill 3 might seem far removed from mastery of a first grade—or eighth grade—curriculum. So, a head scratcher for many tied to conventional schooling is, why are the "soft" outcomes in education, like problem solving and social learning, important?

Progressing with the DLS increases children's ability to engage in and gain meaning from all life experiences—and certainly during childhood at school. Progress with the DLS frees up children's mastery motivation. In other words, the developmental dynamic empowered by attaining the safety-needs DLS shows itself in children's being willing and able to problem-solve, and so progress in learning readiness. When I write of readiness, I refer not to a state of knowledge but to a state of mind. The closer learning experiences are to being developmentally appropriate, the more we educators teach for further gains in the DLS and assist children to use their readiness and problem-solving powers successfully at school.

Anecdotes and Reflections

Anecdote 1: Individual Domain

Some years ago in a Head Start classroom, student teacher Sharon and a child were about to read a picture book about the first snow. For a course paper, Sharon recorded her contact talk with Lindsey, 54 months, which started even before the two started reading. The conversation went longer than appears here (and even included Lindsey's account of making snow angels with her dad). The anecdote focuses on the individual aspect of DLS 3, with a teacher's facilitation.

> Before reading the book, Sharon and Lindsey look at the cover together.
>
> **Sharon:** I wonder what makes it snow?
>
> **Lindsey:** Well, I think that Santa brings the snow in his sleigh and drops it over us—the clouds tell him when to. He has a machine on the back that shoots it out.
>
> **Sharon:** Wow! I didn't know that was how it snowed. Santa is sure busy.
>
> **Lindsey:** Yeah, but Rudolph and Clixen and all those guys help. (*Whispers.*) Do you know who fixes the snower when it's broke? Mrs. Claus does, and my mom says girls can do that.
>
> **Sharon:** It's good that Santa has all that help, and I bet Mrs. Claus is good at fixing things.
>
> **Lindsey:** Yeah, but Santa doesn't bring it everywhere, 'cause my grandma lives in Azizona, and she said they don't ever get snow there.
>
> **Sharon:** Why do you think they don't get snow in Arizona? (*Models the pronunciation.*)
>
> **Lindsey:** It's too far for Santa to drive. My mom says it's too far for us to drive. I wanted to go last night. We went one time on a big airplane—it was scary, but only a little.
>
> **Sharon:** It is a long way to Arizona. Your grandma must be a pretty important person to you, and I bet you miss her.
>
> **Lindsey:** She's my favorite.

Sharon: What is your favorite thing about your grandma?

Lindsey: But . . . I think there might be another way it snows.

Sharon: I'd like to hear about it. Could you tell me about the other way it snows?

Lindsey: Maybe the clouds just melt 'cause they move in front of the sun, and the sun is hot and then they melt.

Sharon: That's neat. Maybe the sun does melt the clouds. It's pretty sunny in Arizona. Do you think that if it got cloudy there that it might snow?

Lindsey: (*Laughs.*) No! There's too much cactuses. Didn't you know there are cactuses everywhere there? We saw big ones that were bigger than my dad, and they had really sharp prickles on 'em.

Sharon: (*Pauses.*) How do the cactus keep it from snowing?

Lindsey: Because, silly, snow doesn't like the prickles on the cactuses! When the snow gets on a prickle, it hurts 'em and they don't like that. So that's why.

The conversation ends, and the two read the book.

Reflection. The whole contact talk took about five minutes (before the two even started the book). Sharon had not talked with Lindsey before. Later that day at circle time, Lindsey sat on Sharon's lap. Lindsey had built a relationship with this caring adult in just a few minutes. By attuning herself to Lindsey via the contact talk, Sharon made the learning environment reliable for the child. With the security Sharon offered her, Lindsey felt free to express her thinking, to share the unique sense of reality of a young child, which is so different from an adult's.

Is a child thinking intelligently if she tells you that Santa sprays the snow out of a sprayer that Mrs. Clause can fix, just not in "Azizona" because of the cactuses? A lot of adults would think this is silly, childish gibberish. A definition of intelligence, stemming from Howard Gardner (2006), is that intelligence is the ability to make something new, physical or intellectual. In this supportive conversation, Lindsey was creating a fantabulous

story. Think about the development in this child's thinking in this one conversation. At the beginning she says snow is caused by Santa and the sprayer; by the end she muses that maybe snow happens when clouds get too close to the sun and melt. Quite a leap.

Young children's thinking is quick and imaginative. They interpret the world as they perceive it and creatively use their imaginations to fill in the gaps. In Piaget's terms, preschoolers are growing from the **developmental egocentrism** of early childhood toward a more concrete grasp of reality in later childhood. When conversing with young children, adults should make any factual corrections light and matter of fact, as Sharon did when she modeled the adult pronunciation of "Arizona." More pointedly correcting Lindsey's childlike sense of reality might not only stifle the conversation but also likely undermine how the young child perceives herself in the world.

In my view, when adults disregard or reject reality for a young child, they undermine mastery motivation and learning readiness. Responsive TT members cross the adult-child reality gap. They grant to a 54-month-old a 54-month-old's worldview. That sense of reality will be different when she is 80 months, though we hope with imaginative intelligence still intact. How did Lindsey know that Sharon would be an empathetic listener? It probably had something to do with Sharon's first question and how she responded to Lindsey's first answer. By the way, what does make it snow?

Communication Practices for Building Relationships

Democracy needs citizens who can initiate, cooperate, negotiate, mediate, and reconcile. TTs coach for and facilitate these communication abilities in young children. Communicating effectively is a product of learning the DLS. For this reason, in this chapter and throughout the book, we emphasize assisting children to communicate.

Acknowledge and Pause Redux

Acknowledge and pause is perhaps *the* fundamental communication-starter practice in relation to DLS 3. Young children's creations tend to be nonrepresentational or early representational. Generally, young kids can't make things that closely depict reality. At the same time, they have an idea of what reality is supposed to look like. (An analogy is knowing that shoelaces need to be tied, but not being able to tie them yet.) From their experience, children tend to expect us to judge their work by how well they represent reality, and so are hesitant to talk about what they are creating. Most children are sensitive about their in-progress creations, as most all artists are.

Teachers use acknowledge and pause when they join a child before or during creative activities. The *acknowledgment* serves as a nonintrusive greeting. The greeting alleviates the pressure put on a child that comments like "What are you going make?" or "Tell me about your picture" do. Instead, the acknowledgment tells the child that the teacher cares enough to pay attention: "You look like you are thinking hard before you start working" or "You are really working hard on that . . ."

The *pause* gives the child time to process a reply. Especially in an early developing brain, much effort is needed to interpret the acknowledgment, think of a response, decide on words to voice the response, and express the words. When children trust their teachers, the pause for teachers often is exciting, waiting to hear what the child is going to say: "This is John Deere green!" or "This is my dad swimming with his swimsuit on."

· ·

Suggestion: Acknowledge *what* a child is making *only* when you are sure about what it is; otherwise acknowledge details in the effort. Darwin had drawn a picture of his family for a "Families Album." I said of the little figure on the left, "I bet that's your baby brother." "Uh-uh, Dan," Darwin said as he shook his head. "That's my dog."

· ·

Keep Up Those Contact Talks

At an early childhood center, Janie couldn't find her mitten. She drew a picture of a kid with one mitten and a frown. Teacher Sylvia commented on the one mitten. The child said the other was lost, and the two had a contact talk about the frustration of losing things. Later teacher and child looked in the lost and found box. No luck, but the TT got two copies of *The Mitten Book* by Jan Brett and read the book in their two small groups. They talked with the groups about losing things. Janie got to share. Some children later made story pictures about "a time when somebody lost something," like "My mom lost her keys."

For many children, it is a special experience to have someone listen to them. Like Lindsey in the previous anecdote, they get it all out while they can. The support children receive during these talks goes a long way emotionally. Contact talks benefit children in multiple ways, as they gain experience with

› Listening to others

› Information processing

› Comprehension of situations

› Sequencing of events

› Concept formation

› Concept-to-expression skills

› Vocabulary development

› Understanding of the art and science of conversing

› Perspective taking

› Accommodating differences in opinion and viewpoint

› Confidence in communicating with others

› Enjoyment of a shared human experience

TTs know that some children are more loquacious, and others more quiet. On the first day, teacher Felix noticed that Jimmy (52 months) arrived on a two-wheeler to preschool! (He lived a few houses away.) The teacher acknowledged the fact to him, and Jimmy said, "Yep, me and my brother ride all over." Jimmy then walked by the teacher and into the classroom. From then on, the teacher watched for Jimmy. The next day, Jimmy arrived and said, "Rode real fast today, teacher," and again went right into the room. Jimmy was a biker, not a talker. But he and the teacher had a long-enough contact talk each morning—a good start to their growing relationship.

A helpful idea is to have a system to track contact talks so that nobody is missed. After one of my workshops, a third grade teacher reported that he made a list and had a designated contact talk with every child once a week. (He had other talks as well, more often than before the workshop.) Jay reported that he found he got to know the children better, and they got to know him as well, including that his dog had tangled with a skunk!

Anecdote 2: Solving Problems Together with Others

This anecdote comes from the Head Start classroom of Deb, Shane, and Loretta—whose setting we visited in the previous chapter (the wands and the puppet play). Children between ages 4 and 5 years were in their setting. The anecdote began as an informal transcription from a video clip, with added material, and focuses on the social dimension of Skill 3. The three boys, in their mid-4s, were using a jumbo-sized building set with wooden hammers, pegs, and large wooden and plastic pieces. They were being building engineers, the kind of STEM (science, technology, engineering, and mathematics) activity that should in no way stop when children enter kindergarten.

> Brent and Isaiah, wearing yellow construction hats, sat on the carpet in the construction area of the classroom. Using a toy hammer, Brent pounded a large green peg into a long plastic piece. Brent said, "We're gonna make a house." Sitting next to him, Isaiah added, "Yeah, a big one."
>
> Dakota joined the two, sitting on the other side of the parts bin. Dakota said, "Now I need that—the hammer. Now I need it." When Brent set the hammer down to look for more parts in the bin, Dakota grabbed it and smiled. Brent objected. "Hey, I need it!"
>
> Dakota said, "I need it to snap this in," and hammered a blue rod into a wooden piece. He quickly finished and handed the hammer back to Brent: "Here you go." Brent said, "Thank you." Dakota said, "Yup." Isaiah frowned at Dakota. "That is ours."

The two boys continued working separately from Dakota. After a few minutes, Dakota moved around the bin and picked up another structure Brent had been working on. "You make this?" Brent grabbed at it with his free hand and said, "Don't, you. Don't!" Brent jumped up, shook the piece he was holding at Dakota, and made jabbing gestures and threatening noises.

Dakota put down the structure and backed away: "Don't, it's going to break and hit people." Brent moved his "weapon" away from Dakota. Dakota cautiously sat down and said, "Okay." Brent also sat. Isaiah said, "Stop taking our stuff." Brent looked at his mate and said, "It would be better if Dakota could play too."

Dakota gingerly moved over beside Brent, and the two boys began to join their structures together. Looking unhappy, Isaiah joined his own structure to the bigger one, sitting as far from Dakota as he could. Brent, now singing to himself, hammered in the last connector and said, "There you go." Together, all three boys carried the finished structure, which was as big as they were, to show the teacher. Isaiah beamed. Another child walked up to them, looked at the structure, and said, "Cool!" "It's rad," answered Dakota.

Reflection. This event happened on a day in April. When Deb saw the video clip, she might have teared up. She commented that Dakota had come a long way since September. If Brent had threatened him like that earlier in the year, an angry Dakota would have pounced on him. The TT had been working hard to help Dakota manage his anger.

When children have a conflict, if one can de-escalate the situation, that child often can get the others to resume cooperative play. In this case, the three children began playing more inclusively after Dakota calmed Brent down. Because of Dakota's actions, Brent felt disposed to include him in the construction. By staying calm, Dakota motivated Brent to manage his mistaken behavior and move from limited to more inclusive cooperative play.

For his part, Isaiah was showing loyalty to Brent and worked hard to follow his mate's lead. To his credit, in my view, Isaiah stayed with the project. Dakota clearly shows here his mastery of DLS 3 in the social dimension—and he brought Brent along.

Levels of Mistaken Behavior

When Brent thought that Dakota would take his other structure, he said, "Don't, you. Don't!" He jumped up, made jabbing gestures with the structure he was holding, and growled at Dakota. This was a Level One experimentation mistaken behavior involving a property dispute. Brent was engaged in serious construction and felt distress that his original structure might be taken. As I see it, Isaiah was showing Level Two socially influenced mistaken behavior. Out of allegiance to his mate, Brent, Isaiah was motivated to try to exclude Dakota from the constructing. When the two boys resolved the conflict and decided to build together, Isaiah decided to join them.

Conflicts like this are common, I would say natural, in encouraging early learning communities, where most young children are transitioning from safety-needs skills to growing-needs skills. If young children who have mostly gained DLS 2 are engaged in developmentally appropriate activity, they don't want to be arguing. They want to be doing! Growing needs have come to the fore. Brent allowed Dakota to resolve the conflict because the engineering experience was important to him. Dakota worked to resolve the dispute for the same reason. Isaiah was still struggling a bit with gaining DLS 2, and so his mistaken behavior seemed to be socially influenced. In the end he went along to get along, and he remained part of a team that created that remarkable structure.

Anecdote 3: Individual and Cooperative Problem Solving

The following anecdote from way back (during my second year at Head Start) begins with an informal large group meeting. The meeting is of a TT and a group of mixed-age preschoolers planning a group-made bulletin board (the best kind). The anecdote follows the events of the meeting and afterward. It illustrates how large group meetings can contribute to children's progress toward DLS 3 in both the individual and cooperative dimensions.

It was December. The holiday open house for families was coming up. We wanted to decorate the room, especially one large, high bulletin board (not placed well for young children). It was time for a group meeting. The assistant teacher and I asked the group of 2½- to 6-year-olds: "What could we put on the bulletin board that would look nice for when your parents visit?"

After a few moments of thought, Rita (age 58 months) said, "We could do 'Night before Christmas.'" (We had read the book the day before.)

I said that sounded fine, but how would we do that? Joey (age 62 months) said, "I will make Santa. I need cotton." Two girls (about 4½) said they would make "a big tree, with lights even." Janelle (67 months) volunteered to make the sled and some reindeer, "but not all of them. It's dark so you can't see them." Karen, 58 months, said, "I will make Rudolph" (different story but no worries.) Rita volunteered to "make the guy coming down the stairs." And Virgil, 56 months, offered, "I will make the stairs, and the chimney."

Five (on-average) 3-year-olds didn't say anything. But at the end of the meeting, they all went to the art center, cut out small pieces of paper, and drew crisscrosses on them. I went over, curious to see what they were doing. Darwin said, "We're makin' presents, Teacher." (There were a lot of presents!) For her part, Karen carefully made Rudolph, but with a yellow nose!

The assistant teacher and I put black corrugated paper (it's what we had) on the bulletin board. The kids brought us their various pieces as they finished them. We asked them where they thought each piece should go and tacked the pieces up for them. I recall that all the children contributed something. One of the TT made a sign that said, "The Night Before Christmas."

On the big day, the families, who were used to commercial, professional-looking bulletin boards, arrived. They looked at this one, saw immediately what it was, and had big smiles all around. The kids pointed out their own pieces. The families and their children were very pleased.

This is not the end of the story. On the first day back to Head Start in January, I had started to take down the bulletin board when the children came in from the buses. "What are you doing, Teacher?" asked Rita. I told her and the others that I was taking the bulletin board down because the holiday season was over. "No," Rita said. "We made it. We take it down." And with me spotting for Rita and Joey as they stood on a table, the children did.

The anecdote above took place years ago. Today, as TTs strive to make holiday events inclusive and responsive to diverse cultures, the same flow of a large group meeting into a class project into an open house could be done around other themes. A class-made bulletin board is emergent curriculum at work, based on the children's interests and cultures. Early pictorial bulletin boards are cool. As Rita demonstrated, they belong not just to the teacher, but to the whole community.

Reflection. My thinking has long been that adults underestimate the significance of young children's early pictorial art. Too often, we dismiss early art as cute or charming and rarely realize that children often tell stories through it (Schickedanz & Collins 2012). Behind the stories, young children's problem solving can be amazing. An example in Anecdote 3 was Karen's drawing of Rudolph. When I acknowledged in a low-key tone, "Karen, you made Rudolph with a yellow nose," without much of a pause she replied, "That's so Santa can see better." (Think about it. The kid improved on the whole concept. Karen's Rudolph is one of my most shared anecdotes in and of itself.)

I will never forget this experience. We did it together. I think that wonderful early pictorial bulletin board upped everybody's game for the rest of the year. By this, I mean we all realized what we were capable of and didn't go back. On that day, the whole group showed individual and social DLS 3, the learning skill.

Developmental Guidance: Major Practices

Developmental Large Group Meetings

In Anecdote 3, the informal group meeting that resulted in the idea for the holiday bulletin board was an illustration of developmental guidance. Out of the group's problem solving grew emergent curriculum that was inclusive of all. The meeting and activity came during the second year of Head Start for many of the children—which included summer Head Start in between. The veteran kids—Rita, Karen, Brian, Janelle, Joey, Louella, and Virgil—led the group, and together the group showed amazing self-sufficiency. These Ojibwe preschool kids relished their largely self-selected activities, and they took their learning at Head Start seriously, every day.

Thinking back, I realize most of those children were dealing with poverty and the intergenerational impact of societal oppression. That year we had two kids who struggled mightily with Skills 1 and 2. They weren't there regularly, and the Head Start staff and I didn't have the skills or resources back then to really help them. (In both cases there were signs of abuse, which, using comprehensive guidance and social work intervention today, we could have done something about. Back then, and I put this lack of response largely on myself, not so much.) Bemidji, Minnesota, is close enough to the Red Lake Reservation for me to learn that as adults, one of the two died by suicide and the other was sentenced to prison for life. I grieve for them to this day. Yet for me, the older preschoolers that December were ready for kindergarten right there and then. Except for the two, whom I will always remember, that year was a joy.

Key Intervention Guidance Practices

In Anecdote 2, a property dispute ensued when Dakota picked up Brent's structure and Brent threatened him. Dakota de-escalated and resolved the situation. With Dakota's response, Brent's trust level must have gone up, because he let Dakota gingerly join their structures, and even told Isaiah that it would be better if Dakota played with them. The three boys then built together.

Thanks to Dakota, the boys resolved their conflict themselves, at the top mediation level called *child negotiation*. As Deb said, Dakota had progressed a great deal in that year. Through resolving the conflict, Dakota led the way in solving this problem so that the three could cooperatively problem-solve in their creation.

Why didn't I go for broke and say Dakota was showing not just DLS 3 but Skills 4 and 5 as well? In the book we discuss the skills in relation to the context in which they are shown. The context in the anecdote is solving problems creatively in cooperation with others—in this case a conflict over materials needed for an engineering project. (But I will say, in this anecdote Dakota *did* show DLS 4 and 5.)

Working for Family Engagement

Recall the four benchmarks in family engagement:

1. Benchmark 1: Family members show acceptance of program and staff.

2. Benchmark 2: Family members take new interest in the learning of their child.

3. Benchmark 3: Family members become active in relation to the general program.

4. Benchmark 4: Family members progress in personal and/or professional development themselves as a result of their engagement.

In Anecdote 3, most of the families at the open house showed they were becoming active in the education of their child. They weren't just receiving information. They were taking time out of their day to show an interest in their child and the program. In truth, a few families at the open house were probably curious to see that tall White guy with a mustache who was teaching their young kids. Others probably attended because the assistant teacher, an elder in the community, told them to get themselves there. But, for whatever reason, most were there.

Whatever their levels of engagement, the family members were treated royally by their kids, had a positive learning experience with the bulletin board,

In the early years of Red Lake Head Start, the director and all the teachers were White; all the assistance staff were Ojibwe. When I left, the Head Start director was Ojibwe, and many of the assistants had become coteachers and received increases in duties and salary. A few years after that, with Bemidji State University being one of the first CDA programs nationally, many teachers were also Ojibwe.

and enjoyed the open house. Thinking in terms of the benchmarks, our TT hoped the open house would consolidate engagement at Benchmark 2—perhaps in the future by appreciating the creations their kids brought home and checking out copies of the one culturally relevant picture book that Head Start at the time had to offer. Consolidation in relation to Benchmark 2 was our goal. Progress for some family members toward Benchmarks 3 and 4 was our hope.

Native American families have experienced heartache and alienation because of a history of European American–forced schooling ("socialization") of their children. We at Head Start were working on a clear mission with our families: To help them to see the program as theirs. On the day of the open house, the staff recognized that we were making headway with the mission.

Ensuring an Encouraging Learning Community for All

1. An early childhood setting is developmentally appropriate only if the setting is developmentally appropriate for everyone.

Conventional schooling tends to reward successful students, and withhold rewards from others, in mistaken efforts to motivate all. Examples are star stickers and other tangible rewards given only to some, and other public recognitions selectively bestowed. To my thinking, rather than motivating "the rest," this mistaken strategy is divisive to the group and debilitating to those for whom academic learning is difficult.

In encouraging early childhood communities, teaching for DLS 3 works differently. In the encouraging community, TTs include all as equally worthy members of the group, cultivate the expression of intrinsic motivation through developmentally appropriate activities, and assess progress in nonintrusive ways through *authentic assessment*.

Authentic Assessment

One way to authentically assess learning is to collect samples of children's everyday efforts and achievements and use this data to assess progress in relation to researched normative markers. While authentic assessment does not provide easy scores for comparative purposes, it allows educators to assess children's learning across developmental domains, including emotional-social development. ". . . Assessment should always be authentic—that is, by using age-appropriate approaches, tools and methods that are culturally relevant, and a language the child understands" (Scott-Little, with Reschke 2022, 162).

2. Children need to feel that they are accepted and encouraged in a setting for them to excel at learning and development in the social, physical, cognitive, and linguistic domains.

A primary psychological challenge for young children, and pedagogical challenge for early childhood educators, is the rift between children's own personal timetables for development and the relatively fixed timetables set by society. When the very young should, and actually do, walk, talk, and go potty are only the first of these challenges. With "older" young children, the benchmark behaviors change, but the rifts continue over such matters as when they can and should "self-regulate," give factual rather than fanciful accounts of experiences, read and write sentences, add sums of numerals, sit in seats for long periods of the day, and so on. When TTs teach for DLS 3, they nurture, rather than force or impede, children's individual, diverse biological timetables set by the blueprints ("brain-prints") of their biology.

Developmental puzzle: How is it that some children read fluently at 4 years of age and others not until 7 years—and as adults both individuals graduate from college? How is it that some children can do arithmetic exercises easily at 5 and others not easily until 8—and both individuals become physicists?

Education for Living in a Democracy

What does it take for an adult citizen to speak effectively at a meeting and give an impassioned but articulate and civil plea to right a perceived wrong? Speaking like this requires the previous list of communication skills that early childhood educators work so hard for children to begin to develop:

> Listening to others

> Information processing

> Comprehension of situations

> Sequencing of events

> Concept formation

> Concept-to-expression skills

> Vocabulary development

> Understanding of the art and science of conversing

> Perspective taking

> Accommodating differences in opinion and viewpoint

> Enjoyment (or semi-enjoyment) of a shared human experience

Individuals gain these abilities through rich experiences beginning in early childhood settings via contact talks, peer conversations, guidance talks, and large group meetings. The friendly give-and-take of interaction is at the heart of teaching for DLS 3. Able communicators, good at listening as well as speaking, make for strong democracy.

Solving Problems Creatively—Independently and in Cooperation with Others

Children working on Skill 3 often feel reluctant to initiate an activity. Individually, the child shows concerns that they "can't do it right." The child often asks for help in activities from the TT or even peers. They may abandon new activities quickly. If the child completes a project, they frequently express frustration with the result. To avoid perceived failure, the child repeats using a few familiar materials and doing mainly familiar activities. At an individual level, these tendencies extend to social problem solving with the TT.

When with others, the child blends in, often following the lead of more confident others in social problem solving. They may show communal pride in accomplishments because they are products of the group. When in a group, the child tends to defend decisions made by the leader. Children starting on Skill 3 frequently show Level Two socially influenced mistaken behavior.

As I said in Chapter 4, cultural influences can affect the behaviors mentioned here. And every child from every culture is different.

Typical Child Behaviors

> Tends to stay with a few favorite activities

> May be reluctant to try new activities

> Shows lack of confidence in engaging with many open-ended activities

> Might often ask for help when activities seem difficult

> Often abandons activities that seem difficult

> Forms dependent relations with authority figures, adults, and peers

> Tends to blend in within a peer group

> Supports authority figures in group decision making

> Is often unsatisfied with individual outcomes; more satisfied with group outcomes

Teacher Responses

TTs provide a learning environment in which children can successfully engage in problem solving, independently and in cooperation with others. TTs provide a variety of learning opportunities and work to engage every child. TTs recognize that the process is more important than the product and do not compel children to make predetermined products. They give enough, but only as much, assistance as children need to feel ownership and do the rest themselves. Teachers use private encouragement—acknowledgment, reflective feedback, guiding questions, and open suggestions ("I wonder what would happen if . . .") to support children in their problem-solving efforts. TTs use public encouragement that does not single out individuals but reinforces a sense of belonging and individual worth for all.

Progress Indicators in Relation in Gaining Skill 3

Accessing and engaging in new activities, not just the familiar few; engaging in open-ended activities; showing persistence when working on problems and tasks; solving problems, obtaining results, and creating products in one's own way; showing less dependency on adult and peer authority figures; showing an increase in independent thinking; and finding personal gratification in outcomes of problem solving and activity engagement.

In cooperative problem solving with others, the many indicators above are the same, with the added ingredient of the give-and-take observed in child-to-child communication.

DISCUSSION QUESTIONS

1. If you are a visual learner, write out the key concept from this chapter (listed below and in the glossary) with its definition from the glossary. Then, referring to the section of the chapter where the key concept originated, reflect on what the concept means to you now that you have read the chapter.

2. Various anecdotes in the chapter illustrate TT members working with children to progress with the DLS. Identify one anecdote (and author reflection) that has meaning for you. Reflect on how the anecdote enhanced and/or changed your possible response to a similar situation.

3. Discuss what you might look for that tells you when an individual child is in each of the three phases of problem solving. What about when children are engaged in cooperative problem solving together?

4. What indicators inform a teacher that a child working on DLS 3 needs support, nudging, or to be left alone?

How do you know when to leave a child alone as they are problem solving? When giving support *or* nudging toward new experiences, what would be a similarity and a difference in the specifics of your approach?

5. Explain and evaluate this statement: In teaching for DLS 3, TT members respect each child's intrinsic mastery motivation and pattern and schedule of development.

6. Share a strategy for assisting families to appreciate and become actively supportive of the efforts of their child at gaining DLS 3. (We recognize that not all families need this assistance.)

7. The book is about education for democracy. Identify a new or newly reinforced idea for you from the chapter. Discuss how that idea contributes to your own approach toward teaching for democracy.

8. How have the thoughts and ideas shared in this chapter impacted your thinking about being a professional working with young children?

Key Concept

developmental egocentrism

CHAPTER 8

The Inclusion Skill

DLS 4: Accepting Unique Human Qualities in Others

SUGGESTED GOALS FOR READERS

1. Explain how, when adults ignore acts of exclusion toward vulnerable others, they are showing the power of silence, which is itself discrimination.

2. Demonstrate a working knowledge of guidance practices that teachers use when they counter the mistaken behavior of discrimination and teach for the inclusiveness that is the essence of DLS 4.

3. Self-monitor the biases one brings into the learning community and how these might affect teaching for DLS 4.

4. Demonstrate an understanding of the immediate and long-term importance of children's witnessing and experiencing inclusive leadership toward all in the community.

5. Hypothesize about how experiencing an early learning community that models and teaches for DLS 4 might affect an individual as they come of age in a complex modern democracy

DLS 1	DLS 2	DLS 3	DLS 4	DLS 5
Finding Acceptance as a Member of the Group and as a Worthy Individual	**Expressing Strong Emotions in Nonhurting Ways**	**Solving Problems Creatively— Independently and in Cooperation with Others**	**Accepting Unique Human Qualities in Others**	**Thinking Intelligently and Ethically**

Starter Notes

Teaching for the five DLS means teaching for civil democratic living in adulthood. A current term for this kind of education is that it is teaching for *equity in society*. NAEYC (2020) defines *equity* this way:

> The state that would be achieved if individuals fared the same way in society regardless of race, gender, class, language, disability, or any other social or cultural characteristic. In practice, equity means all children and families receive necessary supports in a timely fashion so they can develop their full intellectual, social, and physical potential (36).

This chapter makes explicit what teaching for each of the DLS, and in particular Skill 4, is imbued with: *equity education.*

Pre-Prejudice, Prejudice, and Discrimination

Two key resources appear often as references in this chapter:

❯ *Anti-Bias Education for Young Children and Ourselves*, 2nd ed., by L. Derman-Sparks and J.O. Edwards, with C.M. Goins (NAEYC, 2020)

❯ *Roots and Wings: Affirming Culture and Preventing Bias in Early Childhood,* 3rd ed., by Stacey York (Redleaf, 2016)

Thanks also to a contribution of Dr. Jason Rafferty (2018). (You'll see why.)

Stacy York traces the biological origins of **pre-prejudice,** and its morphing into prejudice, by identifying researched elements in phases of early development (York 2016, 35–37). To cite selected concepts in her analysis from these pages:

In developing self-awareness, infants

❯ Connect with the adults in their lives through mirror neurons and copy their reactions

❯ Recognize familiar people and show fear of strangers

❯ Develop a sense of trust [or mistrust] in the world

In developing a sense of self as distinct from others, toddlers (to age 3)

❯ Are sensitive to, catch feelings from, and mimic adult behavior

❯ Recognize physical characteristics and color distinctions

❯ Distinguish people by gender and race

In developing racial and cultural distinctions and understandings, children aged 3 to 6

❯ Associate attributes with races and cultures

❯ Show preference for their own race and culture

❯ Begin to formulate stereotypes

❯ Show aggression through insults and name calling

❯ Explore real and pretend, fair and unfair

My interpretation of York's analysis is this: With the amygdala and hypothalamus system already operating in infants and toddlers, a wariness toward new and unfamiliar people is probably universal.

But in addition, infants and toddlers mirror stressful reactions in significant others, caused by family members' own perceived threats and dangers. The very young can outgrow this biologically logical tendency, but if the reactions are repeatedly reinforced by others, they sometimes generalize the wariness as stranger anxiety, a feeling of pre-prejudice toward unfamiliar others.

Beginning *prejudice* is a negative disposition toward a little-known individual, based on the child's stereotypes about groups the other is associated with. Preschoolers are developing the capacity for stereotyping, which allows for the conception of prejudice (York 2016).

Discrimination happens when persons express prejudice in hostile behaviors toward others. Acts of discrimination, seen in the exclusion of vulnerable others, begin in early childhood (Derman-Sparks & Edwards, with Goins 2020; York 2016). Adults as well as children encounter adverse experiences, including experiences that reinforce their biases. These significant others are likely to convey this stress to the young, making it more difficult for them to gain the safety-needs skills. Still, the more infants can develop a general sense of trust, and toddlers and young children gain DLS 1 and 2, the more *inclusive* young people are likely to be toward those with different physical features and cultural characteristics. These comments are supported by our discussion of attachment theory in Chapter 3.

Significantly, York (2016) states this:

> Early childhood programs can prevent and reduce prejudice by intentionally promoting respect for and inclusion of all forms of human diversity. You can provide direct contact with people from other races and cultures, draw attention to individual similarities and differences, and teach empathy and social skills such as sharing, turn taking, problem solving, giving compliments, and helping one another. . . . Remember, the more familiar children are with a particular race or culture, the more positive their attitudes. (43)

This quote pairs well with a selection adapted from the first edition of *Education for a Civil Society:*

> Children reach literal, categorical, and sometimes fanciful conclusions based on their experiences and perceptions. For instance, a child who has a male physician and sees only pictures of male doctors thinks all doctors are male. An early childhood professional who asks a female physician to visit the program fundamentally changes this preoperational stage misperception. (Gartrell 2012, 135)

As *Sesame Street* has done for decades, enlightened children's media such as PBS try to do their part to reduce the **prejudice of ignorance.** While not everyone agrees, in my view, these programs are helping children to open their minds so that they can experience the world around them in nonbiased ways.

Specifically in relation to DLS 4, young children have the propensity to view the new and different as threatening and to settle upon naïve stereotypes as reality. To assist children to gain the skill of inclusion, teachers need to engage in **prosocial nudging,** illustrated in the anecdotes to follow.

Anecdotes and Reflections

Anecdote 1

This vignette comes from the journal of a student teacher at the former Campus Child Care, Bemidji State University (Minnesota), along with my follow-up conversations with both the student and cooperating teacher.

> At lunchtime, 54-month-old Martin, who was White, came to the table reluctantly when he saw that he would be sitting next to Brandon, 52 months, who was Native American. Martin said softly to Rebecca, an experienced student teacher, "I'm not sitting next to Brandon. He got dirty skin."
>
> Rebecca knelt next to Martin, and said, also quietly, "Brandon's not dirty, Martin. He just has more color in his skin than you do. Lots of people have different skin colors, and that's a good thing. What's important in our class is that everyone is friendly to everyone." As she said this, she guided Martin to his chair and continued, "Brandon, could you pass a milk [carton] to Martin?" Brandon did, and Martin reluctantly thanked him. After rest time, Martin and Brandon played together, which put a big smile on Rebecca's face.

Karla, the lead teacher, complimented Rebecca on her handling of the situation. Later that afternoon, when Martin's dad picked him up, Karla noticed Rebecca talking with Dad in the hallway. Afterward, Karla asked Rebecca what the conversation was about. Rebecca said, "I told him that Martin had said that another child who is Native American had dirty skin. I thought Dad would want to know, so he could reinforce what we tell the children in our class: people are born with different skin colors, that's natural, and what's important is that we are all friendly and get along."

The lead teacher reflected about whether a student teacher should be so bold in her comments to a parent. Karla concluded that by talking with the dad so forthrightly, Rebecca had done something she herself would have found difficult to do. When Martin arrived the next morning and played again with Brandon, Karla recognized the positive impact of Rebecca's courageous action. Though Rebecca would finish student teaching at the center in a few weeks, she had become a full member of the teaching team, and Karla would be sad to see her leave.

Reflection. In guiding Martin toward gaining Skill 4, Karla and Rebecca both showed they had mastery of DLS 4 and 5 themselves. A different reaction from the lead teacher would have turned this wonderful teaching and learning experience on its head. Karla took the brave step to fully include her competent student teacher on the teaching team. Rebecca showed the courage to reject *the power of silence* and to stand up for equity.

Anecdote 2

This anecdote comes from the Children's Learning Center at the University of North Dakota some years ago.

In a classroom of 4-year-olds, Stephon, Andrus, and Voshon played "fireman," using the climber for the fire station and the dramatic play area for the house on fire. Stepping onto the ladder, Teagan tried to join the play, but Stephon told her, "You can't be a fireman 'cause you're a girl. Only boys can be firemen." Teagan scowled and nevertheless tried to join them on the climber, but the boys yelled at her. Teagan sat on the floor and looked totally bothered. Veteran teacher Shandra, who had seen the incident, sat on a low chair (because of her knees) next to Teagan and put her hand on Teagan's shoulder. "You look upset, Teagan." She paused.

With tears in her eyes, Teagan exclaimed, "I want to play too! Girls can put out fires."

"Yes, they can, Teagan," Shandra responded. "You are right. Both girls and boys can be firefighters. Let's talk to the boys."

They moved to the climber, and Shandra said, "Hey, guys, do you remember when Mathis's mom came in and put on her firefighting gear? Men and women fight fires together. That's why we call them fire*fighters* instead of fire*men*." Stephon replied, "But this game is for boys, okay, Teacher?" Shandra maintained an even, friendly tone in refuting the statement: "Our classroom agreement is that girls and boys play together. Teagan is unhappy that you don't want her to play with you. How can Teagan help you fight this fire?"

Stephon looked at the other two fire crew members and shrugged: "Teagan can steer on the back of the truck, 'cause you gotta steer there too. Look, a fire!" The four children raced to the wooden bench that was the fire truck. Voshon handed Teagan a helmet. Teagan steered from the back, grinning.

While they were fighting the fire, Teagan noticed two dolls, picked them up, and carried them to the fire truck. "I'm saving the babies," she called out. "Teagan saved the babies!" the other firefighters shouted. On the way back to the fire station, Teagan sat in the middle of the fire truck, proudly holding the babies she had saved. The four firefighters played together until cleanup time.

After cleanup, Shandra had a *guidance talk* with the three boys. The teacher reminded them that men and women do lots of jobs together, like being doctors, police officers, firefighters, and teachers—like their male teacher, Darius. Shandra also made the time for a quick contact talk with Teagan. She started with the compliment, "You knew to save the babies, didn't you?" and paused. They smiled at each other.

The following day, the TT and children had a group meeting and talked about how men and women work together in many settings. The teachers did not mention the incident the day before. Instead, the teachers shared the photos of the mom firefighter in her gear together with the children in the group. They asked the children what other jobs men and women both can do. They reviewed the guideline that boys and girls play together. They also asked the children if they could play with children who are different from them in other ways—older or younger, different color of skin, different abilities. The team was pleased with the discussion. Later that day, Shandra saw four girls playing firefighter! She watched to make sure that the four were inclusive of any boys who want to play.

Reflection. In both anecdotes, the **active discrimination** caught the TT members' attention. In the early childhood setting it should go without saying that active discrimination shown by adults or children against anyone needs to be stopped. But sometimes children and adults are apt to use another type, **passive discrimination**—ignoring, avoiding, distancing, and keeping silence in the face of acts that enforce inequity. This gives permission for the active expression of prejudice to continue and perhaps become worse (Derman-Sparks & Edwards, with Goins 2020; York 2016). A term referring to this passive discrimination is the **power of silence**.

When it comes to discrimination, interventions that teach alternatives, via guidance talks, mediation, and large group meetings, can be uncomfortable for us adults. In deciding whether to use guidance to address prejudice and discrimination, TTs need to be mindful not to show discrimination themselves (Derman-Sparks & Edwards, with Goins 2020).

Communication Practices for Building Relationships

Acknowledge and Pause

A sterling illustration of *acknowledge and pause blending into reflective listening* is from the second anecdote:

In Anecdote 2, Teagan sat on the floor and looked bothered. Teacher Shandra, who had seen most of the incident, sat next to Teagan and put her hand on Teagan's back. She said, "You look upset, Teagan." Then Shandra paused.

Appropriate touch, and at least physical nearness, are important in serious adult-child conversations. Rebecca got down on the floor next to Martin. Shandra sat on a low chair, but got physically close and put a hand on Teagan's back when she talked with the child. Whenever possible, spry-enough teachers get on the floor right next to the kid. An early childhood educator of many years told me she grabbed her special low chair (it had a smiley face on the back) for such conversations because it was easier to get up off of than the floor. No shame in that. The kids called it "teacher's get-up chair."

With tears in her eyes, Teagan exclaimed, "I want to play too! Girls can put out fires."

"Yes, they can, Teagan," Shandra responded. "You are right. Both girls and boys can be firefighters. Let's talk to the boys."

Shandra started just where a teacher should. When assisting a rejected child to be included, listen to the child, calm them, and verify their right to strong feelings about the situation. Then act together to resolve the situation.

Make Contact Talks Happen

Again in Anecdote 2, when children are bullied and otherwise discriminated against, their sense of belonging in the group is threatened. The security they have gained from DLS 1 is shaken. When teachers see this, they mediate to reestablish the child's inclusion, but the intervention alone might not be enough. To my thinking, Shandra did well to have a second talk with Teagan later in the day. Sometimes teachers need to provide that additional support to make sure the child knows that their place in the group is without question. The group meeting the next day both affirmed for Teagan her worthy place in the group, and probably that of other children as well.

Give Encouragement: Sometimes Private, Sometimes Public

Private encouragement should happen in a guidance intervention, often in the form of a compliment sandwich. **Correction by suggestion** (Ginott [1972] 1993) happens when the situation does not allow the teacher to include the two or three supportive notes in a compliment sandwich. In Anecdote 1, when Rebecca commented that people have lots of different skin colors and we all can get along, she used correction by suggestion both with Martin and his father. Whether correction by suggestion is received positively depends on the skill of the adult using the strategy and on the other person. Having a positive relationship with the other greatly helps.

....

Ginott, by the way, has been a mentor of mine over time. He gave voice to adult-child relations ideas as no one before. See his eminently readable *Teacher and Child: A Book for Parents and Teachers* [1972] 1993).

....

Rebecca didn't know the father and took a risk. The student teacher had courage. She also had the good fortune to have Karla accept her initiative. Karla supported her in this case, when Dad did not object to the guidance, and hopefully would have as well if Dad had objected. TTs, like teams of professionals in other fields, need to support each other. A big part of successful student teaching is building a positive relationship with the cooperating teacher. With Karla, Rebecca clearly had done that. But another part is teachers who can appreciate and so nurture brave acts by student teachers, as Karla did.

Remember Names, Contact Talks, and Promises

Snap quiz! You ready?

1. In the first vignette, what was the name of the child who was first sitting at the lunch table?

2. In the second vignette, what were the names of the boys who tried to keep Teagan from playing with them?

3. What compliment did Shandra give to Teagan in their contact talk?

Did I mention this was an open-book snap quiz? How did you do?

Levels of Mistaken Behavior

Discrimination can happen at any of the three levels of mistaken behavior. What level of mistaken behavior is it if a child rejects another by saying they have dirty skin, or that a child can't play because of their gender? A first thought is that it is a Level Three strong unmet-needs mistaken behavior due to a child still working on expressing strong emotions in nonhurting ways. But TT members really have to observe the situation and know the child to tell. It could also be Level Two socially influenced or even Level One experimentation mistaken behavior. In Anecdote 2, the three boys were Stephon, Andrus, and Voshon. Of the three, Stephon took the lead both in initially keeping Teagan from playing and after the mediation, by giving Teagan a role. Stephon showed Level One experimentation mistaken behavior. At both points, Andrus and Voshon went along with Stephon's leadership and were showing Level Two socially influenced mistaken behavior. Notice that Voshon handed Teagan a helmet. Whatever the dynamics there, that was a friendly gesture and showed a degree of independence.

Sometimes, when a mistaken behavior is stark, teachers might wonder whether the behavior is due to the experimentation of Level One, the social influence of Level Two, or the strong unmet needs of Level Three. As mentioned earlier, the teacher needs to know the child. In Anecdote 1, Martin (54 months) came to the table reluctantly when he saw that he would be sitting next to Brandon. Martin said softly but adamantly to Rebecca, "I'm not sitting next to Brandon. He got dirty skin."

Perhaps a key indicator is whether the child shows the mistaken behavior both disruptively and repeatedly. Martin was not prone to emotional outbursts. He had not made any comments like this before to either Karla or Rebecca. Neither did he shout out the comment in a wild abandonment of decorum. Nor did he make the comment again. As well, Martin played with Brandon later that day. Martin was old enough to form a stereotype and act in reaction to it, developmentally typical for a mid-4. On the other hand, teacher Karla was familiar enough with Martin's father to know he was a man of distinct and firmly held views. Strong views conveyed in an absolute manner by parent to child might make reflecting those views a matter of needed security by the child.

For the community, whether the mistaken behavior of discrimination results from Level One, Two, or Three motivation, the teacher's response is always to stop the behavior and teach an alternative. In working with the child, though, understanding the motivation level behind the behavior is important. In terms of the DLS, is the teacher seeking to guide a child who is struggling with Skills 1 or 2, or one who has made some progress with Skill 2 and only needs to make some more?

Developmental Guidance: Major Practices

Developmental Large Group Meetings

In Anecdote 2 the group had already been visited by a woman firefighter who took photos with the children. The visit was an intentional developmental group meeting. A second developmental group meeting, mentioned in the anecdote, had established the guideline that boys and girls can play together. Developmental group meetings that establish guidelines to be reinforced later do much to facilitate anti-bias ideas. Having cooperatively set a guideline like "Boys and girls can play together," the children know that the TT is not being arbitrary when they remind the children of this. The known guideline applies to all.

Key Intervention Guidance Practices

Calming

In Anecdote 2, through the acknowledge and pause of reflective listening, Shandra was able to help Teagan calm down enough to mediate. Shandra kept close to Teagan throughout to assure the child that the teacher was on her side.

Guidance Talks/Correction by Suggestion

We reiterate here a point made earlier. In Anecdote 1 with Martin, Rebecca used **correction by suggestion** rather than a full-blown guidance talk. When teachers use correction by suggestion effectively, the guiding words are accepted by the child.

Illustration. Rebecca knelt next to Martin, and said, also quietly, "Brandon's not dirty, Martin. He just has more color in his skin than you do. Lots of people have different skin colors, and that's a good thing. What's important in our class is that everyone is friendly to everyone." As she said this, she guided Martin to his chair and continued, "Brandon, could you pass a milk [carton] to Martin?" Brandon did, and Martin reluctantly thanked him. This technique has the advantage of being quick, but it is not necessarily easy. When offering correction by suggestion, a teacher does not want the child to become more upset. TTs need to understand the child and situation when using this technique. Without a secure relationship with Rebecca, Brandon might have felt threatened and reacted adversely. The father did not know Rebecca, but likely acted out of respect and adult restraint.

TTs do best when they use intervention techniques that don't outpace their relationships with children. Day-to-day reality means our interventions sometimes backfire. TTs then need to concentrate on salvaging and strengthening the relationship with the child. Maybe you have experienced this predicament? If not, you will; I know I have. We discuss this matter more fully in Chapter 10.

Conflict Mediation

In Anecdote 2, Shandra successfully mediated with Teagan, Stephon, Andrus, and Voshon. Teagan gained entry to the group and as is a hoped-for goal, brought a fresh perspective to the situation by saving the "babies." This mediation might have seemed to readers too easy, except for three factors: (1) These kids, like those in other anecdotes, were used to mediation. Their TTs had been using it with them since day one. (2) The four were engaged in developmentally appropriate activity—creative big body play *in* the classroom! When confronted with the need to mediate—a demanding exercise—kids want to get it over with and continue playing. (3) The three boys saw that they were caught. They knew the guideline and knew that they needed to meet it.

Intervention Large Group Meetings

In Anecdote 2 on the day after the firefighter conflict, Shandra and the TT held an intervention group meeting to reestablish a guideline (not to dwell on previous events). But one or two meetings alone do not counter messages that children have internalized. As part of their emerging cognitive processes of generalization and differentiation, 4-year-olds have gained the ability to stereotype. In some, the attitudinal undertow toward rejection of the different can be strong. So, the TT remains vigilant. With both the developmental and intervention group meetings in Anecdote 2, the importance of group meetings in prosocial nudging toward DLS 4 should become clear.

Working for Family Engagement

Anecdote 3

The following is a composite of two anecdotal observations from a Head Start and a child care center. This matter, and other strong family concerns, are a challenge to early childhood professionals everywhere who want the best for families relative to the benchmarks. Unlike programs in public schools, most private early childhood programs only exist due to the patronage, loyalty, and the goodwill of their customers (the families). Cooperative relations with families is essential—as perhaps it should be at other levels of education as well.

> Cedric, 53 months, had attended the program for about three weeks. Every day, Cedric went into the dramatic play area, put on women's clothes (trimmed to size and washed frequently), and walked around the classroom in flats, carrying a pocketbook and sometimes wearing a (regularly sanitized) hat. He wore this outfit every chance he could and played with others while wearing it. Raelynn and Cassie, the TT, negotiated with Cedric that he could wear

the clothes during choice time, but like all the children, needed to put on his own clothes for the rest of the day. A bit perplexed, they kept director Selma informed about Cedric's habit.

Other children asked about Cedric's wearing "girl clothes." The TT explained that their setting was a place to try things and suggested maybe Cedric wanted to dress like his mother and sisters. This was good enough for the children, but not for Lyra, a parent and an occasional classroom visitor, who complained to director Selma and mentioned the matter to other parents whose children were in the group. Lyra requested a meeting with the staff and director. Selma told the parent that the TT would set up a date for the following week.

Cedric's older sister had been in the TT's group a previous year, and Raelynn and Cassie knew their mom, Zoe, pretty well. The TT spoke with Zoe about Cedric's practice, and Mom seemed unconcerned. She said that at home Cedric wore his two big sisters' clothes, and they thought it was cute. The TT told the mother that they appreciated having Cedric in the group and that he really enjoyed reading, music, and dramatic play. Raelynn and Cassie said Cedric's dressing style didn't bother them, but they wanted Zoe to know about it. The two decided not to mention the upcoming meeting to Zoe.

The next week, the staff met with Lyra and two other parents. The director greeted them and asked them to share their concerns. Lyra stated that she did not want her child in a group where a boy was "cross dressing." She said Cedric was "bad influence" on the group. The other two parents displayed looks of concern, but Lyra did the talking. Director Selma did some calming. The director asked the TT how Cedric was getting along. (The three had decided they would discuss in general terms his behavior in class, which any visitor could observe.) They shared that Cedric had many friends and was doing well in the program. The TT stated that his mom had no problem with how Cedric dressed. They made clear they limited the dress-up to one time during the day. As follow-up, the staff invited the parents to visit the class as long as they were civil to all.

With much discussion, the staff managed to lower the temperature about the situation, but they let the parents know that there was no question that Cedric would stay in the program and could wear what he liked during the one time of the day. The staff heard no more from the other two parents about the child. The third, Lyra, who had called for the meeting, withdrew her child from the program. Cedric kept up his daily pattern and no one else expressed concerns. Cedric got along well in the learning community and was appreciated by all.

Reflection. The staff accepted Cedric for who he was and did not modify the general course of the child's behavior because of the opinion of other parents. A preference to dress in clothes typically associated with another gender is something that that TTs sometimes see in preschoolers. Neither the staff nor I made an assumption here about Cedric's **gender identity**, as distinct from **biological sex**, or sex assigned at birth. Having a transgender/gender fluid adult grandchild, though, I am aware that educators have too little objective information about gender identity. In an online piece from the American Academy of Pediatrics, Dr. Jason Rafferty (2018) provides this information on the development of gender identity:

> Being a boy or a girl, for most children, is something that feels very natural. At birth, babies are assigned male or female based on physical characteristics. This refers to the *sex* or *assigned gender* of the child. Meanwhile, *gender identity* *r*efers to an internal sense people have of who they are that comes from an interaction of biological traits, developmental influences, and environmental conditions. This may be male, female, somewhere in between, a combination of both or neither. . . . By age four, most children have a stable sense of their gender identity.

> During this same time of life, children learn gender role behavior—that is, doing *"things that boys do"* or *"things that girls do."* However, cross-gender preferences and play are a normal part of gender development and exploration regardless of their future gender identity.

> The point is that all children tend to develop a clearer view of themselves and their gender over time. At any point, research suggests that children who assert a gender-diverse identity know

their gender as clearly and consistently as their developmentally matched peers and benefit from the same level of support, love, and social acceptance.

··

A helpful Viewpoint article related to this topic appeared in the Winter 2022 issue of *Young Children*: "When Blue and Pink Are Not Enough: Saying 'Gay' Matters to LGBTQIA+ Families" (Wright 2022b).

··

The Benchmarks of Family Engagement

The family engagement benchmarks are:

> Benchmark 1: Family members show acceptance of program and staff.

> Benchmark 2: Family members take new interest in the learning of their child.

> Benchmark 3: Family members become active in relation to the general program.

> Benchmark 4: Family members progress in personal and/or professional development themselves as a result of their engagement.

In Anecdotes 1 and 3, Martin's father and Cedric's mother were both willing to receive information from the staff (Benchmark 1). The student teacher and the staff of Cedric's group approached the parents with as much sensitivity as they could muster. Martin's father let the boy return to the program the next day. Zoe responded to the information about her son matter-of-factly. Because neither parent stepped forward proactively in this situation, they remained at the comfort level afforded by Benchmark 1. (This is not to say that either one attained only this benchmark in the rest of their relations with the program.)

In Anecdote 3, parent Lyra came into the classroom perhaps only to "observe," but the TT didn't regard the matter involving Cedric the same way she did. By agreeing to the meeting, director Selma extended to Lyra an opportunity to progress from Benchmark 1 to at least Benchmark 2. Lyra saw that her personal concern was not being resolved in a manner acceptable to her, however, and removed herself from the levels completely by taking her child from the program.

What can providers do with parents like Lyra? Their professional best, but not more than that. Raelynn, Cassie, and director Selma stood strong by the first principle of the Code of Ethical Conduct (NAEYC 2011) by not allowing harm to be done to a child. The cost was something the program just had to accept. Losing a child in this way often involves sadness for the staff. They undoubtedly took consolation in hanging together, for the good of the encouraging early learning community. The cost to programs that stand on ethical principles rather than bend to undue pressures from some members of the community can be high. (Derman-Sparks and colleagues [2020] offer concrete suggestions for working with families whose perspectives differ from that of the program. In particular, see pages 71–72.)

Ensuring an Encouraging Learning Community for All

1. An early childhood setting is developmentally appropriate only if the setting is developmentally appropriate for everyone.

In Anecdote 1 after lunch, Martin and Brandon played together. The freedom of choice in the selection and direction of open-ended activities allows for children to not only become acquainted and problem-solve together, but also to reconcile and heal. Brandon did not hear Martin's comment, but Martin knew he said it. Playing with Brandon gave Martin a chance to bring things back together for himself. Rebecca's actions furthered equity for both children.

In Anecdote 2, Shandra and her TT understood that young children learn through their bodies. To allow for big body play opportunities in the classroom is, for me, the epitome of developmentally appropriate practice. All children learn through movement, and most preschoolers need lots of movement. There is a place for activities that are boisterous as well as busy and bucolic. Teachers maximize DAP as they fashion a dynamic mix that meets the activity levels of all in the group—and also ensure that all in the group have access to every activity.

2. Children need to feel that they are accepted and encouraged in a setting for them to excel at learning and development in the social, physical, cognitive, and linguistic domains.

In all three anecdotes, the TTs worked hard to make the communities welcoming for the children vulnerable for discrimination. In the process, the TTs taught for progress toward DLS 4 not just with the three children at the center, but with all. When children witness—not just experience—teachers working together to ensure every child gains DLS 1, they absorb important learning about how people should treat each other (York 2016). Secure in their community, young children can set about the business of schooling success. ("Everything of value I ever learned, I learned in [and before] kindergarten," must have been how Ryan, age 68 months, felt when he asked his teacher if he could spend another year in kindergarten rather than to move to first grade.)

· ·

Developmentally Appropriate Lunch (a Side Trip to a Great Little Café)

In Anecdote 1, Martin did come to the table and Brandon passed a milk carton to him. Even though cartons are a challenge to open, the passing of items, as in family-style meals, is a socially inclusive practice. Too soon, young children are subjected to institutionalized meals with large numbers of children in a lunchroom lining up to get trays, eating food, dispensing their trays, and clearing the room, all on tight schedules.

By eating together in a leisurely family style, each child knows that they belong as a participating member of a (noninstitutionalized) welcoming group. Worldwide, breaking bread together models the inclusivity that is at the heart of DLS 4.

· ·

Anecdote 4

In one Minnesota Ojibwe Head Start classroom, the children, in small groups with their teachers, took turns performing the tasks involved in eating lunch. The class ate at a table in a carpeted area. The teacher sprayed and wiped the tables while the children washed their hands. On a rotating basis in small groups, the preschoolers, with teachers as coaches, set the tables, including utensils, plates, cups, and napkins. The adults oversaw getting the serving bowls of food from the carts to the tables. Eighteen children sat in groups of six at three tables, each with a member of the TT. The adults facilitated the passing of the bowls and children serving themselves. Here's a typical conversation:

Child: "I don't like wild rice."

Teacher: "At Head Start we try everything."

Child: "I'm takin' just a little."

Teacher: "Make that a little more."

Child: "How 'bout this [a spoonful]."

Teacher: "Okay, but no 'feeding the dog.'" (Group joke—no dropping food under the table.)

Each table group had a small bucket and washcloths handy for spills, but fewer spills happened than folks might expect. At the end of the meal, children as young as 3 used small-scale carpet sweepers to clean up under the tables. Of course, the adults cleaned the whole room at the end of each day. (I know all this because I ate there several times—wild rice, a walleye fish fillet, and blueberry pie were my favorites! "I think they need more training over in [the village of] Ball Club" could have been my refrain back then.)

Reflection. For me, there are three great things about the **family-style meals** arrangement. The first is that when the TT starts with a family group lunch routine on the first day, the children rarely complain about the tasks; working in the rotating small group lunch teams simply becomes part of the routine. (The other groups might be in the reading area, looking at books, or washing hands.)

The second is when an adult gets the children at their table group talking about interesting topics with a statement of curiosity like "I wonder what kids like to do outside in the snow" (or "in the park").

Third (which Montessori and Dewey both would have loved), the children are gaining practical life skills, the most important being real-life experience in democratic living. Montessori and Dewey have been telling us for more than 100 years that programs should blend work and play, not separate the two.

Contrast the *community* in the family group setting with the *institutionalization* in most K–12 school lunchrooms. Do you get steamed up about this like I do?

Education for Living in a Democracy

Persons who had to fend for themselves too much in their upbringing and schooling may enter adulthood with a high-stress-induced potential for rejecting those different from themselves (Nelson et al. 2020). With the unfortunate influence of significant others, the developmental tendency in the young to be wary of strangers too readily leads into prejudice and discrimination toward others. A lack of rich experience with diverse others tends to lead to a *prejudice of ignorance* based on acquired and reinforced stereotypes via family members, friends, and influences in the larger community and culture. Any child, from any family situation, who experiences few relationships with members of groups different from them is at risk for the prejudice of ignorance.

Derman-Sparks and colleagues (2020) as well as York (2016) maintain that young children who experience diversity in social relationships under supportive circumstances have greater acceptance of different others as adults. Yet, even in early learning communities with little diversity, TTs provide education for equity by nudging young children toward gaining DLS 4. They do so by proactively introducing diverse aspects of life in intriguing ways. Educational materials that radiate the wonderful differences and similarities among people, especially in books but also in play figures, pictures in the classroom, puzzles, music, and so on, plant the idea that the world is larger than the home community. Visitors who counter common stereotypes—a woman firefighter, a male nurse, a Native American not in traditional dress (thanks, Buffy Sainte-Marie for your years on Sesame Street)—add to children's worldviews, all the better if those visitors include family members.

Democracy in the social sense means everyone in the group is a worthy member and has a right to be heard. When children see and experience, every day, teachers standing up for this right, they are more likely to internalize the principle as a value (Derman-Sparks & Edwards, with Goins 2020; York 2016). Even in settings where there is little diversity, in the broadest sense early childhood teachers still address developmental and social factors that lead to discrimination among children due to differences in race, behavior, age, gender, disability, and family culture. Teachers who strive for inclusiveness themselves instill the quality in the children they lead (Wright 2022a). They teach children to affirm the human worth of everyone, DLS 4. They teach for civil life in modern democracy.

Accepting Unique Human Qualities in Others

Children who have not yet made progress toward DLS 4 view persons who are different from themselves as potentially threatening. They might join in-groups with others like themselves and identify with the subgroup more than with the community group. Typical perceived differences in others that can trigger nascent discriminatory reactions include factors of gender, race, language, disability, age, appearance, and behavior. Children not yet at Skill 4 would be attuned to verbal and nonverbal cues as to who in the group might be subtly favored or potentially ostracized by TT members and/or peers. Because they often depend on peers and significant family members and neighbors, children struggling with DLS 4 show a lot of Level Two socially influenced mistaken behavior—from repeating an expletive the way a significant adult might say it to joining with friends in calling another child names.

Typical Child Behaviors

> Brings mistaken behaviors into the community, learned from significant others, media influences, and cultural stereotypes

> Plays mainly with a few friends, often of same gender and with other similarities to the child

> Is indifferent/standoffish toward others in community who are not members of the in-group

> Shuns and might make fun of members of the community who appear different

> Is unwelcoming to new members in community

> Might favor one member of the TT over others

> Might ignore inclusive materials, activities, and discussions and favor those that reflect the dominant culture, like wanting to play only with a White doll

Teacher Responses

While checking for their own biases, TTs proactively review existing and select new books and other resources that highlight inclusive pro-equity, anti-bias themes. TTs apply friendly leadership through large group meetings to directly teach democratic principles of individual worth and inclusion. They use the lessons of group meetings to prevent and resolve discriminatory acts by individuals (children and other adults) toward others in the classroom. Teachers set up learning activities and small groups where children can have positive interactions with others different from themselves. They use public encouragement to build and sustain an inclusive group spirit. TTs use private acknowledgment with individual children when they show acceptance of others across differences in viewpoints, as well as differing human qualities.

Progress Indicators in Gaining Skill 4

Initiating cooperative activity with children who have differing human qualities; initiating interactions with children and adults in the classroom who may be new; showing inclusiveness and even support for children who may be vulnerable for stigma; asking questions about differences in human qualities, including behaviors and viewpoints with an intent to understand, not judge; and initiating or joining in conversations about human differences with an intent to understand, not judge.

DISCUSSION QUESTIONS

1. Identify three key concepts (listed below and in the glossary). If you are a visual learner, write each out with its definition from the glossary. Then, referring to the section of the chapter where the key concept originated, reflect on what the concept means to you now that you have read the chapter.

2. Various anecdotes in the chapter illustrate TT members working with children to gain the DLS. Identify one anecdote (and the author reflection) that has meaning for you. Reflect on how the anecdote enhanced and/or changed your possible response to a similar situation.

3. From attachment theory, the more that young children feel affirmed in primary relationships, the more open and sociable they tend to be with others. How can teachers of young children provide prosocial nudging to help develop an acceptance of difference in others?

4. Using information from the chapter as reference points, identify some ways to approach working with LGBTQIA+ (lesbian, gay, bisexual, transgender, queer, intersex, asexual, and more) families.

5. Examine your own response to DLS 4. Based on the elements of your own heritage, upbringing, and education, what aspects of inclusive leadership are or might be difficult for you in working with children and families whose "unique human qualities" differ from yours? How could you effectively address those personal concerns?

6. The book is about education for democracy. Identify a new or newly reinforced idea for you from the chapter. Discuss how that idea contributes to your own approach toward teaching for democracy.

7. How have the thoughts and ideas shared in this chapter impacted your thinking about being a professional working with young children?

Key Concepts

active discrimination

biological sex

correction by suggestion

family-style meals

gender identity

passive discrimination

power of silence

prejudice of ignorance

CHAPTER 9

The Democracy Skill

DLS 5: Thinking Intelligently and Ethically

SUGGESTED GOALS FOR READERS

1. Recognize that even faulty attempts at DLS 5 behavior by young children deserve support.

2. Know that actions showing DLS 5 are easier for some and more difficult for others—who nonetheless, with our support, are capable of the skill.

3. Understand the importance of children showing Skill 5 for long-term civility in our modern democracy.

DLS 1	DLS 2	DLS 3	DLS 4	DLS 5
Finding Acceptance as a Member of the Group and as a Worthy Individual	**Expressing Strong Emotions in Nonhurting Ways**	**Solving Problems Creatively—Independently and in Cooperation with Others**	**Accepting Unique Human Qualities in Others**	**Thinking Intelligently and Ethically**

Skill 5, the democracy skill, is aspirational. We teach for it primarily by leading young children to gain Skills 1–4. When children are showing the other growing-needs skills, they are capable of showing DLS 5 and are exhibiting **dynamic mental health**. Every minute of every day, we hope for children to use Skill 5. More so than with the other skills, TTs continue assisting kids to build the framework, but young children continue the building themselves.

Thinking intelligently and ethically is a complex skill—more so when individuals are only months old. DLS 5 becomes even more complicated when individuals try to resolve conflicts that involve not just one other person but two or more. (Any parent with two or more children knows how complex.) In halting attempts to master the skill, children make mistakes in their behavior—Level One experiments that go in unexpected ways. When we support children's even imperfect efforts at DLS 5, we share with them the aspiration to keep trying.

Readers have slogged through the 10 analysis points/headings in four chapters now. All that slogging hopefully provided useful information for how to guide young children to gain DLS 1 through 4. In Chapter 9 you have graduated from most of those headings. (Congratulations, whoo-hoo!) Chapter 9 looks at only four of the analysis points in a relatively integrated way to keep things flowing.

Starter Notes

Piaget's Skill

DLS 5, the ability to think intelligently and ethically—or **autonomy** in Piaget's terms—is the highest of the DLS. Piaget ([1932] 1960) thought this skill should be the goal of all education. A common reaction to the idea of young children thinking intelligently and ethically is this: young children might show instances of use of DLS 5, but certainly they cannot show this skill consistently. Because young children are so dependent on others for continuing development—and because biologically and psychologically they have a lot of developing to do—those who show DLS 5 cannot be expected to be at this level in an enduring and consistent way. (Actually, some children you know probably practice Skill 5 with more consistency than some adults you might know.) The complexities of growing up suggest that only if children continue with secure relationships and developmentally appropriate education will they have the best chance at sustaining Skill 5 (Cozolino 2014; Goleman 2020).

Still, in recognition of Piaget's contributions, let's give a boost to early childhood education here. A Harvard meta-analysis of 22 studies on high-quality early childhood education programs documents that emotional-social benefits gained from program participation last into adulthood (Feldman 2018):

> Children who attended high-quality ECE programs were less likely to be placed in special education, less likely to be retained in a grade, and more likely to graduate from high school than peers who didn't attend such programs. The lead researcher . . . believes there are several reasons for these gains; however, "there is increasing evidence that social-emotional skills may play a role, as they support children's ability to continuously engage in learning environments, manage their own behaviors, and get along well with others."

Years of developmental science suggests that children who show DLS 5 in early childhood have a higher likelihood of sustaining this skill than children who do not (e.g., Cozolino 2014; Goleman 2020). This statement comes down to the neuroarchitecture that children build during early childhood because of secure attachments with significant others who themselves show Skill 5 consistently. By teachers' modeling and teaching for the DLS in early childhood, the receptive **neuroplasticity** of young children's brains allows for the building of the neuroarchitecture that makes consistent use of the skill more likely as individuals grow and mature. Having teaching for the DLS 5 as an intentional goal in early childhood education contributes to the **brain neuroarchitecture** that makes thinking intelligently and ethically easier for children as they grow.

Neuroplasticity

There is a name for the dynamic quality of the brain that builds the neuroarchitecture conducive to DLS 5 becoming part of one's life. The brain has neuroplasticity: the ability of the neuroarchitecture to physically change with experiences, largely through increased neural connections across different operational centers, including the prefrontal cortex and the hippocampus. With ongoing, positive practice in learning to use DLS 5 (any of the DLS), the relevant neuroarchitecture physically grows more complex inside the individual's head. Neuroplasticity via incoming experiences empowers the neuroarchitecture to enhance its hardwiring.

Currently accepted in developmental science is that neuroplasticity is most evident in early childhood but continues throughout life, with neural connections increasing or decreasing depending on an individual's experiences. So long as positive practice can happen, neuroplasticity allows the neuroarchitecture that manages functions in relation to the DLS to remain robust.

Months Old Versus Years Old

The developmental difference between a child who acts at DLS 5 and an adult who does is vast. The young child who meaningfully shows intelligent and ethical thinking experiences positive neuroarchitecture changes in the brain. The neurological changes contribute to emerging executive functions, which strengthens the child's capacity to act similarly in the future. Meaningful experience engenders healthy neurological development across the frontal lobes, prefrontal cortex, thalamus, and hippocampus that sustains the likelihood of future prosocial acts—and vice versa (Cozolino 2014). (Neurological chit-chat ends here.)

Older individuals, in contrast, have years of experience and mostly developed neural architecture to help them with prosocial interactions. They have developed the cognitive functioning to think through possible consequences of their actions. Young children act more intuitively. Adults also communicate from a position of less dependence on others—though rarely with total independence. In the multitude of groups that humans are members of, pressure is often there to "go along to get along." Individuals always face a dilemma in deciding whether and how to share what is in their minds and hearts. This challenge pertains especially to situations when an adult witnesses a hurting behavior—an act of oppression by a person more powerful toward a person less powerful. The danger of not speaking up, the power of silence, lends tacit approval to hurting behaviors, making it more likely that such behaviors will continue. The intellectual challenge of what to do in these situations requires high level use of DLS 5, to be sure—something only an adult can fathom.

Many of us look at historical figures who acted ethically in the face of power and conclude that the principled life is way too hard. Lots of folks show Skill 5 in individual situations, but isn't it true that only certain icons express DLS 5 with real consistency? But education for democracy is about "everyday heroes," people doing little things that are smart and right, sometimes with, sometimes without, the agreement of others. If individuals are educated toward thinking intelligently and ethically from the beginning, conflicts over time become more civil, and people become better able to work together and figure things out.

The only thing as difficult as learning and practicing the DLS is teaching for others to gain them. Early childhood professionals have a most complicated job—and are the most important teachers in the child's life. We tackle this challenge now and in the next chapter.

Anecdotes and Reflections

With a child struggling to gain DLS 1 and 2, TTs work hard to understand mistaken behaviors and help children learn from them. They need to do the same for a child progressing toward DLS 5. To sustain children's efforts, we need to remember key developmental limitations of early childhood. Young children's executive functions and **perspective-taking** abilities are just beginning to develop. Unkind responses by adults to early efforts with this skill can subvert children's continuing efforts. TTs need to be sensitive to children's early efforts in relation to DLS 5, even when their behaviors may be outside of typical adult comfort zones.

Anecdote 1

The following anecdote comes from a public school kindergarten classroom.

> Sixty-five-month-old Sylvia noticed that a visiting parent had sat in a chair with some white glue and glitter on it. Trying to be helpful, she said to the parent, "You have glitter on your butt." The parent gave the child a "how dare you" look. Before she could say something to the child, however, the teacher, who was right there, commented, "What Sylvia means is that you may have sat in a bit of glue and glitter. You can hardly notice it, and it will wash out. Thanks for caring about our guests, Sylvia, and for trying to help out."

Reflection. The teacher could have said, "Sylvia, you need to be more respectful. You just worry about the glue and glitter that is sticking to you. I am sorry, Mrs. Barrett." Instead, the teacher chose to demonstrate a key lesson in teaching for DLS 5. Children progress with the skill when they experience TTs who model it and who support children in their own beginning efforts. Sylvia attempted to make things better here. Even though socially naïve, due to the teacher's support and modeling, the young child

received encouragement for her efforts, making the experience meaningful. Support children's efforts in relation to DLS 5, even when their behaviors go beyond adult expectations about social niceties. As Sousa (2022, 105) states, "Remember that the brain first reacts emotionally to new learning before reacting rationally." (For all of us, and especially children.)

Six more anecdotes illustrate the stumbling blocks and advances children make in progressing toward DLS 5 and the efforts by teachers to further that progress.

••

> Let's refer back to Anecdote 1 in Chapter 6, where three wands were in use and a fourth child wanted to play with one. When more than two people are involved in a conflict, the difficulty in using Skill 5 increases greatly. Each individual in the situation wants to cling to their own perspectives, interpretations, and feelings. This is why the anecdotes in Chapter 9 involve only two people. Children are just beginners.

••

Anecdote 2

This anecdote, from a Head Start classroom, illustrates the developmental egocentrism of early childhood—the fact that young children are just beginning to develop social perspective and responsiveness. Notice teacher Jules's responses to Dimitri as the boy tries to make things better after a conflict with his younger cousin. In helping young children make progress toward DLS 5, the plastic cup is always half full.

> When the temperature hit minus 20 degrees Fahrenheit with windchill, the Minnesota preschool class stayed in and played in the "big muscles room." Sebastian, 44 months, was happily riding his favorite trike in the active playroom. He was at the right place at the right time when an older 4-year-old got off. However, his cousin Dimitri, 62 months, had signed up for the trike at the beginning of the time block. He, not Sebastian, was next on the list.

Dimitri caught up to Sebastian and stood facing him with one leg on either side of the front wheel. He tried to persuade his younger cousin it was his turn. Sebastian yelled, "No," and then screamed as Dimitri grabbed one hand and forced Sebastian off the trike. As Dimitri rode off, he looked over his shoulder and saw teacher Jules tending to Sebastian, whose screams had become yowls.

Dimitri made a U-turn and rode back to Sebastian and Jules. He got off the trike and offered it to Sebastian, explaining to the teacher, "He was crying loud, and he needed it more."

The teacher asked Sebastian if he wanted to ride. Giving his cousin a wary stare, Sebastian nodded and got on the trike. Jules said, "It's Dimitri's turn when you are done." Sebastian nodded as he rode away.

Jules had seen the whole thing. He and Dimitri sat on the floor together and had a guidance talk. Dimitri explained what happened as he saw it. The two conversed about how younger preschoolers are still learning the routines, and they brainstormed what Dimitri could do next time instead of taking the trike. Jules then told Dimitri that his coming back and giving the trike to Sebastian was considerate and a helpful thing to do.

Jules oversaw the transition when Sebastian got tired of riding. The teacher asked Dimitri if there was something he could say to his younger cousin. Dimitri said, "Sorry." Jules asked the same question of Sebastian, who also said he was sorry. After the trike exchange, Jules had a talk with Sebastian explaining that it was really Dimitri's turn and reminding Sebastian to follow the sign-up list next time.

Reflection. Seems like at the beginning Dimitri was not quite at DLS 3. He "solved" the problem creatively, but not cooperatively. One could make the case that Dimitri was thinking mostly about himself and his rightful turn—until he heard his cousin's wails. He tried then to make the situation right, which Jules saw as opportunity to teach for Skill 5. The teacher knew Dimitri well enough to guess that he felt bad about taking the trike (helped to this perception by Sebastian's protestations). Jules also recognized that Dimitri's effort to make restitution showed progress toward DLS 5. The teacher positively acknowledged Dimitri's intent and his effort.

Taking Turns

So long as TTs give everyone an equal chance, the practice of signing up on a turns list for popular activities can bring some order to potential chaos. A usual practice is that a child who has signed up can do the activity for as long as they want for the (hour or more) work time on that day. Until popularity for the activity wanes, kids get one turn to sign up per week.

Another objective selection practice is to use a magnetic whiteboard with every child's name listed alphabetically or from youngest to oldest. TTs move a marker every morning, and the newly named child gets a choice of whether they want to choose the popular activity. (Also, teachers can use the chart and marker to show other children how many days until their turn—a functional calendar activity.) Seems cumbersome, perhaps, but teaching for democracy, and democracy itself, is cumbersome. Deciding who gets to do what next in a fair way should be a recognized part of the education program.

With lengthy engagement in an activity, children can fully engage, explore, and discover—empowering significant learning that stays with the child. Pursuits begun in early childhood often become lifelong. Abbreviated experiences with favorite activities tend to short-circuit children's developing long-term interests (Zosh et al. 2022). Who knows, Dimitri and Sebastian might grow up to be champion bicycle riders!

Jules's decision to let Dimitri ride the trike after Sebastian reflects a **guidance consequence** for the situation. A **logical consequence** of Dimitri's falling into instrumental aggression might have been losing the privilege of riding. This consequence might have been logical to the teacher, but not necessarily to Dimitri.

The guidance consequence was that Dimitri looked honestly at the conflict, learned a better way to handle it next time, and made amends with his cousin. Jules tried to convey to Dimitri that he believed in the boy's progress toward Skill 5. Jules built on the relationship with Dimitri to encourage him to keep making progress.

With this leadership, Jules helped Dimitri move toward thinking intelligently and ethically. Perhaps next time he might do so from the beginning of a conflict . . . and Sebastian might remember to follow the sign-up sheet.

Anecdote 3

The following anecdote comes from a mixed-age group in an urban early childhood center.

> Maurice, just 3, loved peaches in a bowl and was excited to have them for dessert at lunch. He loved them so much that he declared his affinity to the whole room with a sweeping arm motion—that knocked his bowl onto the floor! Maurice wailed and thunked his head down on the table. Teacher Aretha said, "It's all right, Maurice, it was an accident. We'll get this one cleaned up and get you another peach." But as Aretha was on the floor with Maurice trying to help, she realized that this was the last peach! They had had just enough for each child to have one. (It happens.)
>
> Aretha knew what was coming next and took a long time cleaning up the spill. As she slowly got Maurice to the table, he looked down at his place and there was a peach in a bowl! Aretha looked at the peach and then at Hilda, the just-5-year-old who was sitting next to the boy.
>
> "He needed it more than me," Hilda said. "And he was very sad." The teacher double-checked with Hilda to make sure she had wanted to give up her peach. Hilda nodded with certainty, so she asked Maurice if there was something he could say to Hilda. He said, "Thank you, Hilda." The teacher thanked Hilda too, then, and again later when the two were reading a book.

Reflection. After I shared this anecdote at a training, a participant said to me, "The teacher should not have let Hilda do this. A natural consequence of spilling your peach, if that's the last one, is that you don't get any. By letting Hilda give him hers, the teacher was not letting the boy learn to face reality."

By permitting Hilda to give Maurice her peach, I thought the teacher was letting the lesson be learned that there is compassion in life, that people can show caring for one another. Maybe if both kids were older, the teacher might have stressed the reality lesson. But Maurice was not, and Hilda acted

Discussions About Sharing and Good Deeds

Teachers might develop emergent curriculum from an experience like Hilda and Maurice's by reading a book about generosity, such as the classics *The Rainbow Fish* by Marcus Pfister or *The Giving Tree* by Shel Silverstein. TTs might then hold a group meeting about when to share and when it is all right not to. Discussing selected deep topics with young children, in supportive, nonjudgmental ways, has a definite place in encouraging early learning communities. (No child, in this case Hilda and Maurice, should be singled out in such discussions.) Discussions about deep topics assist children to build their understanding of what it means to be an individual in a social world. (See further Derman-Sparks & Edwards, with Goins [2020] for suggestions about holding deep discussions with young children.)

A problem TTs sometimes have is wanting to make a good-deed doer public, praising the child for altruistic acts. Private versus public acknowledgment needs to hold sway. The teacher might even be discrete with informing the children's families. Above all, we want to support the child who thinks intelligently and ethically so as not to set unrealistic expectations in the child for the future and perhaps suppress their personal development.

intelligently and ethically by empathizing with her distraught younger mate. On this day for sure, Hilda showed DLS 5.

Anecdote 4

The next anecdote is from Blackduck Head Start in Minnesota and experienced student teacher Julie, who, like Ansha, a child in the anecdote, "had it together." Julie wrote:

> Ansha and Lena, both not quite 5 years old, hugged each other when they arrived in the morning and hugged each other good-bye when they left in the afternoon. They played together whenever they were not in different groups. The two lived in

Education for a Civil Society

different parts of the area, and we did not think they got together much outside of school. This is why we were tolerant about the two hanging together so much.

Lena's hair was so long it came to her waist. Her mom kept it brushed and usually braided. One Friday afternoon, the two girls hugged good-bye, and Lena went home to her sister who was in her late teens—their mom had gone out of town for the weekend, and older sister was in charge. Well, older sister had begun cosmetology school, and on Monday Lena came to Head Start with a blue buzz cut!

All of us staff stood there with our mouths open. We had no idea what to say. Lena walked over to Ansha and asked, "What do you think of my haircut?" Ansha started to say something, then changed her mind. She said, "I'm still getting used to it."

"Me too," said Lena, and the two went off to play.

We already knew Ansha was a kid who had it together, but we found out how together that morning. Ansha taught all of us in the room what to say!

Reflection. Lena's long hair was so established in everyone's mind that a blue buzz cut shocked this veteran staff. Ansha seemed to know a lot was riding on her response, decided against her initial impulse, and said something that showed both honest smarts and an appreciation for her friend's feelings. Ansha was thinking intelligently and ethically—she was responding at DLS 5. That's what true friends can do, at any age.

Anecdote 5

Besides illustrating Jason's ability to put DLS 5 into action, the next anecdote gives us the chance to briefly discuss the screen life of young children. This anecdote is from a rural family child care program. It happened on a day I was visiting and giving Fern, the provider, some feedback on her very fine teaching.

In a family child care home, Jason, about to enter kindergarten, was by far the oldest and largest child. Jason loved using the computer, which the younger children were not as interested in. Fern had made a deal with Jason. He could use the computer every

On the topic of friendships, do you remember your first friend? Quite likely it was with a child you met during your preprimary years. Maybe you are still friends, maybe not, but you probably still have warm feelings toward that person. Just as lifelong interests get started in the early years, I believe many friendships do too, some of which we are lucky enough to continue throughout our lives. (Being from a small town, I bet Ansha and Lena are still friends after these many years.)

Note here that I am not talking about the injunction many teachers give children: "We are all friends in this classroom." I think it is presumptuous of teachers to think they should define for children who their friends are. A little guy, Gustav, once nailed this thought for me. His teacher made a remark about all children in the class, including Gil, being his friend. Gustav replied, "Gil's not my friend. He's my mate," as in *classmate*. We do need to encourage children to be friendly with all their classmates ("neighbors"?). But children, like the rest of us, should have the right to decide their friendships for themselves.

day during choice time on one condition. Jason needed to invite children who were near to join him in using the computer. He was to share the computer with them, showing them how to do games and so on.

On the morning I was observing, 38-month-old and 40-month-old boys happened by. Jason shared in a game with each, but soon these kids left. Then, 35-month-old Julia sat down next to Jason. Jason began explaining what he was doing and offered to let her play. Julia shook her head, but stayed and watched the game that Jason continued to explain to her for almost half an hour! When Fern announced it was time to go outside, the two stood up together and went to get their coats on—Julia standing about up to Jason's waist, the two of different sizes, genders, and skin colors. Jason helped Julia get on her coat—but let her zip it for herself.

Reflection. Except for choice time in the daily schedule, Jason did not use the computer. From her experience as a parent, Fern believed that screen play can be addicting to children. So, when she was given a computer for the children, she made it available with selected games only during the morning choice time and encouraged children to use it together—*real* social relations should not stop at electronic screens. (For a good deal more information on young children and technology, see NAEYC.org/resources/topics/technology-and-media/resources.) Fern endeavored to provide hands-on activities for Jason. He was into LEGOS and books for beginning readers, and Fern regularly got new books at Jason's reading level from the Head Start resource coordinator. Moreover, Jason enjoyed helping Fern with the younger children. (How many guys get into early childhood education because significant others did child care that included them?) Teacher and child got along well, and this setting facilitated Jason's progressing toward DLS 5. For many reasons, Jason was ready for kindergarten when he began a few months later.

After I retired, the Mahube Head Start program out of Detroit Lakes, Minnesota (near the city of New York Mills—really), asked me to be a part-time coach for some center TTs and affiliated family child care providers. Thanks to other grants Mahube had received, several family child care providers had contracts with the Head Start agency to serve Head Start working families. The family child care providers received special resources, support, and training. Good program.

Anecdote 6

This anecdote comes from an urban kindergarten in St. Paul. Ms. Darcy won an award for Teacher of the Year that spring.

> Elsa was a new student, who with her family had just arrived from Somalia. Elsa spoke Somali more than English and had not been in a school setting before. Ms. Darcy asked Kendra, 68 months, to play a math card game with Elsa. The card previously was called War, but Ms. Darcy changed the game to Match.

> Each child puts down a card from her hand and the higher card takes the lower, but in this classroom the cards went on a common pile.

> Kendra let Elsa play the first card. Then Kendra quickly found a card with a lower number and put it down! She counted the numbers on the cards in English with Elsa. Elsa was pleased to have helped make a big pile. When they finished the game, Elsa asked, "Again?"

> After Kendra's altruism during the card game, Ms. Darcy monitored Kendra's comfort level and asked her to do more "orienting" with Elsa. The two did many things together that kindergarten year, and Elsa, who was big for her age and fearless, repaid Kendra for her friendship. Often Ms. Darcy heard Kendra teaching Elsa new words. Kendra had a large role in helping Elsa learn English.

> Administration checked with Kendra's family that spring about how she would feel about being in the same class with Elsa in the first grade. Kendra's family gave her okay, and the two girls continued to be friends in first grade.

Reflection. Ms. Darcy had long-term hopes for Kendra with Elsa. Did this expectation of a young child put an undue burden on Kendra? The teacher was aware of this possibility and sensitively checked in with Kendra on a regular basis. It is important not to overburden children who give a lot, with giving too much. They need childhoods too!

Along with this question, another is this: In the game of Match, Kendra was intentionally selecting cards with low numbers. Was this okay? Maybe occasionally, putting other people ahead of traditional rules is intelligent and ethical. As adults, we professionals make this decision frequently. To me, putting people ahead of ritualistic rules is just plain a central part of acting intelligently and ethically. In the next anecdote, teacher Nellie bent the rules during rest time, just as 68-month-old Kendra did in the card game.

Anecdote 7

> While talking with teacher Nellie during rest time, Glenda, a soon-to-be 5-year-old, sat up, pulled the hair of the child next to her, and lay back down like she was asleep! Eddy, just 3, sat up, rubbed his head, grumbled, and lay back down. I gave Nellie an inquisitive

look and she, grinning broadly, whispered, "I am not going to do anything. Glenda has shown a need to be 'perfect' all year. Creating a bit of mischief is good for her."

Reflection. Another teacher's reaction might have been to wade through the resting children and scold Glenda for her misbehavior. *A signal that intervention is misplaced is when the act by the teacher is more disruptive than the child's mistaken behavior.* Nellie was a wise and experienced teacher. She saw that Glenda finally was comfortable enough in the program to for the first time show Level One experimentation mistaken behavior. This is one of those cases where—to Nellie and me—the intentional mistaken behavior of a young child actually indicates emotional-social progress. If Glenda's "mischief" continued in other incidents—or had Eddy been really hurt— Nellie might have quietly talked to Glenda. But more important, the teacher knew she could now encourage Glenda to express herself more in new experiences and social interactions.

Education for Living in a Democracy

Some critics might say this: Being sheltered in encouraging learning communities, children guided toward the democracy skill will be too soft and considerate to withstand the competitive hurly-burly of modern adult life. I disagree. Unlike many adults today, these kids would be learning to be assertive without being aggressive, to disagree agreeably, and to take positions based on principle.

In our semisubsidized capitalism—where to me, too many big companies receive tax breaks and too many little people go hungry—there is room for more equity. Teaching for the DLS is not teaching for marshmallow socialism. It is teaching children to be fair and considerate to one another as children *and* as adults. In societal terms, it is the difference between a response by a company that cuts hours and/or wages so all can keep their jobs during a recession or pandemic, and a company that slashes employee positions to keep profit margins high. It is the difference between an energy company intentionally evolving to renewable energy and one conspiring with politicians to keep pollution standards at bay. It is the difference between schools

that put more money into student mental health programs (and conflict resolution) and those that unduly pressure students to get higher scores on standardized tests—or that bend testing procedures to this end. (Think exempting some students from taking tests or altering test results.)

The hope of this book is that with a well-earned presence of mind and sense of self—not to mention well-practiced communication skills and perspective-taking abilities—a new generation of adults educated for the DLS will contribute much to making public discourse more civil, society more civilized, and the biggest of human challenges more resolvable.

Today in most of the major religions, clergy would say that teaching for the DLS is teaching directly to their religion's values. (I have been told this by clergy of differing faiths.) Doesn't matter to me whose rubrics we are meeting, so long as the outcome is adult emotional-social skills that provide sustenance for democratic society. As teaching for the DLS becomes more established, this is an area that I hope research will further explore.

Thinking Intelligently and Ethically

Children not yet at Skill 5 have trouble *taking perspective*, seeing situations as others do. Being just months old, the task of balancing the perspective of another with one's own is daunting. The task becomes even more challenging if a conflict involves not just one other person but two or three! In efforts to practice DLS 5, children will make mistakes. For instance, they may tattle. Well, sometimes we might want to a child to report, such as when another child climbs a fence and heads home! Guidance practices assist children to assess what they have done and, if needed, what to do instead.

Typical Child Behaviors

> Gives up turn or materials to another child who "needs it more"

> Comforts another child who might be sad or upset

> Invites another child to join in an activity or offers joint use of a material

> Offers to help another child or an adult

> Empathetically expresses how another child might be feeling

> Leads others in cooperative problem solving, accommodating other children in the group who have strong opinions

> Forgoes taking advantage of situations or another child for their own gain

> Suggests a solution to a problem that shows thought and takes others' views into consideration—even if the other is showing signs of aggression

Teacher Responses

TTs model friendly relations and building positive relationships with every child in the class and with all adults in the room, set up learning situations where children can have positive interactions with others different from themselves, are accepting of etiquette mistakes children may show in beginning efforts to think intelligently and ethically, use appropriate private acknowledgment with individual children who show prosocial behaviors, and balance their desire for young children to show empathetic leadership with the need of young kids to be healthy.

Progress Indicators in Gaining Skill 5

Giving up turn or materials to another child who "needs it more"; comforting another child who might be sad or upset; inviting another child to join in an activity or offering joint use of a material; offering to help another child or an adult; empathetically expressing how another child might be feeling; leading others in cooperative problem solving; accommodating other children in the group who have strong opinions; forgoing taking advantage of situations or another child for their own gain; and suggesting a solution to a problem that shows thought and takes others' views into consideration—even if the other is showing signs of aggression.

DISCUSSION QUESTIONS

1. Identify three key concepts (listed below and in the glossary). If you are a visual learner, write each out with its definition from the glossary. Then, referring to the section of the chapter where the key concept originated, reflect on what the concept means to you now that you have read the chapter.

2. Consider the anecdote about the peaches. Do you think Hilda was being overly selfless by giving away her peaches? Would you have let her? How would you explain to young children when it okay to share and when it is okay not to share?

3. How do a child's actions typical of DLS 5 reflect acquisition of the previous four skills? Aren't children who show DLS 3 and 4 also showing DLS 5? How and why should we differentiate—or should we?

4. Using technology is a topic of particular concern among professionals in early childhood. How can technology be a tool for furthering progress in any of the DLS?

5. Caring adults need to be sensitive to children's efforts in relation to DLS 5, even when their behaviors might be mistaken. Describe how the ideas in this chapter have affected your thinking about this idea.

6. The book is about education for democracy. Identify a new or newly reinforced idea for you from the chapter. Discuss how that idea contributes to your own approach toward teaching for democracy.

7. How have the thoughts and ideas shared in this chapter impacted your thinking about being a professional working with young children?

Key Concepts

autonomy

brain neuroarchitecture

dynamic mental health

guidance consequence

logical consequence

perspective taking

CHAPTER 10

Teachers and the Democratic Life Skills

SUGGESTED GOALS FOR READERS

1. Recognize the importance of acting as a citizen with others to advocate for adequate resources for early childhood education.

2. Explain how educational, social, and cultural diversity among TT members can benefit children in their work to gain the five DLS.

3. Discuss the value of individual teachers having personal support systems to buffer them against the everyday stressors they face.

4. Consider the big-picture connection between TTs who have adequate personal resources to consistently teach at DLS 3, 4, and 5 and young children gaining the foundation needed to further civil, democratic society as adults.

DLS 1	DLS 2	DLS 3	DLS 4	DLS 5
Finding Acceptance as a Member of the Group and as a Worthy Individual	**Expressing Strong Emotions in Nonhurting Ways**	**Solving Problems Creatively— Independently and in Cooperation with Others**	**Accepting Unique Human Qualities in Others**	**Thinking Intelligently and Ethically**

When teachers tell others they work with young children, a common reply is, "Oh, you must be so patient." Nancy Weber wrote an influential *Young Children* article on this topic back in 1987: Weber maintained that instead of patience, early childhood professionals need to show *understanding*—about the development of young children, about children as individuals, and about themselves. (In today's terms, we might call this intentional effort at understanding *mindfulness*.) Except in Eastern philosophy, when patience and understanding merge, being patient in Western cultures is considered "bearing pains or trials calmly or without complaint" (*Merriam-Webster.com Dictionary,* s.v. "patient" (adj.), www.merriam-webster.com/dictionary/patient). Weber's thesis is that at some point we run out of patience and negatively overreact to our "burdens." Both as a guiding principle and a goal, early childhood professionals don't run out of understanding.

Every day, teachers themselves use the DLS to understand children and to assist them to gain the skills. They do so (to the best of their ability) by leaving their own complicated life situations at the doors of their programs. They teach using Skills 3, 4, and 5 with as much consistency as they can. They regard teaching young children not as a trial but as a calling.

So, what do TTs need to persist and flourish in the challenging life's work of teaching young children? My three essential items: financial resources, inclusive teaming among all staff, and personal support systems. Your list might include more.

More Financial Resources

Relatively few early childhood professionals make professional-level salaries; the few are mostly those with state licensure who are on the master contracts of school districts that have prekindergarten programs. Taxes subsidize school districts enough to pay these teachers on a par with elementary school teachers. In contrast, most early childhood programs are not tied to public school master contracts. A longtime challenge to the field is that TTs subsidize the programs they work in by accepting low salaries.

Low Incomes Confound Most Early Childhood Professionals

Remember the rogues' gallery list of stressors adults face back in Chapter 3? Social scientists generally agree that there is a correlation between many if not most of those stressors and low family income (Dolan 2019; Sampson & Manduca 2019). It is likely that most low-paid early childhood professionals leave more complicated life situations at the door of their classrooms than most better-paid public school teachers do.

Laws that mandate more resources for non-public school early childhood programs are necessary. The threshold between subsistence and professional-level wage levels for TTs requires a whole lot more crossing. More resources are needed to support professional-level wages for all early childhood teachers *and* to enhance program quality. To justify the needed increase in resources, NAEYC along with state agencies and other organizations are working to improve the operation and quality of early childhood services as well as the preparation and qualifications of early childhood professionals. More resources are needed for this effort as well.

Inclusive Teaming

Throughout the book I have used the term TTs, teaching teams, to emphasize the value of early childhood professionals working together. Children gain in many ways when their in-school significant others model cooperation and comradery. Benefits every day include tailoring teaching ideas to individual group members, balancing support and nudging for every child, and modeling practical democracy.

Benefits to staff themselves are less visible but nonetheless essential. Directly related to the DLS, here are two.

The first benefit is collegial friendships. Think we all agree that life is complicated. It is difficult to come to work from a home with a teething baby, unattended plumbing issues, family members struggling with health issues, and an absent partner—and perform as one would like to over a very full day. A key implication is this: not only do relations among front-line staff need to be friendly and steady, relations with administrators and support personnel must be too. Starting with directors, all staff should recognize when a colleague has hit a rough patch and help their fellow team member make it through the day. (Your supporting that person today could turn around to them supporting you tomorrow.) If challenging issues continue for a mate, the team works to help that person get the assistance they need.

The second benefit is that teachers do sometimes encounter those individual children, families, and colleagues who are challenging to understand and work with. In relation to teaching for the DLS, what TTs *don't* do is overlook strained interactions and relationships. They talk honestly and nonjudgmentally as a team and figure out how to (intelligently and ethically—mindfully) address the situation. Maybe another TT member works more with a given child; maybe another staff member can watch to head off adult-adult conflicts and work to alleviate them. Such situations often improve over time, especially in mutually supportive settings. By

Merits and a Waning Shortcoming of Master Contracts in Public Schools

Over the years, master contracts negotiated by local union/association affiliates with individual school districts are largely responsible for standard-of-living improvements made by public school teachers, including public school pre-K teachers. In my view, however, a side-effect shortcoming in the master contract system has existed for too long.

That shortcoming is this. To protect the professionalism of teachers and enhance teacher security, a prevalent pattern in master contracts has been tight definitions of what professionals do in classrooms (and what paraprofessionals cannot do). In contrast to the more democratic teaching team system in many preschools, master contract language has reinforced a model whereby the teacher teaches, and the paraprofessional provides minimally educational support. A "mass class" teaching approach has resulted, in which the teacher stands before the whole group and instructs while the paraprofessional provides help around the edges. High learner-to-teacher ratios have been the consequence, making secure relationships with individual children and personalized, developmentally appropriate teaching difficult.

The title of this sidebar said "waning" because *official* recognition of the importance of assistance staff is beginning to grow in K–12 schools. For example, a spring 2022 contract settlement between the Minneapolis Public Schools and its teachers included agreements about higher wages for education assistants (read that as livable wage improvements) and smaller class sizes—both conducive to teaching for the DLS.

being responsive in terms of relationships among themselves, TTs affirm the encouraging community for everyone.

The following anecdote illustrates how, through on-site training, the staff of an urban early childhood center learned the advantages of working as a team for the children and themselves.

For a graduate practicum class, four students (experienced early childhood teachers) assisted a large urban early childhood center to enhance its program for preschoolers. Housed in a large church basement, the program included 36 preschoolers, four lead teachers, and four associate teachers. Along with the assistant director, the eight teaching staff were taking a one-credit college class. For the class they agreed to participate in enhancing their program.

The grad students, as instructors, conducted the classes for the staff in the form of group meetings. Together, class members came up with a plan. They would establish four home bases in the classroom space, each with movable partitions that would serve family groups and provide an identified interest area during a common work time. (**Family groups** are small, mixed-aged groups that stay together with the same educators across many time blocks during the day.) For each of the family groups, a two-person TT would be primary providers.

When the group discussion turned to the children, several of the staff—agreeing to not mention names—raised concerns about the behavior of (clearly) the same child, Bryce. The graduate team had noticed Bryce having a few dramatic conflicts, but they were surprised at the intensity of the feelings being expressed by the staff. Finally, one teacher offered that the child was trying hard, but he needed assistance with his strong emotions—the most positive thing anyone said.

The assistant director had the job of assigning children to family groups staffed by each of the four teaching teams. Knowing the staff and children, she set up the family groups with a lot of thought. Bryce was assigned to the group of the last teacher who spoke.

In the next class after the new system was up and running, the staff expressed general approval. Some even mentioned how much a particular unnamed child's behavior had improved! (Readers can perhaps figure out why.)

On Being Colleagues, and When to Leave

Programs that find ways to provide training, guidance, and support that highlight positive staff relations and teamwork are to be treasured. Increasing this priority in early childhood programs is to make the fullest use of each staff member's potential and improve program quality (Gartrell 2020). For any staff member, a measure of connection with a program is whether the teachers there can be the persons they want to be. Failing that, many take the route Myrna did. Myrna, a graduate some years ago, emailed me that she had started work at two different early childhood centers in Minneapolis and St. Paul. Myrna did not feel comfortable with how either program operated, including a perceived absence of teaming together. Being young and with courage, she left both centers. She found a position with a third center that was more developmentally appropriate and collegial and told me how happy she was with the position—and that she had persisted in her search.

Older adults tend to have more responsibilities and investment in the jobs they are in. They generally take more risks than recent college graduates when changing jobs. All I am saying is that once in a while, to consider leaving a program might be for the best. (Though it's helpful to try to get that other job first!)

Including Male Staff

For young children there are many benefits from women and men teaming as teachers. Women and men teachers who together comfort, support, guide, celebrate, and play with kids offer a first experience for many children. That women and men can respect each other and perform tasks cooperatively provides a model for girls and boys to also cooperate in tasks. Long-lasting, significant learning might well be the result. (When men willingly dance, boys dance less reluctantly.)

Still, the up-or-out phenomenon, attributed more often to men than women, is well known among teachers. A male takes a position in a program of mainly female staff. Sometimes, after a relatively short time, he is promoted or leaves to advance professionally. The remaining women have a right to complain that they broke the guy in and taught him most of what he knows. (Yes, some women teachers are "up and outers" as well.)

So what makes it worthwhile to have caring men as well as women teachers in a program even if it is for a short time? After all, continuity in primary providers across time is important for young children. True, but what caring teachers of whatever gender have to offer is, to my mind, worth difficult transitions. Here are two vignettes, narrated by teachers Bruce and Jay, respectively, that show their impact on two boys struggling to reach DLS and 2. Both Bruce and Jay remained in their classrooms for more than a few years. These anecdotes come from "Boys and Men Teachers," a Guidance Matters column in *Young Children* (Gartrell 2006).

Bruce: When Darnell entered our program, he was fairly nonverbal and very big (already 75 pounds as a 3-year-old). He lived with his grandparents, and we three teachers guessed they did not hold him in their laps much, let alone pick him up. We could see Darnell craved physical attention; he tried to climb onto our laps and wanted us to carry him all the time. But it was hard to meet his needs because of his size and the way he had of demanding attention. The other teachers tried to encourage Darnell to talk more and to build relationships that way, but he responded very little. It was like he tuned us out. Something more had to be done.

I am not a particularly large guy, but I knew I had to give comfort to this child, at least hold him on my lap a few times a day and carry him once or twice. After several weeks of this, Darnell began to open up. He talked more and began to try things on his own. On the playground he started to run with the other kids and me and play chase. For the first time, we saw Darnell pleased to be part of the group—and he asked to be carried less! He adjusted, and the other teachers did too. They came to accept Darnell as a typical 3-year-old boy who was just learning how to ask for and give affection.

Jay: Scott was a smallish 4-year-old. Every day in class he struggled to be accepted and to get attention. Scott was a whiz at building things and with large motor activities, but he had trouble interacting with others and often resorted to hitting. I worked with him on using words and friendly touches, and the hitting got less. Still, whenever he got upset, he would throw himself backward against a wall and then either totally ignore everyone or storm off in anger.

One day Scott had a struggle with a peer, and I intervened, not letting him hit the other child. Scott started to close down, and I quietly encouraged him to use his words. Just this side of throwing himself against the wall, Scott stopped, clenched his fists, and screamed as loud as he could, "I'm angry at you, Jay!"

I was thrilled, and as I gave him a big hug, I told him so: "That's wonderful, Scott!" He stayed for a moment in the hug and visibly relaxed.

That moment marked a sea-change for the child. Scott used his words fairly consistently after that. He would often come to me and ask for a hug. He had many engaging interactions with his peers, more fully enjoyed the activities he had done so well before, and was enthusiastic about trying new things.

It is wonderful when caring teachers, both men and women, can respond to the two boys the way these guys did. In the anecdotes, each boy experienced a teacher who looked like them being nurturing. Teachers Bruce and Jay modeled for all in their respective communities that men as well as women can be caring and supportive.

Men and women each make up roughly equal-sized portions of the human population. Yet men enter, and stay in, pre-K to grade 12 education in vastly lower numbers than women. The reality is that very few men are TT members in early childhood education. Setting aside all of the politics around this issue, my belief is that it makes sense in so many ways to have men and women teaming together in classrooms. My hat (and most of my toupee) is off to men teachers as well as women, dedicated to working together and following their callings in encouraging early learning communities.

Personal Support Systems

In writing about the importance of personal support systems, I have concerns that this section might sound like it is from "Dr. Dan" on some self-help blog. But here goes.

Friends at work: I remember two kindergarten teachers who were friends as well as colleagues. One was going through a divorce and the other was dealing with difficult family matters, including one child who had lost hearing due to encephalitis and another who had Down syndrome. The teachers arrived at their primary school early every day, and nearly every day walked around the block talking and listening. Sometimes the topic was their classrooms, sometimes school politics, but mostly it was about their home situations. They told me that rough patches were less severe and classroom days better because of their early morning contact talks.

At work and in the home community, having friends is the first tier of a personal support system. Often, life partners are those friends—with whom we can discuss things freely and not be judged. Probably most of us have a combination of family members and friends whom we can talk to. You know that person is there for you when they ask how you are doing, you say fine, and they reply, "And how else are you feeling?" If they ask the second question, answer honestly. We humans need to talk things through to work them out. I dislike the saying, "Been there, done that." There may be a single shoe style that many people own, but each walks in their own shoes and on their own path. A friend who will listen to you about the journey *you* are taking is a true friend, a person who makes things easier at home as well as work.

Activity groups outside of the program: Also central to mental health is making connections with other people around out-of-work activities. You know:

> Church groups, sports teams, and exercise groups

> School activities for your kids (if you—or they—are not overrun by them)

> Hobbies around which you connect with others (reading, music, yarn doings, yard doings, baking)

> Affiliation with various social and benevolent groups

> Volunteering

> Doing things with family members (including pets)

Limit social media. maybe my bias—no, it's my position—but people need to check themselves as to whether frequent social media use is relaxing and not stress producing. Doing things with real people in the here and now is likely to be most restorative in terms of a person's mental health. my comment does not apply to family members FaceTiming with grandkids and other significant others who are far away—or to family members playing some computer games together. When individuals, young or old, turn to computer games or other screen activities rather than face the world, they likely are showing the survival behavior of flight. In children and ourselves, it pays to firmly ration screen time (NAEYC & Fred Rogers Center 2012)—to show we control it; it doesn't control us.

With the family: Besides big experiences like trips, doing things with family members might include everyday activities like together eating meals, playing games, doing outdoor activities, and watching TV (including eating popcorn and drinking beverages of individuals' choices).

I agree with the renowned child psychologist David Elkind (2001): the plethora of formal organized activities available through schools and communities hurries children too quickly through their childhoods. Besides onerous (for many families) participation fees, equipment costs, travel arrangements, and time commitments, organized activities bring undue performance anxiety (stress) to most children and vicariously to many parents. The folks who say that informal play is best for children (in safe spaces) are right. It is good for parents, too, to get away from work by doing informal activities with their children, giving them time—the best gift of all!

Reaching Out for Assistance

Human life is complicated, and many experiences are stress producing—for adults as well as children. When too much stress stays with us for too long, it is easy to become dependent on mistaken flight survival behaviors—stuff we begin putting into our bodies,

doing with our bodies, or doing to others—virtually or in person. At any age, clinical depression in the society is pervasive and takes many forms.

A longtime stigma, just beginning to be addressed, has been in reaching out for assistance to others, especially professionals: clergy, general practitioners, mental health clinics, mental health personnel. It is a challenge in several ways to find a mental health professional we like and can see regularly. Reaching out, though, becomes essential when we can no longer manage the stress that we feel. It is not a weakness to reach out for assistance; it is a strength. Gaining the assistance of a mental health professional is an affirmation to ourselves and to others around us that we are more than our immediate situation tells us we are (Gartrell 2020). (I won't say I've "been there, done that," but I will say that taking an anti-anxiety pill every day for several years has helped keep my sense of friendly humor, including in this book.)

Educating for a Civil Society

Realistically, what can progressive early childhood education accomplish for young children, especially if they move on to years of schooling that does not consistently reinforce the Democratic Life Skills? Here are two responses.

First, foundations may not be everything, but they are foundations. Developmental science, now coming of age, has established that attributes, interests, multilanguage and music skills, and emotional and social abilities that are gained in early childhood stay with individuals into adulthood (Giovannoli et al. 2020). In young children, the dynamic structure of the brain changes to accommodate these learned capacities. If children cannot continue to use them, the capacities might get pushed to the sidelines (sorted via the hippocampus system), but they are there always waiting to be rekindled (Sousa 2022).

Young children who gain the ability to do the following will always have the foundations of these skills ready to build on and use:

> Find acceptance as a member of the group and as a worthy individual

> Express strong emotions in nonhurting ways

> Solve problems creatively—independently and in cooperation with others

> Accept unique human qualities in others

> Think intelligently and ethically

You, dear readers, contribute mightily to these gains.

Second, in the child's future schooling, perhaps not via institutional policy but at least due to relationships with individual teachers, the DLS will be reinforced. As they grow, children will get to use and practice the skills. If a child is fortunate, their family and many teachers will provide this opportunity. The matter comes down to caring adults who listen to children, with nonjudgmental, thoughtful guidance, and encourage children to express their intentions, goals, frustrations, and strategies in nonhurting ways. In progressive schools these practices are a matter of policy; in other schools individual teachers have believed and will always believe in thoughtfully listening and responding to children.

Our society needs individuals who can think of innovative ideas and express them in ways that lead to cooperative problem solving. Empowering civil dialog is the key. If not the whole glorious structure, early childhood education at least provides the foundation for these abilities. And you, dear teachers, are the "first assisters," guiding each child to build that foundation. In teaching for the Democratic Life Skills, you are guiding the young to help democracy survive and flourish.

DISCUSSION QUESTIONS

1. If you are a visual learner, write out the key concept from this chapter (listed below and in the glossary) with its definition from the glossary. Then, referring to the section of the chapter where the key concept originated, reflect on what the concept means to you now that you have read the chapter.

2. Consider the third item from my list of essential resources early in the chapter. Focusing on yourself or an anonymous colleague, how do you cope in relation to having adequate personal resources? What might you or your colleague do to cope even better?

3. Mutually supportive teaming calls for use of the eight communication practices introduced in Chapter 4. Discuss how any four practices might be effective in developing a supportive community for all staff within the early childhood setting.

4. Staff may be diverse in terms of race, gender, culture, education, age, and ability, among other identities. How can TTs having diverse representation on a cohesive staff enrich the expression of DLS 3, 4, and 5 in children and in staff themselves? Discuss any three diversity factors in this regard.

5. The book is about education for democracy. Identify a new or newly reinforced idea for you from the chapter. Discuss how that idea contributes to your own approach toward teaching for democracy.

6. How have the thoughts and ideas shared in this chapter impacted your thinking about being a professional working with young children?

Key Concept

family groups

Appendix

Here is a simple, concise summary of the lists of noteworthy principles and practices from the book.

Five Democratic Life Skills

DLS 1: Finding acceptance as a member of the group and as a worthy individual

DLS 2: Expressing strong emotions in nonhurting ways

DLS 3: Solving problems creatively—independently and in cooperation with others

DLS 4: Accepting unique human qualities in others

DLS 5: Thinking intelligently and ethically

Eight Communication Practices for Building Relationships

Smile and nod.

Acknowledge and pause.

Make contact talks happen.

Use friendly humor.

Use appropriate, friendly touch.

Utilize compliment sandwiches.

Give encouragement: private to individuals, public to the group.

Remember names, contact talks, and promises.

Three Levels of Mistaken Behavior

Level One experimentation mistaken behavior

Level Two socially influenced mistaken behavior

Level Three strong unmet-needs mistaken behavior

Seven Principles of Guidance

Principle 1: Use democratic leadership to create an encouraging early childhood learning community for every member of the group.

Principle 2: Emphasize emotional and social learning through a whole child/personal development perspective, within the context of developmentally appropriate practice.

Principle 3: Foster mastery motivation and the expression and healthy development of executive function.

Principle 4: Practice mutually beneficial communication techniques with both children and adults.

Principle 5: Use a general guidance plan for social problem solving in the community—the five finger formula.

Principle 6: Respond to conflicts using a collection of guidance practices that affirm and teach.

Principle 7: With children experiencing frequent and severe conflicts: collaborate with a team, including staff and families, in the use of comprehensive guidance.

Developmental Guidance: Major Practices

Use developmentally appropriate practices for all.

Use eight communication techniques to build secure relationships with all in the setting.

Rely on developmental large group meetings.

Utilize developmentally appropriate emergent curriculum.

Key Intervention Guidance Practices

Calming methods

Guidance talks

Conflict mediation

Intervention large group meetings

Comprehensive guidance

Five Finger Formula

Thumb: Calm everyone down—yourself, too. Set the scene for the mediation.

Pointer: Guide the children to accept how each person sees the conflict. (Individual perspectives might not be what others thought happened. Understanding this is key to conflict resolution.)

Tall guy: Brainstorm possible solutions. (Provide suggestions for children with limited language or who are dual language learners. Respect nonverbal signs of agreement or disagreement.)

Ringer: Agree to one solution and try it. (The solution may not be what you had in mind, but if it makes sense and all are okay with it, go with this solution.) Sometimes steps 3 and 4 naturally merge.

Pinky: Monitor the solution and positively acknowledge cooperative efforts and acts of reconciliation. Hold guidance talks with individuals as needed. Discuss what children can do next time instead.

Family Engagement Benchmarks

Benchmark 1: Family members show acceptance of program and staff.

Benchmark 2: Family members take new interest in the learning of their child.

Benchmark 3: Family members become active in relation to the general program.

Benchmark 4: Family members progress in personal and/or professional development themselves as a result of their engagement.

Glossary

A

acknowledge and pause: A "golden" (central) communication practice for building relationships with young children and adults. The two-step practice involves first complimenting a specific in the other's effort or achievement and then pausing to listen to and appreciate the other's response.

active discrimination: Prejudice actively asserted toward others who are different from oneself, causing physical and/or psychological oppression for those others.

adverse experience: Perceived harmful experience that can cause acute and chronic unmanageable stress in children, child trauma, and childhood post-traumatic stress disorder (PTSD).

amygdala- and hypothalamus-driven stress response: The amygdalae together with the hypothalamus give emotional interpretation to incoming stimuli and regulate physiological reactions to the stimuli, including sensing and reacting to stress. Upon sensing adverse experiences, the amygdala-hypothalamus function overrides nascent executive function with unmanageable stress and survival behaviors.

anti-bias education: Education programming and practices intended to prevent the development of pre-prejudice and prejudice in relation to race, sex, gender identity, cultural and linguistic factors, individuals with distinct physical appearances and behavior patterns, and other identities. As a movement, anti-bias education is also intended to assist adults to overcome already existing bias and discrimination.

attachment theory: A theory beginning with John Bowlby and Mary Ainsworth that addresses the formation of primary relationships between infants, toddlers, and young children with parents and other significant adults. The theory holds that behavioral mechanisms that young children develop are largely a function of the nature of their relationships with others significant to them. When secure, the attachment is likely to result in enhanced self-esteem and social responsiveness in the child.

attunement: Originating from cross-culture study by Mary Ainsworth, the term describes the state of mind of a primary caregiver who has been able to form a secure relationship with a young child. The successful achievement of mindfulness by the caring adult in responding to a young child over time.

authentic assessment: A type of culturally relevant educational assessment used across a range of domains that samples everyday efforts and tasks of the child and compares this observed data to developmental norms. Less intrusive and more comprehensive than academic standardized assessment. Assessment method of choice in early childhood and progressive education.

authority aversion: Common effect in children subject to the stress-conflict-punishment syndrome, who lose trust in significant adults and develop oppositional attitudes toward them and the institutions they represent. A guidance alternative to the term *oppositional defiant disorder*.

autonomy: Piaget's term for the ability to make ethical, intelligent decisions that balance others' viewpoints with one's own. Different than heteronomy, which is conformity with and compliance toward significant others, tending to result in Level Two socially influenced mistaken behavior.

B

benchmarks for family engagement: Four benchmarks allow early childhood professionals to assess their efforts at empowering family engagement and building partnerships with families. Benchmark 1—Family members show acceptance of program and staff. Benchmark 2—Family members take new interest in the learning of their child. Benchmark 3—Family members become active in relation to the general program. Benchmark 4—Family members progress in personal and/or professional development themselves as a result of their engagement.

biological sex: The sex, sometimes referred to as gender, assigned to an infant at birth based on anatomy.

brain neuroarchitecture. The structures of the brain, forming through neuroplasticity especially during early childhood, that have much to do with a growing individual's response potential. Healthy emotional-social nurturing during the early years builds brain neuroarchitecture with an increased capacity for intelligent and ethical decision making in adults.

C

calming: Guidance action taken during a conflict to de-escalate the situation and prepare individuals to resolve the problem. Getting calm may take a cooling-down time, either in or away from the setting of the conflict.

child negotiation: An indication of the success of a learning community's efforts at using and teaching mediation. Child negotiation happens when children have internalized the steps of conflict mediation and undertake the mediation on their own without adult assistance.

child trauma: A perceived threat of harm or actual harm experienced by a child or immediate others due to one or more direct or witnessed adverse experiences. The adverse experiences cause unmanageable stress to the extent that the child goes into a state of immediate and sometimes long-term feelings of intense fear, helplessness, or horror. Child trauma shows in post-traumatic stress disorder (PTSD) and survival behaviors.

choice time: A time block designed for self-selected, self-directed autonomous learning activity (play). Other interchangeable terms are *work time, play time, work and play time*, and the traditional *free play*. During these times, TTs monitor and facilitate children's engagement and hold contact talks. The times are typically more than a half hour so children can have ample experience with engaging, disengaging, and reengaging. Small group planning beforehand and reviewing afterward contribute to desired metacognition (learning about one's learning) relative to choice time experiences.

coming around phenomenon: The moment when a child feels accepted by, and decides it is safe to be oneself in, the community. This usually evident stepping forward is a prime indicator that the child has gained safety-needs skills sufficiently to begin to grow in psychologically healthy ways. This early moment of demonstrated resilience is an occasion for the celebratory beverage of the teacher's choice.

compliment sandwich: An encouragement technique that provides at least two acknowledgments of effort and progress sandwiched around one request or suggestion for further progress.

comprehensive guidance: A coordinated guidance strategy that is used when children show continuing strong unmet-needs mistaken behavior. TTs formally or informally use an individual guidance plan (IGP). They typically engage administrative staff and families in meetings to develop, use, and assess the IGP. Comprehensive guidance entails working as a team to learn more about the child's situation, improve relationships with the child, rethink the program for the child, and make coordinated use of intervention guidance practices. Almost always, comprehensive guidance involves working cooperatively with families and sometimes involves professionals from outside the program.

conflict: An expressed disagreement between individuals. Conflicts are normal across the entire lifespan. The hallmark of the Democratic Life Skills is the ability to resolve conflicts in nonhurting ways for all parties concerned.

contact talks: Quality time shared between individuals for the purpose of building and sustaining positive interpersonal relationships. Contact talks can be brief, but they need to happen with every child at least once every day. Different from task talk, which is intended to get things done.

conventional discipline: Any act of intervention by adults that slides into punishment as a mistaken consequence for a conflict that a child has caused or fallen into. Punishment, the imposition of pain and suffering, fails to teach children the emotional-social skills we want all children to learn and instead causes and aggravates unmanageable stress that makes it difficult for children to learn those emotional-social skills.

cooling-down time: Time given to individuals in conflict to get calm enough to talk through the problem. Cooling-down times sometimes involve having a child leave the setting of the conflict. These times are different from time-outs because they are not done as a consequence for what a child did, but to calm down to discuss what happened. Teachers act as leaders in helping children to cool down.

correction by suggestion: Derived from a term used by Haim Ginott as an alternative to the punishments of blame and shame. In Ginott's usage, correction by direction has two to three elements: describe what you see, express your feelings about it (optional), and direct the other to what needs to be done to fix the situation. Correction by suggestion means gently directing the other to do what needs to be done.

culture bound: Limitations of study findings and authoritative viewpoints due to sampling error or research methodology and scholarship skewed toward the social/cultural background of the researcher/scholar. Typically but not exclusively, this bias favors White, middle-class, male cultural factors and values, so restricting the generalizability and possibly the validity of findings and viewpoints.

culturally responsive: Early childhood educators' ability to be knowledgeable about and respectful toward cultural characteristics and values of individuals and groups that are different from their own. Understanding and including children's cultural knowledge and practices and prior experiences in the curriculum.

D

Democratic Life Skills (DLS): The skills children need to be healthy individuals and contributing citizens in a modern democracy. Includes: (1) perception of oneself as a worthy group member and individual; (2) expression of strong emotions in nonhurting ways; (3) creative and cooperative problem solving; (4) acceptance of human differences in others; and (5) intelligent and ethical decision making.

developmental egocentrism: Piaget clinically established that children's views of the world lack the complex perceptions of reality of adults. Children tend to see life revolving around themselves in simple, charming, and often anthropomorphic ways. Developmental egotism designates this phase in life of young children's world views.

developmental guidance: The use of guidance to build an encouraging early learning community for every member. In addition to developmentally appropriate practices for all, primary practices include eight individual relationship-building communication practices, large group meetings, and emergent curriculum.

developmental stressors: Everyday stressors that are the result of a child's being only months old in a world run by adults, who are decades old. Writing about this situation, Leontine Young (1966) originated the apt descriptive phrase "life among the giants."

developmentally appropriate practice (DAP): "Methods that promote each child's optimal development and learning through a strengths-based, play-based approach to joyful, engaged learning. Educators implement developmentally appropriate practice by recognizing the multiple assets all young children bring to the early learning program as unique individuals and as members of families and communities" (NAEYC 2020, 5).

dynamic mental health: The state of mind when a child has substantially gained the safety-needs skills and progresses toward gaining the growing-needs skills. The child is responding to intrinsic mastery motivation and is engaging in problem-solving behaviors and healthy development of executive function. A child who has struggled to reach this state is showing *resilience* in the process of personal development.

E

early childhood depression: The state of overwhelmed nascent executive function due to adverse experiences and/or atypical brain development. The child's unmanageable stress results in the survival behaviors of psychological freezing and fleeing, shown by the child to a significant degree. Can be a symptom of childhood post-traumatic stress disorder.

emergent curriculum: Intentionally developing curriculum that builds on children's interests. Early childhood educators pick up on the interests and experiences of young children and with them build creative, multisensory thematic investigations that incorporate interdisciplinary content (Masterson 2022). Teachers watch for emerging new interests that can lead to a next thematic wave.

encouragement (private and public): Supportive statements given to recognize specific effort and achievement. In contrast to evaluative praise, teachers give encouragement to individual children as privately as possible and to groups collectively without singling out individual children, thus avoiding mistaken adult behaviors that set up winner-loser dynamics within the community.

encouraging early learning community: Through the use of developmentally appropriate practice, the community welcomes all as worthy individuals and members of the group. It encourages all members to gain the two safety-needs skills and make progress with the growing-needs skills. It is a place where supportive equity education is the guiding principle. Members want to be there even if sick, as opposed to not wanting to be there when they are well. An encouraging community begins within the minds of teachers.

environmental stressors: Sources of unmanageable stress that the child encounters via the family, the home community, and/or the classroom—undue stress encountered in the experiential world of the child.

equity education: The totality of practices and environmental influences in the encouraging early learning community that convey to children of all races, socioeconomic backgrounds, cultural heritages, abilities, appearances, and behavioral patterns that they are worthy and capable of gaining the five DLS.

establishment aversion: A common consequence in mental attitude of a child's falling into a long-term stress-conflict-punishment syndrome. An attitude generalized beyond authority aversion to general society. A definite factor is educators who did not or could not help children to alleviate unmanageable stress and mistaken survival behavior.

executive function: A complex, coordinated process of cognitive, emotional, social, and physical operations that enable children to stay on task in attending to situations, summoning relevant memories, organizing thoughts, managing feelings, and solving problems. Originating in the cerebral cortex frontal lobes, executive function begins to develop in early infancy, grows dramatically from ages 3 to 5, and does not reach maturity until individuals are in their 20s.

extrinsic motivation: Distinct from intrinsic, mastery motivation, this is the motivation that many adults seek to instill in children, through rewards and punishments, to elicit desired learning behaviors. The more distant classroom activities are from developmentally appropriate practice, the more adults must rely on extrinsic motivation. In settings where adults rely on extrinsic motivation, mastery motivation might survive, but it cannot flourish.

F

family engagement: Describes the coming together of teaching teams and family members for the collaborative benefit of the child. As teachers initiate and sustain actions that welcome and support families, family members participate with teachers in furthering the personal development and education of their children. The relationship involves two-way communication—listening to families and doing "with" them rather than "to" or "for" them.

family groups: Stable small groups of mixed-aged children with a dedicated teacher. These small groups stay together through various designated time blocks during the day. The groups might eat together as well as participate in planned activities like reading and projects during small group times each day. The groups encourage positive relationships among children and a secure relationship with the designated adult group leader.

family-style meals: Family-style meals entail a small group of children and a primary care adult preparing the meal setting, sharing food, and talking together. Distinct from cafeteria-style meals prevalent in schools.

five finger formula for conflict resolution: Used more formally in conflict mediation and less so in guidance talks and large group meetings, the five steps of this general social problem-solving approach are (1) calming and set-up; (2) both parties coming to agreement on how each sees the issue; (3) brainstorming possible solutions; (4) deciding on and implementing a solution; and (5) monitoring and guiding for successful resolution—often including one or more guidance talks.

G

gender identity: The gender each child comes to identify with through a brain-driven developmental process that begins around age 2. *Gender-diverse identity* refers to a child's identification with gender characteristics different from the sex assigned at birth. Gender-diverse identity is a complex internal brain process that develops parallel to gender identity that is in congruence with a child's assigned sex.

greeting meetings: Friendly orientation meetings of staff with parents when families first start programs. When families join on a staggered basis, meetings might be held on a periodic basis.

growing-needs skills: DLS 3, 4, and 5, which children address after making substantial progress with the safety-needs skills, DLS 1 and 2. For children who have struggled with DLS 1 and 2, the growing-needs skills are indicators of resilience. Children work on the growing-needs skills simultaneously but make gains in each according to their individual personalities and circumstances.

guidance: A way of teaching that nurtures each child's unique potential through consistently positive, sometimes firm but always friendly and flexible, interactions. Classroom management that teaches rather than punishes. Guidance happens in two dimensions, developmental and intervention. When employed during conflicts, it is restorative, not punitive. It is teaching for healthy personal development, teaching for the five Democratic Life Skills.

guidance talks: An individual conversation with a child who shows mistaken behavior at any level and needs to learn an alternative behavior. The teacher scaffolds from the mistaken behavior toward a less hurtful conflict response. The teacher and child discuss how the child saw the conflict, how the other person might have felt, what the child can do to make things better (different from a forced apology), and what they could do differently next time.

guidance consequence: A "logical consequence" is an act of "correction" that "fits" a mistaken behavior and is imposed by an adult (Dreikurs & Grey [1968] 1993). In contrast, a guidance consequence has implications for the teacher as well as the child. For the teacher, the consequence is to calm and teach in order to resolve the conflict and guide toward a less hurting response next time. The consequence for the child is to participate in the conflict resolution and learn as much as they can at that time about how to respond in a future conflict more civilly.

guidelines, not rules: Typically, rules instruct children what not to do. Rules tend to limit teachers' reactions to ignoring or enforcement, which restricts guidance possibilities during teachable moments. Guidelines identify friendly cooperative standards for relations and behavior that, when children show mistaken behavior, teachers can guide children toward. Example: Rule: "No hitting." Guideline: "Friendly touches only."

H

happygrams: Notes of encouragement and examples of children's successes shared with families and sometimes read to children. Especially important when children begin programs and as a part of comprehensive guidance. Might be conveyed as printed messages; through texts, emails, or communication apps; or in phone messages as arranged with family members.

I

individual guidance plan (IGP): A coordinated strategy of intervention and assistance developed by a teaching team when encountering sustained Level Three mistaken behavior by a child. The team works with the family and secures additional assistance, often from an administrator (or, in a larger program, specialized staff) and possibly consultants and professionals from outside the program.

institution-caused mistaken behavior: Mistaken behavior by children in reaction to stress from unrealistic (not developmentally appropriate) or biased expectations put on them by teachers and/or the program.

instrumental aggression: Verbal and physical aggression that a child shows toward others intentionally, on purpose. This aggression is still mistaken behavior in that the child is reacting to the stress of unmet needs for belonging and a sense of self-worth. From previous conflicts the child has learned mistaken strategies of coping through attempting to control situations by domination, and perhaps evading detection for the conflicts intentionally caused.

intervention guidance: During conflicts that lapse into mistaken behavior, intervention guidance starts with calming techniques and includes any combination of guidance talks, conflict mediation, large group meetings, and comprehensive guidance to sustain the encouraging early learning community. Its purpose is to resolve conflicts in restorative ways that retain secure relationships and to teach for and reinforce children's sense of attainment of the safety-needs skills.

invisible child: A child who is using the mistaken survival behaviors of psychological freezing and fleeing and seeks to become invisible in the group. They have been successful in the mistaken survival behavior when TT members overlook or fail to notice the child.

L

large group meetings: Different from circle times, these community-wide meetings constitute developmental and intervention guidance practices that manage daily programming and resolve public issues cooperatively. Because they provide regular and perhaps long-term experiences at listening to others, sharing thoughts and feelings, and cooperative problem solving, large group meetings provide consummate opportunities for children to gain communication, language arts, and social competence, and direct preparation for civil and productive life in democracy.

Level One experimentation mistaken behavior: Mistakes in behavior as the individual encounters new situations. Can be intentional (controlled experiments) or unintentional (uncontrolled experiments) that in either case go in unexpected directions. A mark of mental health in young children who are only months old. The "preferred" mistaken behavior in encouraging early learning communities.

Level Three strong unmet-needs mistaken behavior: Mistaken survival behavior that individuals show to relieve themselves of unmanageable stress. Can be atypical behaviors that reflect a need either to become invisible or to act out to defend oneself. Most dramatically, it takes the form of reactive or instrumental aggression shown verbally and/or physically. Level three mistaken behavior has deep emotional underlays and tends to be repeated over time.

Level Two socially influenced mistaken behavior: Mistaken behavior by individuals who are influenced by significant others, peers, or the media. Might be due to individual influence, such as repeating a swear word heard in the home or community or media, or to group influence—a mistaken behavior that catches on and is repeated by members of the group. Mistaken behavior due to conformity with influential others that results in conflicts.

liberation teaching: In the guidance context, the term refers to the will and consequent leadership of the teacher to (1) assist a child to make unmanageable stress manageable, and (2) nudge the child toward healthy personal development. In the language of the book, liberation teaching refers to guiding the child to gain

DLS 1 and 2 and willingly engage with attaining DLS 3, 4, and 5. In everyday language, it refers to never giving up on a child.

logical consequence: Rudolf Dreikurs (Dreikurs & Grey ([1968] 1993) identified a logical consequence as a measured action taken by an adult as a consequence of something a child has done. In plain language, imposing a consequence is "making the punishment fit the crime." From the guidance perspective, a problem with Dreikurs's formulation is that the consequence is often more logical to the adult than to the child, due to their differing senses of reality. An example with older children is an adult who confiscates a cell phone rather that ensures that it is zipped up and left in a backpack. Setting and reinforcing guidelines with the group facilitates the use of guidance consequences, which tend to make consequences fairer for both child and adult.

M

managing emotions: The guidance theory alternative to self-regulation. In the presence of secure relationships, managing emotions refers to an individual's developing ability to balance stress-based impulses with executive functioning to resolve conflicts in nonhurting ways.

mastery motivation: Mastery motivation is a term for the universal brain dynamic for learning and psychological growing intrinsic in every child. Mastery motivation is distinct from the extrinsic motivation many adults rely on through rewards and punishments to get the behaviors they seek. As a key dynamic in the healthy development of executive function, mastery motivation requires nurturing and nudging by significant others in developmentally appropriate settings. Mastery motivation shows in a child's willing engagement with DLS 3, 4, and 5, which in turn is a prime indicator of healthy executive function and of healthy personal development.

mediation: An approach to conflict resolution with children that follows the five finger formula. With limited language users, children working on DLS 1 and 2, and beginners in the process, teachers use high-level coaching. With children experienced in the procedure and making progress with DLS 2, teachers change to low-level facilitation. With experienced children who have moved from safety-needs skills to growing-needs skills, teachers observe as children negotiate between themselves to resolve the conflict.

mistaken behavior: Errors in judgment and actions that cause or are the result of conflicts. Includes actions done on purpose, as the dynamic behind all mistaken behavior is unmanageable stress that the individual does not know how to relieve in nonhurting ways.

morning greeting talks: Contact talks that a significant adult in the program holds when a child first arrives for the day. For a child fighting unmanageable stress, arrival can be a particularly difficult time. The purpose of the talks is to ease the child into the day by helping them adjust to the transition, thereby buffering high stress. For programs, the meetings are challenging to hold because arrival is a busy time for staff. When TT members recognize that the meetings tend to reduce disruptive conflicts by the challenged child, they can look at them as an investment in the day.

N

neuroplasticity: The ability of the actual physical structure of the brain to change with experiences, largely through increased neural connections across different operational centers. For instance, language-related neuroarchitecture of young children who speak two or more languages has more synapse connections and physical neural functioning in the language centers of the brain than that of young children who speak one language. Currently accepted in developmental science is that neuroplasticity is most evident in early childhood but continues throughout life, with neural connections growing stronger or weakening and dying depending on an individual's experiences.

P

passive discrimination: The ignoring of active discrimination by others toward vulnerable individuals. Passive discrimination thus enables and gives covert permission for continued oppression of individuals in the setting, making it a discouraging place not just for the individuals who are victimized, but for all.

personal development: Empowered by positive emotional development (largely attaining DLS 1 and 2), personal development identifies the process of healthy development in all domains together: social, physical, cognitive, linguistic, and existential/spiritual.

perspective taking: The ability to understand a situation as another person does, often interpreted in two dimensions. Perceptual perspective taking refers to the ability to understand how another person sees and hears events in physical space. *Conceptual (or empathetic) perspective taking* is the ability to understand a person's psychological experience, thoughts, and feelings in a situation. *Perspective taking* is an essential ability increasing as the child progresses with the DLS. With only beginning executive function, young children show perspective taking more perceptually and intuitively than analytically.

physiological stressors: Sources of stress within an individual due to neurological and/or physical conditions. These can include autism spectrum disorder, attention deficits, disabling injuries, illnesses, and gene-based conditions. Physiological stressors make life challenging not just for the child but also for the family and other significant adults close to the child. For this reason, physiological stressors often become compounded by environmental stressors.

post-traumatic stress disorder (PTSD): A marked pattern of stress-related behaviors in children who have experienced adverse experiences that rise to the level of child trauma. Such behaviors can vary, but prevalent are general worry and anxiousness, emotional outbursts, being inattentive, and remoteness in relationships. PTSD can show itself immediately after the traumatic event or for a long period thereafter.

power of silence: The choice of educators to say nothing when they see acts of oppression by members of the community toward others. Contributes to the development of prejudice in children toward vulnerable individuals and groups. Contributes to a bully-victim dynamic that undermines the encouraging early learning community. The power of silence is passive discrimination that gives tacit permission for active discrimination to continue.

prejudice of ignorance: The prejudice that persons develop toward other individuals and groups because of a lack of actual experience and relationships with individuals from those groups. Common sources are attitudes conveyed by significant others and stereotypical portrayals conveyed by media. Can be passed on across generations.

pre-prejudice: Due to very limited development and experience, as well as attachment influences, infants and toddlers often react negatively to certain human differences before they can conceptualize why. As preschool children more consciously associate negative feelings with diverse individuals and groups, their pre-prejudices can morph into early but real prejudices.

preschool expulsion: The act of requesting a family to remove their child from a program. More prevalent in preschool than K–12 schools, acts of preschool expulsion happen most often to older preschool boys, and Black boys in particular.

preschool push-out: A less raw term than preschool expulsion, preschool push-out labels the widespread practice in preschool programs of expelling children whom staff label as "not fitting in" or "not being ready for" their programs. Preschool push-out happens most often in programs lacking sufficient resources to assist children struggling with DLS 1 and 2. Teacher bias is a factor too: older preschool boys, and especially Black boys, are particularly at high risk of being expelled.

progressive education: Education that respects diversity, promotes equity, and teaches to the whole child. Balances the needs of the developing child with the curriculum. Often project oriented, incorporating children's experiences, knowledge, and relationships from their home, community, and cultural contexts. Staff proactively model and teach the principles of democracy to prepare individuals to function in and contribute to dynamic modern society—and to mark the place of progressive education in the perpetuation of democracy.

prosocial nudging: The gentle leadership of a caring adult that encourages children toward productive social interactions, relationships with other children, and meaningful learning experiences. Together with support, nudging is crucial in assisting children to progress with all the DLS.

R

reactive aggression: Children experiencing unmanageable stress feel threatened by everyday situations that might not be threatening to others. To defend themselves, these children act out in impulsive ways, physically and/or verbally. In the encouraging early learning community, these are acts of mistaken survival behavior and should not be used to label the character of the challenged child.

readiness: Not simply knowing the basics, readiness is the state of mind of a child who is willing to undertake new learning experiences. In developmentally appropriate programs, these children have gained the safety-needs skills and have the cognitive as well as affective resources to pursue Skills 3, 4, and 5. Readiness means competence and confidence in one's ability to learn.

reflective listening: A communication practice in which an adult supportively acknowledges a perceived emotion of a child. Reflective listening by the adult is an act of both perceptual and conceptual perspective taking. The highest use of acknowledge and pause. The foundation of guidance teaching.

resilience: The capacity of a child to overcome the impact of adverse experience and trauma and to proactively engage with life. The demonstrated ability of a child to progress from struggling with DLS 1 and 2 to gaining the safety skills sufficiently to work on attaining DLS 3, 4, and 5. The wellspring of resilience is a secure relationship with one or more significant others who buffer the child from sources of trauma to the degree that they can make unmanageable stress manageable.

S

safety-needs skills: Democratic Life Skill 1: Finding acceptance as a member of the group and as a worthy individual; and Democratic Life Skill 2: Expressing strong emotions in nonhurting ways

secure relationship: A consistent pattern of interaction between an adult and child that is based on mutual acceptance, appreciation, and trust. The secure relationship enables children to gain DLS 1 and 2 and to progress to gaining DLS 3, 4, and 5. Within the context of the early childhood program, the secure relationship begins with outreach by a caring teacher. That initial person might not be the leader of a TT, but instead be a member of the TT who intuitively relates well with the child.

self-regulation: The ability to self-manage feelings and behaviors in nonhurting ways toward others and oneself. A preference in the guidance approach is to think in terms of management rather than self-regulation. Management implies figuring out what *to* do, rather than just controlling one's emotions and *not* doing.

significant learning: A term originated by Carl Rogers, this is learning that yields new meaning important enough that it stays with an individual over time. Every act of learning has an affective as well as a cognitive dimension. When learning is significant, the overall affective dimension is positive to the degree that the cognitive gains are personally meaningful. An illustration is when a child for the first time reads all of the words of a book, reads it again and again thereafter, and as an adult reads it to their own children.

significant others: Parents, caregivers, and other adults who are close to the young child, and through attachment and relationship have a profound influence on the child's attitudes, behavior, development, and education. Includes adults who have primary relationships with children outside of the family setting.

stigma: A stated or implied label that leads others to disparage an individual, so causing that individual to be negatively separated from the group. Examples: Child initiated: "Poopy butt Charley. You can't play." Adult initiated: "You hit again! Caroline, go to the time-out chair!" Stigmatized children internalize negative messages about themselves, other persons, and the setting.

story pictures: Materials include paper, often 8½ × 11 inches, that is blank at the top for art and has lines for writing on the bottom; washable markers; crayons; and pencils. Children create story pictures when they use early art with early writing to tell a story of personal significance to them. Not being bound to the conventions of representational art, writing, and reading, story pictures allow young children to express a wide range of thoughts and feelings in authentic, creative ways. Stapled together, story pictures form individual journals or class books. (Children's writing on the top, and pictures on the bottom, are accepted, of course.)

stress-conflict-punishment syndrome: A repeating dysfunctional emotional/behavioral pattern that children fall into when they feel unmanageable stress, show mistaken survival behavior (often aggression), and receive punishment as a consequence. Children then internalize negative self-messages, feel alienated from the setting, and act out again to cope with reinforced unmanageable stress. The syndrome can follow individuals throughout schooling and into adulthood.

stress response: Mistaken survival behaviors that the child shows because of feeling unmanageable stress caused by adverse experiences up to and including trauma. Similar to PTSD in that unless alleviated, the stress response can be a motivating factor in behavior long term.

support and nudge: The two-fold response of teachers to children who are working on any of the DLS. In interactions with a child, teachers keep the dual motivations for safety and for psychological growing in mind. They respond to the child with a ratio of support and prosocial nudging that they judge necessary to help the child feel supported enough to take steps toward engaging in a new experience.

survival behaviors: Behaviors triggered by the amygdala-hypothalamus system to protect the child from perceived threat and danger. Traditionally, survival behaviors were thought of as the famous two: fighting or fleeing. In recent years, psychologists have added a third behavior, "freezing." In early childhood settings, fighting means that a child shows aggression, verbal and/or physical and reactive or instrumental. Fleeing shows in the psychological symptoms ranging from psychosomatic ill health to childhood depression—actual fleeing by a young child is generally unrealistic. Freezing is seen in children's attempts to become inconspicuous to the extent of "being invisible" in the group. The child's initial reaction to any attention is to feel threatened. In the encouraging early childhood learning community, we refer to mistaken survival behaviors as mistaken because young children do not know how to otherwise ask for help, and the behaviors put them at risk for negative reactions by some adults.

T

task talk: The common type of conversation between an authority figure and child when things need to get done. Can be at any intensity: suggesting, requesting, or commanding, with varying impacts on the child. Distinct from contact talk, which is open-ended individual time between an adult and a child. A guidance talk is task talk and so is a conversation that involves a compliment sandwich.

teacher role, parent role: An early childhood professional should remain less emotionally attached to, and possessive of, children than their parents. A strong parent-child bond lasts throughout the parent's life. As well, the parent's relationship is primarily with their own children. Limited in time from perhaps months to a few years, the teacher's relationships with children are inclusive of all in the encouraging early learning community.

time-out as temporary expulsion: An example of discipline sliding into punishment, time-out is the isolation of a child from the group because of a conflict the child has caused or fallen into. Contrasted with a "cool-down time," in which an adult removes a child from a conflict so the child can calm down and the conflict can be resolved.

toxic stress: Term for the impact on the child of one or more adverse experiences, especially if those experiences rise to child trauma. Causes amygdala- and hypothalamus-generated neurochemical reactions that result in survival behaviors, including aggression. Toxic stress overwhelms frontal cortex centers in the brain, undermining healthy cognitive and social functioning as well as long-term development of executive function.

turns list: A method used in early childhood settings to provide fair access to turns with popular materials and activities. With a TT's help, children sign up on the turns list to use the material or do the activity. To encourage full exposure and significant learning, an individual's turn is usually as long as they want during the choice time period on a given day. (Turns list opportunities might be once a week.) Lifelong interests begin with the significant learning that comes from in-depth experiences. Turns lists rather than forced brief turns give recognition to this understanding.

U

unmanageable stress: Sometimes termed *toxic stress*. The product of a child's encountering one or more adverse experiences that cause amygdala-hypothalamus survival reactions. The term *unmanageable stress* reflects the gradations of reactions to adverse experiences that children might feel, in contrast to the polarization implied in the term *toxic stress* ("either it is, or it isn't"). *Unmanageable stress* is the term of choice in the book.

V

veteran preschoolers: A term for preschoolers who have become totally familiar with the setting and in the time before kindergarten might show a "been there, done that," bored reaction to programming. Unless accommodated, the attitude can result in mistaken behavior that is challenging for the community.

W

welcome booklets: Guidebooks for families and new staff offering invitations for engagement and laying out key policies and practices that provide opportunities for discussion and relationship building.

welcome conferences: Beginning conferences for families when their children join the program. They are most effective when held within two weeks of the family's start date. Designed for staff and families to get to know each other, learn about the child beginning the program, and generally invite and welcome family engagement. Holding the conferences in the home of the family, where possible, is beneficial.

References

A Semi-Lively Introduction

Broughton, A. 2022. "Black Skin, White Theorists: Remembering Hidden Black Early Childhood Scholars." *Contemporary Issues in Early Childhood* 23 (1): 16–31.

Dye, H. 2018. "The Impact and Long-Term Effects of Childhood Trauma." *Journal of Human Behavior in the Social Environment* 28 (3): 381–92.

Farquhar S., & E.J. White. 2014. "Philosophy and Pedagogy of Early Childhood." *Educational Philosophy and Theory* 46 (8): 821–32.

Gartrell, D.J. 2000. *What the Kids Said Today: Using Classroom Conversations to Become a Better Teacher.* St. Paul, MN: Redleaf Press.

Gartrell, D.J. 2012. *Education for a Civil Society: How Guidance Teaches Young Children Democratic Life Skills.* Washington, DC: NAEYC.

Gartrell, D.J. 2014. *A Guidance Approach for the Encouraging Classroom.* 6th ed. Belmont, CA: Wadsworth Cengage Learning.

Maslow, A. [1962] 1999. *Toward a Psychology of Being.* 3rd ed. New York: Wiley.

NAEYC. 2022. *Developmentally Appropriate Practice in Early Childhood Programs Serving Children from Birth Through Age Eight.* 4th ed. Washington, DC: NAEYC.

Chapter 1

Baker, M.C. 1966. *Foundation of John Dewey's Educational Theory.* New York: Atherton Press.

Benarroch, E.E. 2020. "Physiology and Pathophysiology of the Autonomic Nervous System." *Continuum: Lifelong Learning in Neurology* 26 (1): 12–21.

Dewey, J. [1897] 1990. *The School and Society and The Child and the Curriculum.* Chicago: University of Chicago Press.

Dewey, J. [1916] 1966. *Democracy and Education: An Introduction to the Philosophy of Education.* New York: The Free Press.

Dewey, J. [1938] 1997. *Experience and Education.* New York: Touchstone.

Gartrell, D.J. 2000. *What the Kids Said Today: Using Classroom Conversations to Become a Better Teacher.* St. Paul, MN: Redleaf Press.

Gartrell, D.J. 2012. *Education for a Civil Society: How Guidance Teaches Young Children Democratic Life Skills.* Washington, DC: NAEYC.

Hymes, J.L., Jr. [1953] 1974. *Effective Home-School Relations.* New, rev. ed. Sierra Madre, CA: Southern California Association for the Education of Young Children.

Kellogg, R. [1969] 2015. *Analyzing Children's Art.* New York: Girard & Stewart.

Mancilla, L., & P. Blanco. 2022. "Engaging in Reciprocal Partnerships with Families and Fostering Community Connections." In *Developmentally Appropriate Practice in Early Childhood Programs Serving Children from Birth Through Age 8,* 4th ed., NAEYC, 145–57. Washington, DC: NAEYC.

Maslow, A. [1962] 1999. *Toward a Psychology of Being.* 3rd ed. New York: Wiley.

Montessori, M. [1912] 1964. *The Montessori Method.* Trans. A.E. George. New York: Schocken Books.

NAEYC. 2022. *Developmentally Appropriate Practice in Early Childhood Programs Serving Children from Birth Through Age Eight.* 4th ed. Washington DC: NAEYC.

PEN (Progressive Education Network). n.d. "Our Mission." Accessed December 19, 2022. https://progressiveeducationnetwork.org/mission.

Shonkoff, J.P., & D.A. Phillips, eds. 2000. *From Neurons to Neighborhoods: The Science of Early Childhood Development.* National Research Council and Institute of Medicine. Washington, DC: National Academies Press.

Westbrook, R.B. 1995. *John Dewey and American Education.* Ithaca, NY: Cornell University Press.

Chapter 2

Benarroch, E.E. 2020. "Physiology and Pathophysiology of the Autonomic Nervous System." *Continuum: Lifelong Learning in Neurology* 26 (1): 12–24.

Bustamante, A.S, E. Dearing, H.D. Zachrisson, D.L. Vandell, & K. Hirsh-Pasek. 2021. "High-Quality Early Child Care and Education: The Gift that Lasts a Lifetime." Education Plus Development, Brookings, November 4. https://www.brookings.edu/blog/education-plus-development/2021/11/04/high-quality-early-child-care-and-education-the-gift-that-lasts-a-lifetime.

CCTASI (Center for Child Trauma Assessment, Services and Interventions). n.d. "What Is Child Trauma?" Northwestern University Feinberg School of Medicine. Accessed December 18, 2022. https://cctasi.northwestern.edu/child-trauma.

CDC (Centers for Disease Control and Prevention). 2022. "New CDC Data Illuminate Youth Mental Health Threats During the Covid 19 Pandemic." Centers for Disease Control and Prevention. www.cdc.gov/media/releases/2022/p0331-youth-mental-health-covid-19.html.

Crime and Justice Research Alliance. 2019. "School Suspensions Related to Subsequent Offending." Science X, July 12. https://phys.org/news/2019-07-school-suspensions-subsequent.html.

Dewey, J. [1900] 1969. *The School and Society.* Chicago: University of Chicago Press.

Dye, H. 2018. "The Impact and Long-Term Effects of Childhood Trauma." *Journal of Human Behavior in the Social Environment* 28 (3): 381–92.

Erikson, E.H. [1963] 1993. *Childhood and Society.* New York: W.W. Norton and Company.

Feldman, M. 2018. "New Harvard Study Reveals Lasting Benefits of Quality Early Childhood Education." First Five Years Fund, Harvard Graduate School of Education, March 23. www.ffyf.org/new-harvard-study-reveals-lasting-benefits-quality-early-childhood-education.

Freire, P. 1970. *Pedagogy of the Oppressed.* Trans. M.B. Ramos. New York: Continuum.

Froebel, F. [1826] 1887. *The Education of Man.* Trans. W.N. Hailmann. New York: D. Appleton and Company.

Gartrell, D.J. 2020. "Instead of Discipline, Use Guidance." *Teaching Young Children* 13 (3): 14–17. www.naeyc.org/resources/pubs/tyc/feb2020/using-guidance-not-discipline.

Gunnar, M.R., A. Herrera, & C.E. Hostinar. 2009. "Stress and Early Brain Development." In *Encyclopedia on Early Childhood Development* [online], eds. R.E. Tremblay, R.G. Barr, R. Peters, & M. Boivin, 1–8. Montreal, Quebec: Centre of Excellence for Early Childhood Development.

Harvard Medical School. 2020. "Understanding the Stress Response." Harvard Health Publishing, July 6. www.health.harvard.edu/staying-healthy/understanding-the-stress-response.

Harvard University. n.d. "What Is Executive Function? And How Does It Relate to Child Development?" Center on the Developing Child. Accessed January 8, 2023. https://developingchild.harvard.edu/resources/what-is-executive-function-and-how-does-it-relate-to-child-development.

Lupien, S.J., R.P. Juster, C. Raymond, & M.F. Marin. 2018. "The Effects of Chronic Stress on the Human Brain: From Neurotoxicity, to Vulnerability, to Opportunity." *Frontiers in Neuroendocrinology* 49: 91–105.

Masten, A.S., & A.J. Barnes. 2018. "Resilience in Children: Developmental Perspectives." *Children* 5 (7): 98.

Meek, S.E., & W.S. Gilliam. 2016. "Expulsion and Suspension in Early Education as Matters of Social Justice and Health Equity." *NAM Perspectives.* Discussion paper, National Academy of Medicine, October 31. https://nam.edu/expulsion-and-suspension-in-early-education-as-matters-of-social-justice-and-health-equity/#:~:text=Recent%20findings%20from%20the%20Department%20of%20Education%20%282016%29,receive%20one%20or%20more%20suspensions%20as%20white%20preschoolers.

Montessori, M. [1949] 2007. *The Absorbent Mind.* Radford, VA: Wilder Publications.

NAEYC. 2011. "Code of Ethical Conduct and Statement of Commitment." Position statement. Washington, DC: NAEYC. www.naeyc.org/resources/position-statements/ethical-conduct.

NAEYC. 2020. "Developmentally Appropriate Practice." Position statement. Washington, DC: NAEYC. www.naeyc.org/resources/position-statements/dap/contents.

NAEYC. 2022. *Developmentally Appropriate Practice in Early Childhood Programs Serving Children from Birth Through Age Eight.* 4th ed. Washington, DC: NAEYC.

Pallas, A.M. 2000. "The Effects of Schooling on Individual Lives." In *Handbook of the Sociology of Education*, ed. M.T. Hallinan, 499–525. Boston: Springer.

Piaget, J., & B. Inhelder. 1969. *The Psychology of the Child*. New York: Basic Books.

Rogers, C.R. 1961. *On Becoming a Person*. Boston: Houghton Mifflin.

Shonkoff, J.P., A.S. Garner, B.S. Siegel, M.I. Dobbins, M.F. Earls, L. McGuinn, J. Pascoe, & D.L. Wood. 2012. "The Life-Long Effects of Early Childhood Adversity and Toxic Stress." *Pediatrics* 129 (1): e232-46. https://publications.aap.org/pediatrics/article/129/1/e232/31628/The-Lifelong-Effects-of-Early-Childhood-Adversity?autologincheck=redirected.

Shonkoff, J.P., & D.A. Phillips, eds. 2000. *From Neurons to Neighborhoods: The Science of Early Childhood Development*. National Research Council and Institute of Medicine. Washington, DC: National Academies Press.

Stanford Medicine Children's Health. n.d. "Posttraumatic Stress Disorder (PTSD) in Children." Accessed December 18, 2022. https://stanfordchildrens.org/en/topic/default?id=post-traumatic-stress-disorder-in-children-90-P02579.

US Census Bureau. 2015. "Census Bureau Reports at Least 350 Languages Spoken in U.S. Homes." News release no. CB15–185, November 3. www.prnewswire.com/news-releases/census-bureau-reports-at-least-350-languages-spoken-in-us-homes-300171345.html.

Vygotsky, L.S. [1935] 1978. *Mind in Society: The Development of Higher Psychological Processes*. Ed. and trans. M. Cole, V. John-Steiner, S. Scribner, & E. Souberman. Cambridge, MA: Harvard University Press.

Wright, B.L. 2022. "Creating a Caring, Equitable Community of Learners." In *Developmentally Appropriate Practice in Programs Serving Children from Birth Through Age 8*, 4th ed., NAEYC, 111–44. Washington, DC: NAEYC.

Chapter 3

Ainsworth, M., M.C. Blehar, E. Waters, & S.N. Wall. 1978. *Patterns of Attachment: A Psychological Study of the Strange Situation*. Hillsdale, NJ: Erlbaum.

Atwool, N. 2006. "Attachment and Resilience: Implications for Children in Care." *Child Care in Practice* 12 (4): 315–330.

Bowlby, J. 1969. *Attachment and Loss*. New York: Basic Books.

Bowlby, J. 1988. *A Secure Base: Parent-Child Attachment and Healthy Human Development*. New York: Basic Books.

CCTASI (Center for Child Trauma Assessment, Services and Interventions). n.d. "What Is Child Trauma?" Northwestern University Fenberg School of Medicine. Accessed December 20, 2022. https://cctasi.northwestern.edu/child-trauma.

Dye, H. 2018. "The Impact and Long-Term Effects of Childhood Trauma." *Journal of Human Behavior in the Social Environment* 28 (3): 381–92.

Ginott, H. [1972] 1993. *Teacher and Child: A Book for Parents and Teachers*. New York: Scribner.

Masten, A.S., & A.J. Barnes. 2018. "Resilience in Children: Developmental Perspectives." *Children* 5 (7): 98.

Mesman, J., M.H. van IJzendoorn, & A. Sagi-Schwartz. 2016. "Cross-Cultural Patterns of Attachment: Universal and Contextual Dimensions." In *Handbook of Attachment Theory, Research, and Clinical Applications*, 3rd ed., eds. J. Cassidy & P.R. Shaver, 852–77. New York: Guilford Press.

National Scientific Council on the Developing Child. 2004. "Young Children Develop in an Environment of Relationships." Working Paper No 1. Cambridge, MA: National Scientific Council on the Developing Child. https://developingchild.harvard.edu/resources/wp1.

Nelson, C.A., R.D. Scott, Z.A. Bhutta, N. Burke Harris, A. Danese, & M. Samara. 2020. "Toxic Stress and PTSD in Children/Adversity in Childhood Is Linked to Mental and Physical Health Throughout Life." *The BMJ*. https://www.ncbi.nlm.nih.gov/pmc/articles/PMC7592151.

Purnell, C. 2010. "Childhood Trauma and Adult Attachment." *Healthcare Counselling and Psychotherapy Journal* 10 (2): 1–6.

Spock, B.L. [1946] 2018. *Baby and Child Care/Dr. Spock's Baby and Child Care*. 20th ed. New York: Gallery Books.

Stern, J.A., O. Barbarin, & J. Cassidy. 2022. "Working Toward Anti-Racist Perspectives in Attachment Theory, Research, and Practice." *Attachment & Human Development* 24 (3): 392–422.

Stupica B., B.E. Brett, S.S. Woodhouse, & J. Cassidy J. 2017. "Attachment Security Priming Decreases Children's Physiological Response to Threat." *Child Development* 90 (4): 1254–71.

Young, Leontine. 1966. *Life among the Giants: A Child's-Eye View of the Grown-Up World.* New York: McGraw-Hill.

Chapter 4

Carlson, F.M. 2006. *Essential Touch: Meeting the Needs of Young Children.* Washington, DC: NAEYC.

Gartrell, D.J. 2000. *What the Kids Said Today: Using Classroom Conversations to Become a Better Teacher.* St. Paul, MN: Redleaf Press.

Gartrell, D.J. 2006. "The Beauty of Class Meetings." Guidance Matters. *Young Children* 61 (6): 54–55. Accessed January 4, 2023, from https://drjuliejg. files.wordpress.com/2015/02/7-nov-06-yc-gm-class-meetings1.pdf.

Gartrell, D.J. 2007. "Tattling: It Drives Teachers Bonkers." Guidance Matters. *Young Children* 62 (1): 46–48. Accessed January 4, 2023, from https:// drjuliejg.files.wordpress.com/2015/02/8-jan-07-yc-gm-tattling.pdf.

Gartrell, D.J. 2012. *Education for a Civil Society: How Guidance Teaches Young Children Democratic Life Skills.* Washington, DC: NAEYC.

Gartrell, D.J. 2014. *A Guidance Approach for the Encouraging Classroom.* 6th ed. Belmont, CA: Wadsworth Cengage Learning.

Gartrell, D.J. 2020. *A Guidance Guide for Early Childhood Leaders.* St. Paul, MN: Redleaf Press.

Gonzalez-Mena, J. 2014. *50 Strategies for Communicating and Working with Diverse Parents.* 3rd ed. London: Pearson.

Harlow, S.D. 1975. *Special Education: The Meeting of Differences.* Grand Forks, ND: University of North Dakota.

Koralek, D., K.N. Nemeth, & K. Ramsey. 2019. *Families and Educators Together: Building Great Relationships that Support Young Children.* Washington, DC: NAEYC.

Mancilla, L., & P. Blanco. 2022. "Engaging in Reciprocal Partnerships with Families and Fostering Community Connections." In *Developmentally Appropriate Practice in Early Childhood Programs Serving Children from Birth Through Age 8,* 4th ed., NAEYC, 145–58. Washington, DC: NAEYC.

Masterson M. 2022. "Planning and Implementing an Engaging Curriculum to Achieve Meaningful Goals." In *Developmentally Appropriate Practice in Early Childhood Programs Serving Children from Birth Through Age 8,* 4th ed., NAEYC, 215–51. Washington, DC: NAEYC.

NAEYC. 2022. *Developmentally Appropriate Practice in Early Childhood Programs Serving Children from Birth Through Age 8,* 4th ed. Washington, DC: NAEYC.

Vance, E. 2014. *Class Meetings: Young Children Solving Problems Together.* Rev. ed. Washington, DC: NAEYC.

Chapter 5

Butcher, K, & J. Pletcher. 2015. "Teacher/Family Partnerships: How Teachers View Parents." *Michigan State University Extension Newsletter,* April 24. www. canr.msu.edu/news/teacher_family_partnerships_ how_teachers_view_parents.

Gartrell, D.J. 2008. "Comprehensive Guidance." Guidance Matters. *Young Children* 63 (1): 44–45.

Gartrell, D.J. 2014. *A Guidance Approach for the Encouraging Classroom.* 6th ed. Belmont, CA: Wadsworth Cengage Learning.

Gunnar, M.R., A. Herrera, & C.E Hostinar. 2009. "Stress and Early Brain Development." In *Encyclopedia on Early Childhood Development* [online], eds. R.E. Tremblay, R.G. Barr, R. Peters, & M. Boivin, 1–8. Montreal, Quebec: Centre of Excellence for Early Childhood Development. www.child-encyclopedia. com/documents/Gunnar-Herrera-HostinarANGxp. pdf.

Harvard Medical School. 2020. "Understanding the Stress Response." Harvard Health Publishing, July 6. www.health.harvard.edu/staying-healthy/ understanding-the-stress-response.

Katz, L.G. 1977. *Talks with Teachers: Reflections on Early Childhood Education.* Washington, DC: NAEYC.

National Center on Early Childhood Health and Wellness. 2022. "Understanding and Eliminating Expulsion in Early Childhood Programs." Early Childhood National Centers. https://eclkc.ohs.acf. hhs.gov/publication/understanding-eliminating-expulsion-early-childhood-programs.

Shonkoff, J.P., A.S. Garner, B.S. Siegel, M.I. Dobbins, M.F. Earls, L. McGuinn, J. Pascoe, & D.L. Wood. 2012. "The Life-Long Effects of Early Childhood Adversity and Toxic Stress." *Pediatrics* 129 (1): e232-46. https://publications.aap.org/pediatrics/article/129/1/e232/31628/The-Lifelong-Effects-of-Early-Childhood-Adversity?autologincheck=redirected.

Chapter 6

Ansbacher, H.L., & R.R. Ansbacher. 1956. *The Individual Psychology of Alfred Adler: A Systematic Presentation in Selections from His Writings.* New York: Basic Books.

Blair, C. 2002. "School Readiness: Integrating Cognition and Emotion in a Neurobiological Conceptualization of Children's Functioning at School Entry." *American Psychologist* 57 (2): 111–27. https://doi.org/10.1037/0003-066X.57.2.111.

Blair, C., & A. Diamond. 2008. "Biological Processes in Prevention and Intervention: The Promotion of Self-Regulation as a Means of Preventing School Failure." *Development and Psychotherapy* 20 (3): 899–911.

Bodrova, E., & D.L. Leong. 2007. *Tools of the Mind: The Vygotskian Approach to Early Childhood Education.* 2nd ed. Upper Saddle River, NJ: Merrill/Prentice Hall.

Elliot, R. 2003. "Executive Functions and Their Disorders." *British Medical Bulletin* 65 (1): 49–59.

Florez, I.R. 2011. "Developing Children's Self-Regulation Through Everyday Experiences." *Young Children* 66 (4): 46–51.

Galinsky, E. 2010. *Mind in the Making: The Seven Essential Life Skills Every Child Needs.* New York: HarperCollins.

Gartrell, D.J. 2012. "From Rules to Guidelines: Moving to the Positive." Guidance Matters. *Young Children* 67 (1): 56–58. Accessed July 26, 2022, from https://drjuliejg.files.wordpress.com/2015/02/19-jan-12-yc-gm-rules-to-guidelines.pdf.

Luby, J.L. 2009. "Early Childhood Depression." *American Journal of Psychiatry* 166 (9): 974–79. https://ajp.psychiatryonline.org/doi/epdf/10.1176/appi.ajp.2009.08111709.

Vance, E. 2014. *Class Meetings: Young Children Solving Problems Together.* Rev. ed. Washington, DC: NAEYC.

Chapter 7

Dombro, A.L., J. Jablon, & C. Stetson. 2020. *Powerful Interactions: How to Connect with Children to Extend Their Learning.* 2nd ed. Washington, DC: NAEYC.

Gardner, H. 2006. *Multiple Intelligences: New Horizons in Theory and Practice.* Rev. ed. New York: Basic Books.

Schickedanz, J., & M.F. Collins. 2012. *So Much More than the ABCs: The Early Phases of Reading and Writing.* Washington, DC: NAEYC.

Scott-Little, C. With K.L. Reschke 2022. "Observing, Documenting, and Assessing Children's Development and Learning." In *Developmentally Appropriate Practice in Early Childhood Programs Serving Children from Birth Through Age Eight,* 4th ed., NAEYC, 159–80. Washington, DC: NAEYC.

Chapter 8

Derman-Sparks, L., & J.O. Edwards. With C.M. Goins. 2020. *Anti-Bias Education for Young Children and Ourselves.* 2nd ed. Washington, DC: NAEYC.

Gartrell, D.J. 2012. *Education for a Civil Society: How Guidance Teaches Young Children Democratic Life Skills.* Washington, DC: NAEYC.

Ginott, H. [1972] 1993. *Teacher and Child: A Book for Parents and Teachers.* New York: Scribner.

NAEYC. 2011. "Code of Ethical Conduct and Statement of Commitment." Position statement. Washington, DC: NAEYC. www.naeyc.org/resources/position-statements/ethical-conduct.

NAEYC. 2020. "Developmentally Appropriate Practice." Position statement. Washington, DC: NAEYC. www.naeyc.org/resources/position-statements/dap/contents.

Nelson, C.A., R.D. Scott, Z.A. Bhutta, N. Burke Harris, A. Danese, & M. Samara. 2020. "Toxic Stress and PTSD in Children/Adversity in Childhood Is Linked to Mental and Physical Health Throughout Life." *The BMJ.* https://www.ncbi.nlm.nih.gov/pmc/articles/PMC7592151.

Rafferty, J. 2018. "Gender Identity Development in Children." American Academy of Pediatrics. www.healthychildren.org/English/ages-stages/gradeschool/Pages/Gender-Identity-and-Gender-Confusion-In-Children.aspx.

Wright, B.L. 2022a. "Creating a Caring, Equitable Community of Learners." In *Developmentally Appropriate Practice in Programs Serving Children from Birth Through Age 8,* 4th ed., NAEYC, 111–44. Washington, DC: NAEYC.

Wright, B.L. 2022b. "When Blue and Pink Are Not Enough: Saying 'Gay' Matters to LGBTQIA+ Families." *Young Children* 77 (4): 36–43.

York, S. 2016. *Roots and Wings: Affirming Culture and Preventing Bias in Early Childhood*. 3rd ed. St. Paul, MN: Redleaf Press.

Chapter 9

Cozolino, L. 2014. *The Neuroscience of Human Relationships*. 2nd ed. New York: Norton and Company.

Derman-Sparks, L., & J.O. Edwards. With C.M. Goins. 2020. *Anti-Bias Education for Young Children and Ourselves*. 2nd ed. Washington, DC: NAEYC.

Feldman, M. 2018. "New Harvard Study Reveals Lasting Benefits of Quality Early Childhood Education." First Five Years Fund, Harvard Graduate School of Education, March 23. www.ffyf.org/new-harvard-study-reveals-lasting-benefits-quality-early-childhood-education.

Goleman, D. 2020. *Emotional Intelligence*. 25th anniversary ed. New York: Bloomsbury Publishing.

Piaget, J. [1932] 1960. *The Moral Judgment of the Child*. 2nd ed. Glencoe, IL: The Free Press.

Sousa, D.A. 2022. *How the Brain Learns*. 6th ed. Thousand Oaks, CA: Corwin.

Zosh, J.M., C. Gaudreau, R.M. Golinkoff, & K. Hirsh-Pasek. 2022. "The Power of Playful Learning in the Early Childhood Setting." In *Developmentally Appropriate Practice in Early Childhood Programs Serving Children from Birth Through Age 8,* 4th ed., NAEYC, 81–107. Washington, DC: NAEYC.

Chapter 10

Dolan, E.W. 2019. "Study Provides New Details on How Stress Processes in Low-Income Families Could Affect Children's Learning." PsyPost, March 5. www.psypost.org/2019/03/study-provides-new-details-on-how-stress-processes-in-low-income-families-could-affect-childrens-learning-53258.

Elkind, D. 2001. *The Hurried Child: Growing Up Too Soon*. 3rd ed. Cambridge, MA: Perseus Press.

Gartrell, D.J. 2006. "Boys and Men Teachers." Guidance Matters. *Young Children* 61 (3): 92–93. Accessed January 4, 2023, from https://drjuliejg.files.wordpress.com/2015/02/4-may-06-yc-gm-boys-and-men-teachers.pdf.

Gartrell, D.J. 2020. *A Guidance Guide for Early Childhood Leaders*. St. Paul, MN: Redleaf Press.

Giovannoli, J., D. Martella, F. Federico, S. Pirchio, & M. Casagrande. 2020. "The Impact of Bilingualism on Executive Functions in Children and Adolescents: A Systematic Review Based on the PRISMA Method." *Frontiers in Psychology* 11. www.frontiersin.org/articles/10.3389/fpsyg.2020.574789/full.

NAEYC & Fred Rogers Center for Early Learning and Children's Media. 2012. "Technology and Interactive Media as Tools in Early Childhood Programs Serving Children from Birth Through Age 8." Joint position statement. Washington, DC: NAEYC. www.naeyc.org/resources/topics/technology-and-media/resources.

Sampson, R., & R. Manduca. 2019. "Punishing and Toxic Neighborhood Environments Independently Predict the Intergenerational Social Mobility of Black and White Children." *Proceedings of the National Academy of Sciences* 1116 (16): 7772–77.

Sousa, D.A. 2022. *How the Brain Learns*. 6th ed. Thousand Oaks, CA: Corwin.

Weber, N. 1987. "Patience or Understanding." *Young Children* 42 (3): 52–54.

Glossary

Dreikurs, R., & L. Grey. [1968] 1993. *The New Approach to Discipline: Logical Consequences*. New York: Plume Books.

Masterson M. 2022. "Planning and Implementing an Engaging Curriculum to Achieve Meaningful Goals." In *Developmentally Appropriate Practice in Early Childhood Programs Serving Children from Birth Through Age 8*, 4th ed., NAEYC, 215–51. Washington, DC: NAEYC.

NAEYC. 2020. "Developmentally Appropriate Practice." Position statement. Washington, DC: NAEYC. www.naeyc.org/resources/position-statements/dap/contents.

Young, Leontine. 1966. *Life among the Giants: A Child's-Eye View of the Grown-Up World*. New York: McGraw-Hill.

Index

expressing strong emotions in
nonhurting ways and, 100
finding acceptance as a member
of the group and as a worthy
individual and, 86
solving problems creatively—
independently and in
cooperation with others and, 113
thinking intelligently and
ethically and, 139
Elkind, David, 148
embarrassment, 26
emergent curriculum, 60, 61–62
emotional-social development, 3
encouragement, 57–58, 80, 122
encouraging early learning
community, 11, 85–86, 99–100,
112–113, 126–128
environmental stressors, 40–42
equity, 118
Erikson, Erik, 20
establishment aversion, 28
executive function, 24–25
experimentation mistaken
behavior, 59
expressing strong emotions in
nonhurting ways, 10–11, 46, 90–101

F

families, working cooperatively
with, 13–14
*Families and Educators Together:
Building Great Relationships that
Support Young Children,* 69
family engagement, 56, 69–72
accepting unique human
qualities in others and, 124–126
benchmarks for, 70–72
expressing strong emotions in
nonhurting ways and, 97–99
finding acceptance as a member
of the group and as a worthy
individual and, 84–85
solving problems creatively—
independently and in
cooperation with others and, 112
family groups, 146
family-style meals, 126
*50 Strategies for Communicating
and Working with Diverse
Parents,* 69
finding acceptance as a member
of the group and as a worthy
individual, 9–10, 45–46, 76–87
fight-or-flight response, 20–21
five finger formula, 62, 81–82

foundational skill. *See* finding
acceptance as a member of the
group and as a worthy individual
Freire, Paulo, 33
Freud, Sigmund, 91
friendly humor, 55–56, 80
Froebel, Friedrich, 14, 15

G

gender identity, 125
Ginott, H., 122
good deeds, 136
group punishment, 67
growing-needs skills, 8, 9
guidance
accepting unique human
qualities in others and, 123–124
comprehensive, 3, 22, 32, 68–69,
83–84
developmental, 3, 30–31, 60–62,
96, 111, 123
expressing strong emotions in
nonhurting ways and, 96–97
finding acceptance as a member
of the group and as a worthy
individual and, 83–84
functions of, 28–29
intervention, 3, 31–32, 60, 62–69,
80–84, 96–97, 111–112, 123–124
principles and practices of, 29–33
solving problems creatively—
independently and in
cooperation with others and,
111–112
using, 29
guidance consequence, 135
guidance talks, 63–64, 82, 97, 123

H

happygrams, 99
Harlow, Steven, 58
humor, 55–56, 80
Hymes, James, 14

I

inclusion skill. *See* accepting
unique human qualities in others
inclusive teaming, 145–147
individual guidance plan (IGP), 68
individuality, 34–35
inferiority complex, 91
institution-caused mistaken
behavior, 42
instrumental aggression, 23, 94–95

intervention guidance, 3, 31–32, 60,
62–69
accepting unique human
qualities in others and, 123–124
expressing strong emotions in
nonhurting ways and, 96–97
finding acceptance as a member
of the group and as a worthy
individual and, 80–84
large group meetings as, 67–68,
97, 124
solving problems creatively—
independently and in
cooperation with others
and, 111–112
intrigue phase, problem solving, 104

K

Katz, Lilian, 3, 84–85

L

large group meetings, 30, 60–61
accepting unique human
qualities in others and, 123, 124
expressing strong emotions in
nonhurting ways and, 96, 97
developmental, 60–61
finding acceptance as a member
of the group and as a worthy
individual and, 83
as intervention guidance, 67–68
solving problems creatively—
independently and in
cooperation with others and, 111
learning skill. *See* solving problems
creatively—independently and in
cooperation with others
liberation teaching, 4, 23, 33
logical consequence, 135
Luby, Joan L., 92

M

male teachers, 146–147
Maslow, Abraham, 1, 8, 9, 20, 91
mastery motivation, 9, 24–25, 30–31
mediation. *See* conflict mediation
mindfulness, 62–63
mistaken behavior, levels of, 11, 21
accepting unique human
qualities in others and, 122–123
expressing strong emotions in
nonhurting ways and, 95–96
finding acceptance as a member
of the group and as a worthy
individual and, 80
institution-caused, 42